EVALUATING PERFORMANCE OF CRIMINAL JUSTICE AGENCIES

Volume 19. **Sage** Criminal Justice System Annuals

EVALUATING PERFORMANCE OF CRIMINAL JUSTICE AGENCIES

Gordon P. Whitaker
Charles David Phillips
Editors

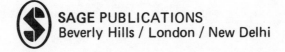

SAGE PUBLICATIONS
Beverly Hills / London / New Delhi

For information address:

SAGE Publications, Inc.
275 South Beverly Drive
Beverly Hills, California 90212

SAGE Publications India Pvt. Ltd.
C-236 Defence Colony
New Delhi 110 024, India

SAGE Publications Ltd
28 Banner Street
London EC1Y 8QE, England

Printed in the United States of America

Library of Congress Cataloging in Publication Data

Main entry under title:

Evaluating performance of criminal justice agencies.

    (Sage criminal justice system annuals ; v. 19)
    Contents: Introduction. / Gordon P. Whitaker, Charles David Phillips—The police and crime control. / Mary Ann Wycoff and Peter K. Manning — The police and noncrime services. / Stephen Mastrofski— [etc.]
    1. Police—United States—Addresses, essays, lectures. 2. Courts—United States—Addresses, essays, lectures. 3. Correctional institutions—United States—Addresses, essays, lectures. I. Whitaker, Gordon P. II. Phillips, Charles David. III. Series.
HV8141.A53 1983   350.74'0973   83-11056
ISBN 0-8039-2048-2
ISBN 0-8039-2049-0 (pbk.)

FIRST PRINTING

CONTENTS

PART III: The Performance of Prisons

EDITORS' INTRODUCTION

COMPLEXITY IN PERFORMANCE EVALUATION

Social scientists have now labored for over two decades at systematically analyzing the performance of agencies administering the criminal law. During this time they have neither formulated nor stumbled on a satisfying set of general statements about performance. They have, however, discovered a few simple truths, the simplest and most frustrating of which is that performance measurement is exceedingly difficult and almost dishearteningly complex. To most of the questions that we pursue here, there will be no satisfying answers for a long time. At this stage, all that we can reasonably and responsibly hope to do is reveal this complexity and make some fledgling attempt to deal with it.

This is the task to which the authors in this volume have applied themselves. For each of the three types of agencies on which we focus (local police, state courts, and correctional institutions), we commissioned papers that we felt would demonstrate the three basic sources of complexity that so frustrate progress in this area of research: the political, conceptual, and technical obstacles that beset all efforts to analyze performance in criminal justice agencies. With the term *political* complexity, we refer to the difficulties that arise because of the fact that all the agencies that administer our criminal laws have multiple goals. Frequently, each of a number of external constituencies has its own goal for an agency, and goal conflicts within agencies are common. By *conceptual* complexity, we mean the problems in devising a model that draws appropriate connections between the actions of agency employees and the attainment of any chosen goal. Most goals for criminal justice agencies involve social conditions subject to economic and social determinants outside an agency's control. Also, one agency's effectiveness is often dependent on the actions of other agencies and actors. Our models of social process must identify the effects of individual agency actions in this tangled web of causality. After one has decided on goals and models, *technical* complexities arise in the form of the methodological and statistical issues that then loom so large.

In each section of this volume, the chapter topics demonstrate the political complexities inherent in administering the criminal law. Mary Ann Wycoff and Peter Manning discuss crime control as a goal, Stephen Mastrofski discusses the noncrime services the police provide, while concern for the equity of police services is the topic of Elinor Ostrom's work. None of these studies, of course, captures the breadth of the demands placed on the police in America. Together, they still fail to exhaust the important goals that people have for police. We did not, for example, include a chapter on due process. Nevertheless, these studies give us a clear sense of the multidimensional nature of the police mandate.

Having a variety of goals is not a situation unique to the police. Sheldon Ekland-Olson and his colleagues discuss the courts as distributors of a social cost (punishment) that is expected to generate a social benefit (deterrence), but it is just as appropriate for Kenneth Hardy to analyze court performance by studying discrimination in the distribution of that social cost. Many different demands are also made of corrections agencies. Mary Ellen Marsden and Thomas Orsagh address the political complexity of goals for prisons, analyzing the demise of the general goal of rehabilitation and its replacement with a broader, and often more punitive, array of social goals. Administrative and organizational goals are also important aspects of public sector performance, and it is such goals that Gloria Grizzle and Ann Witte address in their contribution to the section on corrections agencies.

In the diversity of these works lies a clear and important message, which many of our contributors themselves voice — that any attempt to confine discussions of performance in criminal justice agencies to a single dimension of performance does very real violence to serious social inquiry about how well these agencies meet their responsibilities.

The various dimensions of performance collectively addressed by the chapters in this volume demonstrate the political complexity inherent in analyses of criminal justice agencies. The specific foci of many of these contributions, however, are the conceptual complexities in this field of research. The major concern of some of the chapters that follow is with the problems that arise when researchers attempt to devise models linking agency activity to crime reduction. The authors are profoundly troubled by the conceptual inadequacies they find in many studies purporting to investigate the deterrence doctrine. Wycoff and Manning, for example, find almost all of the previous research on the deterrent power of the police to be fundamentally flawed. They argue that researchers must begin to make the critical conceptual distinction between police involvement in presumably crime-related activities and the effects of these activities on crime levels. They further argue that we must begin making theoretically sound distinctions among the various crime-reduction techniques used by police, and among statements about the special effects that we can expect from these programs.

The work of Douglas Smith and Jody Klein follows one thread of this argument by looking at the production function for one of the classic measures of police performance — arrests. They discover that arrest behavior is fairly impervious to organizational or agency characteristics (for example, professionalization and bureaucratization), being determined largely by situational factors and encounter characteristics. Such a finding suggests that certain agency technologies that have received a great deal of attention in deterrence studies (for example, arrest rates) may not be policy-manipulable.

Ekland-Olson and his associates present a similar line of argument concerning studies of the relationship between sanction severity and crime. They argue that deterrence studies must delve more deeply into the perceptual aspects of sentence severity. Each individual will make behavioral choices based on his or her perceptions of the probability and costs of punishment. Ekland-Olson et al. suggest that one key to understanding these differing perceptions lies with individual differentials in the amount of perceived disruption to social networks that might be wrought by punishment. Robert Bursik's analysis of the effects of juvenile court outcomes on recidivism presents an analogous argument for studies of special deterrence; he investigates whether environmental or contextual factors affect youths' responses to sanctions.

It is not only deterrence studies that present troublesome conceptual problems. As Ostrom clearly demonstrates, conceptualizing equity issues in policing is far from simple. The available studies base their conclusions on analyses of different stages in the service distribution process while implicitly, and sometimes unknowingly, using strikingly different formulations of the meaning of equity. Studies of discrimination in the allocation of punishment suffer many of the same deficiencies. Hardy shows that these analyses usually contain two fundamental flaws: They fail to investigate discrimination at every stage in the adjudiction process, and they fail to recognize that discrimination can be the result of a series of higher-order interactions, as well as a simple direct effect.

All these authors point to generic problems resulting from a set of fairly common tendencies among researchers analyzing criminal justice agencies. All too frequently, researchers fail to pay due respect to the complexity of the processes generating agency outcomes, and to the complexity of factors influencing the targets of agency activity. Outcome measures are often simply measures of aggregate behavior; hence, targets are rarely seen as diverse or differentially responsive. Programs, too, are rarely viewed as multistage processes interacting within a complex and largely uncontrollable environment. Thus, neither researchers nor administrators can speak with any degree of certainty about the specific mechanisms that generate specific results. A "black box" mentality still reigns supreme too often.

The technical complexity of performance analyses in criminal justice agencies may seem the most mundane of the issues addressed in this volume. Most discussions of methodological and statistical issues tend, at best, to be enervating, and at worst, soporific. In this area of inquiry, however, such analyses are terribly important. The unreliability of official data discussed by Wycoff and Manning, and the feedback issue outlined by Ekland-Olson and his colleagues, are perennial, as yet unresolved problems that taint the findings of much of the cross-sectional deterrence research.

Even when researchers use field experimental or quasi-experimental designs, they still face an impressive array of unresolved methodological problems, while many of the most serious technical problems in performance research are intricately intertwined with the conceptual inadequacies noted above. As Charles Phillips and his associates demonstrate in their analysis of the effects of institutionalization on juveniles, different operationalizations and strategies of analysis may lead researchers to dramatically different conclusions about agency performance. Phillips et al. also point out that the focus on behavioral outcomes, to the exclusion of attitudinal and processual data, and in addition to the failure to specify the mechanisms that generate special deterrence, make the results of sophisticated, quasi-experimental studies highly suspect.

Several other measurement problems are raised here, further illustrating the technical complexity inherent in analyzing the performance of criminal justice agencies. Mastrofski discusses some of the problems in defining meaningful measures of police activity, while Grizzle and Witte address a different sort of measurement problem: estimating the efficiency of prisons. Both chapters suggest promising measurement strategies, but the authors correctly caution that their work is exploratory and that considerable refinement is needed.

Those who believe that research will soon produce definitive analyses on which policy decisions can be based, or who believe that such information is currently available, may find our discussion (and much of the contents of this volume) unduly negative in tone, but we find nothing disheartening about the volume. On the contrary, the recognition of these complexities and the scholarly attention that they are receiving are most encouraging. Knowledge in this field will continue to grow by a slow process of accretion, and because any definitive answers to our most important questions lie far in the future, true progress can only be made by grappling with the complexities of the issues that we research, not by ignoring them.

—Gordon P. Whitaker
Charles David Phillips

I

POLICE PERFORMANCE

Chapter 1

THE POLICE AND CRIME CONTROL

MARY ANN WYCOFF
PETER K. MANNING

Measurement of the police's impact on crime has long been the *sine qua non* of those endeavors that might be loosely dubbed "police performance measurement." Recently, however, some researchers have come to question the reliability of the most commonly employed measures of police effectiveness in combating crime. Both practitioners and researchers have argued that such measures lack face validity —that measures of crime-related police effectiveness, no matter how statistically reliable they might be, cannot reflect the actual breadth of the police function. This chapter first reviews these arguments briefly; it then argues that most of the existing effectiveness measures are inadequate for assessing even the narrow, crime-focused functions of police. Progress in measuring the impact of police on crime depends on developing a clearer conceptualization of these effects, one approach to which is outlined here.

AUTHORS' NOTE: *This chapter is based in part on research supported by grants 78-NI-AX-0056 and 79-NI-AX-0095 from the National Institute of Justice. Points of view or opinions expressed in this document are those of the authors and do not necessarily represent official positions or policies of the U.S. Department of Justice.*

CURRENT ASSESSMENTS OF POLICING

Studies of police effectiveness in reducing crime commonly employ dependent variables such as the level (or change in the level) of recorded crime, reported victimizations, numbers of arrests, and numbers of clearances or convictions. The use of these indicators to measure police performance has been severely criticized, however, on both technical and conceptual grounds.

Technical Problems

Elsewhere, we have reviewed and summarized some of the technical problems associated with the use of statistical indicators (Wycoff, 1982a; Manning and Wycoff, forthcoming). Thus, we will review these issues only briefly. Reported crime rates and arrest rates, because of their easy availability for numerous jurisdictions, are the most frequently used indicators of police effectiveness, and yet many scholars have written about the unreliability and noncomparability of official crime rates (for example, Bell, 1960; Wolfgang, 1963; Skolnick, 1966; Biderman and Reiss, 1967; Black, 1970; Zimring and Hawkins, 1973; Skogan, 1974; Maltz, 1975; Pepinsky, 1975; Seidman and Couzens, 1975; Cook, 1977; McCabe and Sutcliffe, 1978; Nagin, 1978). Their research indicates that many victimizations go unreported, and that many are recorded differently by different officers and across different jurisdictions. Some analysts (for example, Hatry, 1975; Greenwood et al., 1977; Nagin, 1978) have focused on the limitations of clearance rates, while others (for example, Sherman and Glick, 1982) have demonstrated the noncomparability of arrest statistics across jurisdictions. Such problems leave us convinced that these indicators should not be used for comparative or aggregate analyses of the crime-fighting effectiveness of the police, and used only with caution for analyses within jurisdictions. It should also be noted that reported victimization rates, although not without problems, are better indicators of crime levels than officially recorded statistics; however, the high cost of victimization surveys greatly limits their availability for use by most researchers and police agencies.

The validity and reliability hazards of official data are compounded when such data are used in aggregate analyses, where it is impossible to account for all the local variances in the data and/or for local conditions that might alter the relationship between predictor and outcome variables. In the aggregation, relationships between measured police efforts and crime-related outcomes may be buried. Aggregate analyses based on purely cross-sectional data are especially problematic because of the inability to determine the direction of causation in such data sets. Some hope has been placed in the use of simultaneous equations (for example, Ehrlich, 1973) as a means of avoiding these problems, but Greenberg (1977) and Nagin (1978) have argued that we know too little about crime and its causes to permit the appropriate and effective application of simultaneous equations in aggregate analyses.

Conceptual Problems

On technical grounds alone, the traditional measures of crime effectiveness seem to lack usefulness as measures of police performance. It might well be argued, however, that the technical issues are less of a stumbling block than the basic conceptual problems. Foremost among these is the fact that crime-focused measures of police effectiveness — no matter how reliable they may be — do not represent the entirety, or even the greatest part, of the police function. This argument has been most thoroughly and convincingly made by Whitaker and his colleagues (1982) in a work that builds on the earlier observations and research of a variety of scholars (Banton, 1964; Wilson, 1968; Bercal, 1970; Reiss, 1971; Pate et al., 1976; Goldstein, 1977; Manning, 1977; Vanagunas, 1977; Lilly, 1978; Scott, 1979). All of these researchers argue that the police activities clearly related to crime matters constitute less than half of the total activities of patrol officers, while clusters of "service" and "order maintenance" activities may account for as much as two-thirds of patrol time. Morris and Hawkins (1977) argue that crime-focused police functions are the most important aspects of police work, and therefore the ones that ought to be evaluated, but this perspective has been challenged by a number of other observors (for example, Bittner, 1970; Goldstein,

1977; Manning, 1977; Wilson and Kelling, 1982). These scholars argue that police responses to crime are only one means by which the police work to maintain community order, and that it is the maintenance of order that is the more important, and more encompassing, of the two functions.

The reliance on crime-focused measures as indicators of overall police performance is, in part, a consequence of the same pressures that caused the crime-fighting functions of police to be viewed as central in recent decades. The sources of these pressures have been reviewed by Manning (Manning and Wycoff, forthcoming). It has also been argued (Wycoff, 1982b), however, that the use of such measures may also *cause* the tendency to view the police role solely in terms of crime-related activities. Researchers have simply measured what they could measure; official crime data are often the only data available within the resources of a research budget or the schedule of a research project. As study after study has evaluated the police in terms of their crime-related activities, the impression has grown that these are their most important functions. If it were not so, why would they be virtually the only ones measured? Such a process feeds on itself; constant assessment of the police in terms of their crime functions tends to distort everyone's perception of the police role.

This is not an irremediable problem. Whitaker and his associates (1982) argue that no single dimension of policing can be considered representative of police performance, and that no single perspective on individual performance issues can provide an adequate assessment of performance on these separate dimensions. Rather, any realistic approach to police performance measurement must be complex, dealing with individual performances rather than with performance as a whole. It makes no sense to ask: "How good a job is your police department doing?" when what we need to know is: "How good a job is it doing with respect to which problem, from whose perspective, and at what costs?"

Developing such specific measures will be an expensive and time-consuming task. It will be done only when the research community finally rejects the use of crime-focused indicators as surrogates for accurate monitors of police performance. Only when researchers stop saying, "We know there are serious problems with these data, but we are going to use them anyway, since we don't have anything else," will there be a strong demand for the resources necessary to develop these better performance measures.

To argue that police performance must be measured in ways other than through the assessment of crime-focused activities is not to argue that there is no place for the measurement of such activities. Indeed, reliable and valid measures of crime-focused police performance will be essential in the necessary multiplex of police performance measures. It is not enough, however, simply to put crime-related measures in their proper place. We would argue that not only do the existing measures misrepresent the broader police role, but that they also misrepresent the more narrowly conceived crime-related functions. Just as there is more to the police role than fighting crime, so is there more to the crime-control function than making arrests and attempting to reduce the number of crimes committed. The development of measures that validly represent the entirety of the crime-control function depends on the development of a more adequate conceptualization of that function. Before presenting our proposal for such a conceptualization, we turn briefly to our understanding of the terms "police" and "performance."

NOTES ON "POLICE" AND "PERFORMANCE"

Police

In much of the police performance literature, the police are often referred to as the hypothetical collective of all municipal police agencies in the United States, or at least the collective of all the agencies in cities of some minimum size. The term "the police" is seductive, tempting the researcher to believe that there is an actual collective, defined and united by critical commonalities. It is this belief that leads to the aggregation of data across agencies, while the internal character of the agencies or the organizational contexts in which they operate may be so different as to obliterate any statistical relationship that might be found within some specific subset of agencies. On occasion, one even finds the performance of "the police" discussed when data have been gathered from only one agency. Again, the researcher is tempted to generalize to all police agencies, which are assumed, because they are "the police," to be more similar than dissimilar. In fact, though, there is great variety among police departments — even in cities of similar size — and there are often justifiable grounds for arguing that the performance characteristics of one agency will not necessarily be the same as those of another, "similar" agency. It becomes important, then, to be as precise as possible about the conditions under which any aspect of performance is being tested and to avoid unsubstantiated generalization.

When we conceptualize the crime function, we too will speak in terms of the police as a hypothetical collective. When we link measures to our concepts, however, we will distinguish between this collective and the individual agencies, because the type of research and the relevance of performance measurement differ, depending on the level of analysis.

Performance

Our conception of performance is not the standard formulation, which tends to equate it with the outcome, effects, or consequences of inputs, programs, or strategies. We adhere to a narrower definition of performance as the execution of work: To perform is simply to do, independent of the consequences. Performance may thus be characterized solely in terms of quality, independent of consequence. For example, in the case of an officer arresting an intoxicated driver, the arrest would be the content of the officer's performance. If the arrest were competently and courteously conducted, and with probable cause, we would judge it to be of high quality. The quality of the performance could be demonstrated independent of the consequences of the arrest. The arrest might not deter other intoxicated drivers. In fact, it might not even keep the driver off the street long enough to prevent him or her from continuing to drive while intoxicated; nevertheless, the officer may have delivered a good performance in the conduct of the arrest. Whether the content of the performance (the arrest itself) would be given high marks could depend on departmental policy, or on the most current knowledge about how police should handle intoxicated drivers. While the content and quality of this behavior constitute the performance of an individual officer, the performance of an agency, although more complicated, can be conceptualized in an analogous way.

The effects or consequences of a performance may be calculated independent of that performance. One can determine its effect on an intended objective, its costs, and its consequences for other organizational goals, and this distinction — between behaviors and outcomes — is important for articulating the process by which organizational (or individual) inputs are (or are not) translated into desired outcomes. Without an emphasis on this distinction, some researchers have found it too easy to slip into the "black box" syndrome, examining only inputs and outcomes with no attention to how, or indeed to whether, certain inputs may be used to effect a predicted outcome. This conceptual and methodological shortcut offers another temptation to aggregate data across dissimilar contexts. When inputs and outcomes bear the same names in a variety of settings, it is easy to overlook the possibility that within each of these settings, they may be related only through highly dissimilar processes and have very dissimilar consequences.

Performances, then, are to be conceptualized and measured independently of outcomes. This is a distinction that we would make in thinking about the performance and effects of behaviors in any organization, and one that we will discuss in more detail below.

MEASURING POLICE PERFORMANCE AND EFFECTS

There are two approaches to improving the measurement of either police performance or the effects of policing. One involves improving the technology or methodology of measurement, and the other involves improving our conceptualization of that which is to be measured. We will deal briefly with the first, and more extensively with the second.

Methodology

The use of official crime, arrest, or other organizational data should be avoided in either comparative studies or in those in which data are to be aggregated across communities. Enough is now known about the ways in which these data are compiled for one to be certain that they are substantially noncomparable. In general, the aggregation of data about police performance or the effects of policing should be avoided, unless the researcher is in a position to consider the contextual factors that may affect these measures differently in different communities. Among these variables are legal constraints, community characteristics (socioeconomic, historical, cultural, and political), the quality of other community services, and the type and degree of public participation in policing.

The most reliable analyses will be experimental studies conducted on a site-by-site basis. Based on results derived from such analyses, it will be possible to take into account those contextual or organizational characteristics that may influence either police performance or the effects of policing. The next most reliable method will be longitudinal studies, again done site-by-site, with particular attention to contextual and organizational factors. In site-by-site studies, whether experimental or longitudinal, the use of official records is less hazardous than in comparative or aggregate analyses. Nevertheless, attention must still be given to any changes that may occur over time in the way that such data are compiled.

Conceptualization

Perhaps the greatest improvement in measurement will result from clearer thinking about what is (or should be) measured. As indicated previously, many studies of police effectiveness have viewed their impact on crime in a very simple and direct fashion: A link was hypothesized between some police input (for example, number of personnel or size of budget) or output (for example, arrests or citations) and the level of crime, but with little attention to the process that translates inputs or outputs into outcomes. At the same time, little regard was given to the conceptual complexity of crime itself. As Manning has written: "Crime is a definition; it is not a thing," based on the conviction that "there are many forms of crime, many manifestations of crime, and many ways to attack crime" (Manning and Wycoff, forthcoming). The multiple forms, manifestations, and strategies cannot be captured in the simple proposition of a relationship between a particular input and the outcome of "crime."

Just as there are many forms of crime, so are there many causes of crime. Few of these causes are as yet well understood, but many are now believed to be beyond the exclusive control of the police. Early studies of police crime-fighting effectiveness failed to take into account, even conceptually, that the outcome variable — crime — was one in which much of the variance was due to conditions that the police could not affect. For example, police have little influence over the social conditions that foster some crimes, or over the factors that cause citizens to bring crime to the attention of the police. They also have little access even to those crimes that are known about and predictable to some degree (for example, domestic assaults).

The commission of a crime, regardless of how it is defined, is a condition generally removed from the direct observation or control of the police; rather, it is affected by numerous factors other than a system of formal control. Yet crime has seldom been conceptualized in ways that acknowledge these limitations or allow for the determination of whether police are doing *that which it is in their power to do* in response to crime. While a few studies have taken into account the likelihood that police can have greater effects on some types of crime than on others (for example, Press, 1971; Kelling et al., 1974; Boydstun, 1975), a great many have simply combined all Part I crimes into one outcome variable against which a particular police input or effort might be pitted. Unfortunately, the use of one such global outcome variable has made it unlikely that these types of studies will be able to detect a significant police impact on the incidence of crime.

At the same time, the focus on a single outcome — the incidence of crime — ignores the fact that police forces and cities tend to have more than one goal with respect to crime. The need to help citizens feel comfortable in their communities, even in the face of whatever crime may exist, is a legitimate and important goal of police agencies, and one toward which they are constantly working. It is also one, however, that is rarely acknowledged in the literature dealing with police effectiveness in responding to crime. We will posit two ultimate goals of the police response to crime: (1) the reduction of the incidence of crime, and (2) the increased comfort of citizens. These are the goals toward which all crime-related police activities are directed. But these are not only police goals; these goals and the responsibility for attaining them are shared by several other criminal justice agencies, as well as other social and political organizations in the community. At the same time, both goals are affected by multiple influences, some of which are beyond the control of even the most powerful agency or organization. For this reason, indicators of either the incidence of crime or of levels of citizen comfort are very "messy" measures with which to gauge the effectiveness of police efforts.

We suggest that there are three intermediate goals of crime-related police activities. These are located conceptually between police activities, or inputs, and the ultimate goals of crime reduction and increased citizen comfort. We believe that these goals can serve as more suitable outcome variables against which to measure the effectiveness of police efforts. These intermediate goals can be labeled as *preventing* crime, *managing* crime, and *penalizing* crime. Crime prevention is a familiar and rather straightforward concept that reflects the belief that police can anticipate the occurrence of particular crime patterns and take steps to change those patterns. Penalizing crime refers to all police efforts to make the commission of a crime a costly undertaking for an offender. The sense of being hunted, the fear of being caught, the costs associated with arrests, the threat of being convicted — all of these are penalties that police levy against suspected offenders.

These intermediate goals — preventing and penalizing crime — are defining characteristics of what Reiss (1980) has identified as two different systems of law enforcement — the *compliance* system, and the *penalty* system. Both systems contribute to the attainment of the ultimate goals of crime reduction and increased citizen comfort. While prevention efforts may actually reduce the incidence of some crimes, which may in turn increase citizen comfort, they also perform the symbolic function of signaling to citizens that someone in power is aware of their problem and is paying attention to them. Similarly, penalty-inducing behaviors may also deter crime — either directly, through the removal of an offender from society, or indirectly, through the discouragement of potential offenders — at the same time demonstrating to law-abiding citizens that they live in a community that does not tolerate the types of behaviors that provoke hunts and arrests.

The third intermediate goal may be less obvious. The idea of "managing crime" stems from the reality that some crime will always exist, despite the best efforts of the police and society in general. In the absence of complete crime prevention, something must be done to reduce the social costs and consequences of crime. This might be done through efforts to physically contain crime (as in the case of rioting, looting, or prostitution), to recover lost goods, to give assistance to victims, and to offer reassurance to the public, either by teaching them how to better protect themselves against particular crimes, or by demonstrating that the police are making efforts to apprehend suspects and prevent future crimes.

Each of these three intermediate goals, to a much greater degree than the ultimate goals, can be operationalized as intermediate outcomes that are within the capacity of the police and that can be linked directly to particular police strategies or activities. It is the direct conceptual link between police efforts and the goals that are theoretically tractable through those efforts, that makes the measurement of police performance with respect to crime-related goals a meaningful endeavor. By defining the goals that are within reach of the police, it becomes logically and empirically possible to ask to what extent police succeed in doing that which it is reasonable to expect of them.

Measurement depends, of course, on the specification of both a goal and the effort made to accomplish it. Although the intermediate goals of crime-focused police activities can be reduced to three, the activities directed toward them are far more numerous, limited only by the imagination and resources of the police organization, and by the legal and social constraints on it. Nevertheless, it is possible to create a typology of police efforts by examining the intersection of crime-related goals and the targets of crime-related police activities.

One can view the crime-focused activities of police as addressing three types of targets: *acts* – units of clusters of behavior considered to be a problem for police concern; *actors* – entities that play social roles (for example, persons, groups or corporations); and *opportunities* – conditions that increase or reduce the probability of an illegal act (Manning and Wycoff, forthcoming):

This scheme of targets is not based upon formal police taxonomies of crime, or types of crime as they are listed in the

UCR, or subclassified. Instead, it is based upon a sociologi-
cally derived analytic of acts, actors and opportunities. We use
acts because the long history of criminology has focused on
positivistic or behavioristic explanations for crime, e.g., the
biological views of Lombroso, the psycho-social views of
Freudians and Neo-Freudians, and the symbolic interactionis-
tic theories of Sutherland and others. We focus on actors
because the cumulated history of criminology also suggests
that the effects of labelling, association and socialization tend
to reinforce patterns of attitudes and build up histories or
biographies of "criminality." These, in turn, are histories,
formal and informal, known to the police and from which they
derive their common-sense theories of suspiciousness, incon-
gruity, dangerousness and all those implicit clues which lead to
stops, questioning, and field interrogations which are the prelude to many arrests for minor violations (see Brown, 1981 but
also Rubenstein, 1973; Ericson, 1981, 1982; and Muir, 1977).
Finally, the opportunities to commit crimes have [long] been
the concern of theorists of crime such as Cloward and Ohlin
(1960), and the more recent theorists of defensible space
(Newman, 1972), behavioral design to prevent crime (Jeffrey,
1971), and "situational" crime prevention (Clarke, 1980).
[Acts, actors, and opportunities, then] . . . can be considered
theoretically derived targets for police intervention based
upon previous research findings.

This matrix of intermediate goals and the targets of goal-directed
police behaviors is presented in Table 1.1. The means of attaining
these goals and the police activities required can be analyzed in
greater detail by dividing each cell in the table into those activities that
are covert and those that are overt (following the work of Marx, 1980,
1981). This distinction is useful for anticipating measurement issues.
It also alerts both the police and the public to a variety of legal and
ethical issues of which they should be aware. For example, Cell 1
(Prevent Crimes/Acts) might include covert activities such as "sting"
operations and overt activities such as guarding potential crime
targets, marking goods that might be stolen, and teaching crime
prevention strategies to citizens. Cell 2 (Prevent Crimes/Actors)
might include either overt or covert surveillance of suspected offen-

TABLE 1.1   Means of Crime-Focused Policing

	Goals		
Targets	Prevent Crimes	Manage Crimes, Criminals, Victims	Penalize Crimes
Acts	1	4	7
Actors	2	5	8
Opportunities	3	6	9

ders. It might include the covert infiltration of groups of suspected offenders, or it might include youth athletic programs overtly designed to motivate potential juvenile offenders to devote their energy to noncriminal activities.

Examples of strategies or activities within other cells include the following: Cell 3 (Prevent Crimes/Opportunities): enforcement of curfew laws, advice on architectural planning or other security measures; Cell 4 (Manage Crimes/Acts): investigation, collection of evidence, recovery of stolen property; Cell 5 (Manage Crimes/Actors): arrest of suspect, assistance to victim and witnesses; Cell 6 (Manage Crimes/Opportunities): containment of demonstrations, riots, and the like, and use of suspect interception plans around likely crime targets; Cell 7 (Penalize Crimes/Acts): publicizing crimes, offering rewards for information; Cell 8 (Penalize Crimes/Actors): surveillance, arrest, and interrogation of suspect; Cell 9 (Penalize Crimes/ Opportunities): enforce laws (for example, housing codes concerning locks and lighting) designed to increase security.

Clearly, these examples are only a few of the many that could be proposed for each of the cells; these are currently recognized as police activities directed toward crime. One advantage of this goal/target matrix is that it suggests broad categories of approaches that imaginative police strategists and criminologists could use, though they may not be as familiar. The matrix also provides a way of summarizing various approaches to crime. More importantly, from a researcher's perspective, it focuses the measurement of crime-related police efforts on specific activities that can be linked to particular intermediate goals, thus eliminating the use of broad categories of input (for example, budgets, numbers of personnel) and outcome variables (for example, level of crime). Instead, the matrix focuses attention on particular outcomes over which specific police actions can be expected to have some degree of control.

At the same time, this type of matrix conceptually separates activities from goal attainment, allowing measurement to be directed separately at the performance of an activity and the attainment of a goal (effectiveness). Goal measurement must be accompanied by the measurement of agency activity, because program failure may simply result from the unsuccessful implementation of what might otherwise be an appropriate strategy. For example, Wycoff and her colleagues (forthcoming) evaluated a special unit designed to target personal robberies. The researchers concluded that the unit's strategies were so poorly implemented that it was impossible to make statements about the likely impact of the strategies on robberies. This is a significantly different statement from a conclusion that the planned strategies were likely to have no impact on robberies. Such a distinction would not be possible if performance had not been measured separately from its effects.

WHEN TO MEASURE WHAT

We have argued that any effort to measure the effectiveness of crime-focused activities should be accompanied by measurement of the performance of those activities. However, it may not always be necessary, appropriate, or possible to accompany measurements of activity with measurements of effectiveness. When city officials or police administrators are concerned with accountability, they are concerned with whether the police are doing what they have been instructed to do, and they need measures of activity performance to determine this. Measurement of most activity performance alone is within the means of city governments and should be the routine responsibility of police managers and supervisors, with occasional monitoring by a city inspections office. The measurement of effectiveness, however, is a different matter.

We have argued that the measurement of effectiveness, if it is to be done properly, may require both longitudinal and experimental research. This is not always feasible. If it were expected that the effectiveness of every major strategy would be so assessed, impossible demands would be placed on most city budgets (see Goldstein and Susmilch, 1982, for a discussion of this issue). For the most part, policymakers at the local level must determine strategies based on the best available knowledge as to what is likely to be effective, given the conditions prevailing in their community. It is the responsibility of the research community, working in cooperation with police agencies, to establish that knowledge. The availability of large-scale resources designated solely for research purposes, and the access to a variety of agencies working within differing contexts, create the necessary conditions for testing the general effectiveness of police strategies.

The fact that practitioners must rely on this knowledge as a partial basis for decision making increases the responsibility of researchers to provide as much information as possible about both performance and context. Contextual information helps local planners determine whether particular strategies are likely to be as effective in their setting as they may have proved to be in other settings. The performance of a police executive may be judged in part by his or her knowledge about the demonstrated effectiveness of various strategies. Similarly, the performance of a police agency should be determined by the extent to which it successfully implements a selected strategy. Until more is known about the causes of crime, the selection of effective strategies may be as much a matter of guesswork and common sense as of science. Nevertheless, the measurement of performance, and hence the establishment of accountability, could quickly become much more rigorous if performance were conceptualized as activity rather than as outcome.

SUMMARY

We have argued that traditional measures of police effectiveness in fighting crime are not only inadequate for measuring the performance and effectiveness of the broader police role, but also for even the more narrow, crime-focused functions of the police. The measurement of these functions can be improved methodologically, but the greatest improvement will come from reconceptualizing the goals of crime-focused activities. We must specify intermediate goals that the police can attain and specify strategies that are directly linked to those goals. The assessment of crime-control strategies within the context of a matrix of targets and goals will eventually make it meaningless to speak generally of the crime-related performance or effectiveness of the police, and this should lead to a more useful focus on the effectiveness of particular strategies in the pursuit of particular goals.

REFERENCES

BANTON, M. (1964) The Police in the Community. London: Tavistock.

BELL, D. (1960) "The myth of crime waves," in The End of Ideology. New York: Free Press.

BERCAL, T.E. (1970) "Calls for police assistance: consumer demands for governmental service." American Behavioral Scientist 13: 681-691.

BIDERMAN, A.D. and A.J. REISS, Jr. (1967) "On exploring the 'dark figure' of crime." Annals of the American Academy of Political and Social Science 374: 1-15.

BITTNER, E. (1970) The Functions of the Police in Modern Society. Washington, DC: Government Printing Office.

BLACK, D. (1970) "Production of crime rates." American Sociological Review 35: 733-748.

BOYDSTUN, J.E. (1975) San Diego Field Interrogation: Final Report. Washington, DC: Police Foundation.

BROWN, M.K. (1981) Working the Street. New York: Russell Sage Foundation.

CLARKE, R.V.G. (1980) "Situational crime prevention: theory and practice." British Journal of Criminology 20: 136-145.

CLOWARD, R.A. and L.E. OHLIN (1960) Delinquency and Opportunity. New York: Free Press.

COOK, P.J. (1977) "Punishment and crime: a critique of current findings concerning the preventative effect of punishment." Law and Contemporary Problems 41 (Winter): 164-204.

EHRLICH, I. (1973) "Participation in illegitimate activities: an economic analysis." Journal of Political Economy 81: 521-565.

ERICSON, R. (1982) Reproducing Order: A Study of Police Patrol Work. Toronto: University of Toronto Press.

——— (1981) Making Crime: A Study of Detective Work. Toronto: Butterworth.

GOLDSTEIN, H. (1977) Policing a Free Society. Cambridge, MA: Ballinger.

——— and C.E. SUSMILCH (1982) Experimenting With the Problem-Oriented Approach to Improving Police Service. Madison: Law School, University of Wisconsin.

GREENBERG, D.F. (1977) "Deterrence research and social policy," pp. 281-295 in S. Nagel (ed.) Modeling the Criminal Justice System. Beverly Hills, CA: Sage.

GREENWOOD, P.W., J.M. CHAIKEN, and J. PETERSILIA (1977) The Criminal Investigation Process. Lexington, MA: D.C. Heath.

HATRY, H. P. (1975) "Wrestling with police crime control productivity measurement," pp. 86-128 in J. L. Wolfe and J. F. Heaphy (eds.) Readings on Productivity in Policing. Washington, DC: Police Foundation.

JEFFREY, C. R. (1971) Crime Prevention Through Environmental Design. Beverly Hills, CA: Sage.

KELLING, G. K., T. PATE, D. DIECKMAN, and C. E. BROWN (1974) The Kansas City Preventive Patrol Experiment. Washington, DC: Police Foundation.

LILLY, J. R. (1978) "What are the police now doing?" Journal of Police Science and Administration 6 (March): 51-60.

MALTZ, M. D. (1975) "Crime statistics: a mathematical perspective." Journal of Criminal Justice 3: 177-194.

MANNING, P. K. (1977) Police Work: The Social Organization of Policing. Cambridge, MA: MIT Press.

————— and M. A. WYCOFF (forthcoming) Crime-Focused Policing: Final report for U.S. Department of Justice, grant 79-NI-AX-0095.

MARX, G. (1981) "Statement regarding police undercover activities and guidelines for the FBI hearings on FBI oversight." Washington, DC: Judiciary Committee, House of Representatives.

————— (1980) "The new police undercover work." Urban Life 8: 399-446.

McCABE, S. and F. SUTCLIFFE (1978) Defining Crime: A Study of Police decisions. Oxford, England: Basil Blackwell.

MORRIS, N. and G. HAWKINS (1977) Letter to the President on Crime Control. Chicago: University of Chicago Press.

MUIR, W. K., Jr. (1977) Police: Streetcorner Politicians. Chicago: University of Chicago Press.

NAGIN, D. (1978) "General deterrence: a review of the empirical evidence," in A. Blumstein et al. (eds.) Deterrence and Incapacitation: Estimating the Effects of Criminal Sanctions on Crime Rates. Washington, DC: National Academy of Sciences.

NEWMAN, O. (1972) Defensible Space. New York: Macmillan.

PATE, T., A. FERRARA, R. A. BOWERS, and J. LORENCE (1976) Police Response Time. Washington, DC: Police Foundation.

PEPINSKY, H. E. (1975) "Police decision-making," in D. M. Gottfredson (ed.) Decision-Making in the Criminal Justice System. Rockville, MD: National Institute of Mental Health.

PRESS, S. J. (1971) Some Effects of an Increase in Police Manpower in the 20th Precinct of New York City. Santa Monica, CA: Rand Corporation.

REISS, A. J., Jr. (1980) "The policing of organizational life." Presented to the Nijenrode International Seminar on Management and Control of the Police Organization, Breukelen, the Netherlands.

————— (1971) The Police and the Public. New Haven, CT: Yale University Press.

RUBENSTEIN, J. (1973) City Police. New York: Farrar, Straus & Giroux.

SCOTT, E. J. (1979) Calls for Service: Citizen Demand and Initial Police Response. Bloomington: Workshop in Political Theory and Policy Analysis, Indiana University.

SEIDMAN, D. and M. COUZENS (1975) "Getting the crime rate down: political pressure and crime reporting." Law & Society Review 8: 457-493.

SHEARING, C. and J. LEON (1977) "Reconsidering the police role: a challenge to a challenge of a popular conception." Canadian Journal of Criminology and Corrections 19: 331-345.

SHERMAN, L. W. and B. D. GLICK (1982) "The regulation of arrest rates." Presented to the American Sociological Association, San Francisco.

SKOGAN, W. G. (1974) "The validity of official crime statistics: an empirical investigation." Social Science Quarterly 55: 20-38.

SKOLNICK, J. H. (1966) Justice Without Trial: Law Enforcement in Democratic Society. New York: John Wiley.

VANAGUNAS, S. (1977) "Socioeconomic class and demand for urban police services not related to criminal incidents." Journal of Police Science and Administration 5: 430-434.

WHITAKER, G. P., S. MASTROFSKI, E. OSTROM, R. PARKS, and S. PERCY (1982) Basic Issues in Police Performance. Washington, DC: National Institute of Justice.

WILSON, J. Q. (1968) Varieties of Police Behavior. Cambridge, MA: Harvard University Press.

——— and G. L. KELLING (1982) "Broken windows." Atlantic Monthly 249 (March): 29-38.

WOLFGANG, M. E. (1963) "Uniform crime reports: a critical appraisal." University of Pennsylvania Law Review 11: 708-738.

WYCOFF, M. A. (1982a) "Evaluating the crime-effectiveness of municipal police," in J. R. Greene (ed.) Managing Police Work. Beverly Hills, CA: Sage.

——— (1982b) The Role of Municipal Police: Research as Prelude to Changing It (Technical Report). Washington, DC: Police Foundation.

——— C. BROWN, and R. PETERSEN (forthcoming) Birmingham Anti-Robbery Unit Evaluation Report. Washington, DC: Police Foundation.

ZIMRING, F. E. and G. J. HAWKINS (1973) Deterrence. Chicago: University of Chicago Press.

Chapter 2

THE POLICE AND NONCRIME SERVICES

STEPHEN MASTROFSKI

Recalling his years as a newspaper reporter, H. L. Mencken (1942) wrote of early twentieth-century police:

> In those days that pestilence of Service which torments the American people today was just getting under way, and many of the multifarious duties now carried out by social workers, statisticians, truant officers, visiting nurses, psychologists, and the vast rabble of inspectors, smellers, spies and bogus experts of a hundred different faculties either fell to the police or were not discharged at all. An ordinary flatfoot in a quiet residential section had his hands full. In a single day he might have to put out a couple of kitchen fires, arrange for the removal of a dead mule, guard a poor epileptic having a fit on the sidewalk, catch a runaway horse, settle a combat with table knives between husband and wife, shoot a cat for killing pigeons, rescue a dog or a baby from a sewer, bawl out a white-wings for spilling garbage, keep order on the sidewalk at two or three funerals, and flog half a dozen bad boys for throwing horse-apples at a blind man.

AUTHOR'S NOTE: *An earlier version of this chapter was presented at the 1982 annual convention of the American Society of Criminology in Toronto. The author appreciates the comments of Charles Phillips, Douglas Smith, and Gordon Whitaker on that earlier draft.*

Police work has changed since Mencken's time, but the patrol officer's day still brims with noncrime matters.

Noncrime police duties have persisted despite numerous efforts to focus the police mandate exclusively on crime control (Manning, 1977: ch. 4; Walker, 1977; Fogelson, 1977). In fact, the noncrime workload of police may be growing at a much faster rate than the crime workload. Figure 2.1 illustrates this for Chicago during the period 1970-1978. Uniform Crime Report offenses remained fairly stable, while noncrime incidents increased at an average annual rate of 3.1 percent.[1] The size of the police force also remained stable. If the Chicago pattern is at all representative, it suggests that noncrime services are becoming an increasingly important part of police work.

Today the crime-fighting and noncrime public service functions coexist uneasily in the police profession. The former dominate training curricula, career incentives, and organization evaluations, while the latter permeate the workload. Pressure to shift more police resources to handle serious predatory crimes continues and is heightened by sensitivity to public sector resource limitations and escalating crime statistics (Morris and Hawkins, 1977). In contrast, some have proposed giving full credence to the array of problems that the public routinely asks the police to handle (Goldstein, 1977; Silberman, 1978: 328).

The debate over how police should deal with noncrime problems can be traced to the emergence of the contemporary police organization of the mid-to-late 1800s, but relevant empirical evidence has been notably absent. This chapter will discuss three issues relevant to those who would evaluate police noncrime services. First, the crime-noncrime distinction is scrutinized. Second, the relationship between police performance in both noncrime and crime matters is explored. Third, the distribution of the supply and demand of noncrime services is examined to assess the likely distributional impacts of altering the police role in noncrime services. Because reformers and researchers have given little consideration to these issues, we have scant empirical evidence on the wisdom and feasibility of reforms to change the noncrime role of police. The studies reviewed and the empirical analysis presented in this chapter do not provide conclusive answers, but they do suggest avenues for future performance evaluation.

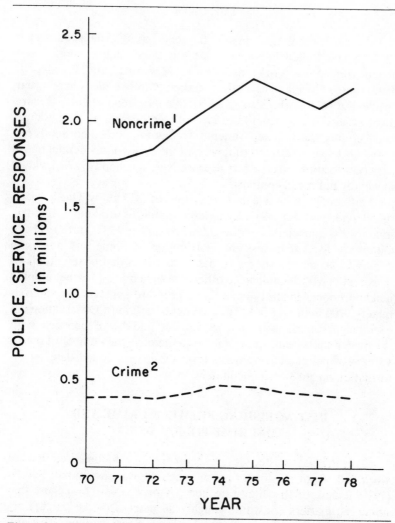

Figure 2.1   Chicago Police Radio Dispatch Responses, 1970-1978

1. Includes "miscellaneous" calls for service and traffic.
2. Includes Part I and II UCR offenses.

SOURCE: Chicago Police Department records.

THE DATA

The empirical analysis in this chapter is based on data collected in 1977 by the Police Services Study[2] in three metropolitan areas: Rochester, New York; St. Louis, Missouri; and Tampa-St. Petersburg, Florida. The project studied patrol services in 60 urban residential neighborhoods served by 24 police departments. Departments varied in size from 13 to 2050 officers, including 21 municipal and 3 county sheriff's departments. One or more neighborhoods per jurisdiction were selected to represent the array of residential patrol service conditions in each jurisdiction. Neighborhoods varied widely in wealth and racial composition.[3]

This chapter uses two data sets from the 1977 study. One is based on telephone interviews with a random sample of residents — approximately 200 households per neighborhood (over 12,000 total). These data were used to assess the distribution of crime and noncrime demands. A second source of data was the coded observations of researchers who accompanied officers assigned to patrol the sampled neighborhoods. In all, 500 patrol officers were observed for approximately 7200 hours (15 full shifts per neighborhood). Observations in each neighborhood were matched for shift and day of the week, with the busier shifts being oversampled to increase the number of observations of police-citizen encounters. Observers coded detailed information on 5688 such encounters.[4]

DISTINGUISHING BETWEEN CRIME AND NONCRIME POLICE WORK

Over the last two decades, researchers have documented that the workload of patrol officers is overwhelmingly noncriminal. Scott's (1981) review of this literature and his own research suggest that noncrime matters constitute roughly 80 percent of the public's requests for police intervention. However, Scott cautions that the literature distinguishing noncrime from crime police work lacks consistency. Activities that some researchers regard as noncrime services, others consider crime-related. This fuzziness arises from a failure to come to grips with two conceptual issues: First, the classification or labeling of events by police must be viewed as a complex process of uncertainty reduction. Second, the distinction between crime and noncrime police service should not be based solely on the label applied by police. These assertions are elaborated below.

In policing, what is noncrime is the residue from the process of identifying and classifying crime incidents. What is criminal is a matter of police discretion, with those lowest in the department hierarchy (communications personnel and patrol officers) having the most to say about whether an incident is classified as a crime, since it is they who organize available evidence into a form that the "slotting routines" of the department and criminal courts can process (Prottas, 1978).

Classifying a situation as a crime is a multistaged process of uncertainty reduction. When a citizen calls in a request for service, he or she is in the key position to shape the police response by means of the information provided, although the complaint operator and dispatcher actually decide how to classify the call. Communications personnel may decide to give the call a crime classification and dispatch an officer, but the officer knows that this classification is provisional. The officer is then expected to confirm or modify this classification once he or she has investigated the situation.

If the crime-labeling process were strictly determined by criminal statute, the police would simply apply the information available about the incident to the elements of relevant criminal offenses. Several extralegal factors, however, shape the labeling process as well: the agency's official and unofficial guidelines (Prottas, 1978), perceived organizational incentives (Brown, 1981), the perceived seriousness of the situation (Brown, 1981: 187), earlier labeling decisions of police communications personnel (Pepinsky, 1976), the workload pressure on officers at the time of police response (Maxfield, 1979), and the nature and preferences of civilian participants in the incident (Black, 1980: ch. 3).

If the responding officer decides to apply an official crime classification to the incident, he or she completes a crime report. This report is subject to further modification by supervisors, detectives, records personnel, or by citizens who subsequently change their minds or report new information that persuades police to "unfound" the crime (Coleman and Bottomley, 1976). Thus, whether the police treat an incident as a crime often varies from one stage to the next, depending on the legally relevant information available and the play of the many extralegal factors involved.

The complexisty of the labeling process, no matter how compelling, is rarely reflected in the data available to performance evaluators. Consequently, some reasonable simplification of the process must be performed. The police work culture provides the basis for such a simplification, in that the expectations of the responding patrol officer pervade the police response to work incidents. Officers believe that incidents with certain characteristics have a far greater crime-fighting payoff than others, even though it is widely accepted that even the most innocuous circumstances may be crime-related. For example, a citizen's robbery complaint may be treated with great "crime potential" even if the officer ultimately classifies it as a non-crime dispute between two inebriated individuals. The reverse may also be true: A routine neighbor complaint that ultimately results in an arrest may have been approached initially as an unlikely law violation. Naturally, expectations vary with individuals and circumstances, but research on street-level police suggests that there are widely shared values — or a police culture — about which situations produce the greatest opportunity for crime fighting and which have a much lower payoff for this aspect of police work (Rubinstein, 1973: ch. 8; Van Maanen, 1974; Brown, 1981: ch. 6; Skolnick, 1975: ch. 9).

The expectations that form the police crime-fighting culture are those of arrest, prosecution, and conviction in the criminal courts. The manifestations of the crime-fighting role in the patrol officer's encounters with the public are making arrests, interrogating suspects, questioning witnesses, and gathering evidence, albeit far less frequently than popular accounts of policing suggest (Black, 1980: ch. 4; Reiss, 1971: 74; Smith and Visher, 1981; Whitaker, 1982). Brown's (1981: ch. 6) research on patrol officers' crime-fighting expectations indicates that officers expect felony violations, minor violations, and field interrogations (suspicion stops) to be the productive areas for anticrime work.

A somewhat modified version of these crime-expectation incidents is offered in Table 2.1, where violent crimes, nonviolent crimes, morals crimes, and suspicious circumstances are subcategories. The examples given for each subcategory represent the most frequent incidents encountered by patrol officers in the Police Services Study.

Noncrime incidents are those where officers' crime-fighting expectations are low. Noncrime subcategories are also listed in Table 2.1. Traffic offenses are misdemeanor or summary offenses but patrol officers and the public typically consider them minor violations. They are considered part of the crime-fighting role only when intervention is motivated by the intention to apprehend violators for more serious offenses (Goldstein, 1977: 40). Disputes, nuisances, and dependent persons are generally regarded as order maintenance, not criminal law enforcement matters, although criminal statutes and local ordinances may be applicable in a given case (Wilson, 1975: ch. 2). The remainder — medical, information requests and offers, general assistance, miscellaneous, and gone on arrival — are usually classified in the miscellaneous service category, constituting problems that some have argued might easily be handled in the private sector (Wilson, 1975: 5).

The distribution of encounters recorded by Police Services Study observers is consistent with patterns noted in previous research. The vast majority (71 percent) are noncrime,[5] with the largest single noncrime category, accounting for almost one-fourth of all encounters, being traffic. Among crime encounters, nonviolent incidents account for the majority and constitute the second largest category overall.

Of course, the distribution of encounters according to incident categories does not show the complete picture of crime and noncrime police services. The classification that an incident receives often fails to reflect what an officer actually does. An officer may ultimately give an incident a noncrime classification, but in the course of the encounter, he or she may have pursued the possibility that a crime had occurred, questioning witnesses, interrogating potential suspects, and/or searching persons before deciding not to file a crime report. On the other hand, an officer may classify an incident as a crime but still perform many order maintenance and assistance activities outside the traditional crime-fighting role.

Grouping police behavior in public encounters into three categories — enforcement, coercion, and assistance — helps to distinguish crime-fighting activity from other service functions. Enforcement subsumes both arrest and investigation activities, with the former including a statement of arrest by the officer, removing a suspect from the scene involuntarily, and asking someone to sign a complaint.[6] Investigation activities include frisks and personal

TABLE 2.1   Crime and Noncrime Incidents and Their Distribution
in Police Services Study

	Percentage of All Encounters[a]
Crime Incidents	
Violent crimes. Murder, robbery, assault, kidnapping, rape, child abuse.	3.0
Nonviolent crimes. Theft, selling or receiving stolen goods, breaking and entering, burglary, vandalism, arson, fraud, leaving the scene, false report, nonsupport	15.0
Morals crimes. Drug violations, gambling, prostitution, obscene behavior, pornography.	1.3
Suspicious circumstances. Reports or observations of prowlers, gunshots, screams, suspicious persons or conditions.	9.8
Total	29.1
Noncrime Incidents	
Traffic (regulation and enforcement). Violation of traffic laws, traffic flow problem, accidents, abandoned vehicles.	24.1
Disputes. Fights, arguments, disturbances involving interpersonal conflict.	8.6
Nuisances. Annoyance, harassment, noise disturbance, trespassing, minor juvenile problem, ordinance violation.	10.7
Dependent persons. Drunks, missing persons, juvenile runaway, mentally disordered, other person unable to care for self.	3.4
Medical. Injured accident victims, suicide and attempts, deaths, others needing medical attention.	1.9
Information request. Road directions, referral, police or government procedures, miscellaneous requests where no additional police action mentioned	4.0
Information offer. Return property, missing or stolen property, false alarm report, complaint or compliment about police, general information provision.	2.8
General assistance. Animal problem, lost or damaged property, utility problem, fire or other disaster, assist motorist, lockouts, companionship, irrational or crank call, house check, escort, transportation.	9.2
Miscellaneous. Internal legal procedures, assistance request, officer wants to give information, officer wants information, officer assists, courier.	4.4
Gone on arrival. Dispatched calls where parties to the problem are not at the scene	1.8
Total	70.9

a. N = 5688

searches, property searches, questioning potential witnesses and suspects, and protecting a crime scene. Frisks and personal searches are often conducted to ensure the officer's safety, and sometimes to harass citizens. In each case, the fruits of the search may have direct implications for the quality of the arrest and prosecution, and are therefore considered enforcement activities. Most patrol investigations fail to produce an immediate arrest. Some result in the decision not to classify the incident as a crime, but while the possibility of a crime is being pursued, the officer is fulfilling a crime-fighting role.

Coercion — the capacity that dominates the police function, according to many scholars (Bittner, 1974; Brown, 1981; Muir, 1977) — is doing or threatening harm to others. Arrest and certain investigative behaviors are coercive, but they are usually legitimated by the officer's responsibility to bring offenders to justice in the formal criminal process. Here I refer to "coercive" as involving the use or threat of physical force or the threat of enforcement activities.[7] These are the most severe manifestations of order maintenance.

Assistance, the third category of police behaviors, is unambiguously dissociated from crime fighting in that it benefits specific individuals, not society, and "exhausts the value of the service" (Wilson, 1975: 5). Included in this category are the innumerable personal services that the police provide, such as first aid, transportation, summoning additional assistance, making referrals, settling arguments, offering comfort, providing information, finding lost property and people, and other physical aid.

The extent to which incident categories fail to distinguish adequately between crime and noncrime police activity is demonstrated in Table 2.2. Overall, there is little difference between crime and noncrime incidents in terms of the relative frequency with which assistance was rendered. Police provided assistance in slightly less than half of the crime encounters (49 percent) and in slightly more than half of the noncrime encounters (54 percent). Among noncrime encounters, such assistance was virtually certain for information requests and quite likely in disputes, dependent-person cases, and encounters concerning medical problems. As noted earlier, nonviolent crimes account for the majority of crime problems where such assistance is rendered.

Crime and noncrime incidents differ little in the probability that police will coerce someone, being 15 and 13 percent, respectively. As one might expect, coercion is most frequent among noncrime problems in encounters involving disputes and nuisances. The particularly high frequency of coercion in the morals crime category (47 percent) is understandable, given that these were predominantly officer-initiated actions where none of the citizen participants supported the intervention. In the majority of encounters where coercion was applied, the police made no arrest (60 percent for crime and 75 percent for noncrime). This suggests that most of the coercion reported here focuses on order maintenance, not apprehension.

Crime and noncrime encounters show the greatest differences in the likelihood of enforcement activity. Investigation activities are almost twice as likely for crime as for noncrime incidents (43 and 22 percent, respectively). The fairly high probability that officers will undertake some enforcement action (usually investigation) in disputes, nuisances, dependent-person cases, and citizens' information offers suggests that officers do not usually dismiss noncrime matters without first exploring their crime-related possibilities.

Investigation into incidents for crime possibilities is part of a broader diagnostic function performed by police in nearly every matter in which they intervene. In these data, when forms of police inquiry not specific to enforcement[8] are combined with enforcement-related investigation activities, some form of police inquiry was noted in 92 percent of the crime incidents and 82 percent of the noncrime incidents (not shown in table). Of all the activities noted here, then, general inquiry for the purpose of problem diagnosis was by far the most common.

The last column of Table 2.2 indicates the percentage of incidents where an officer made an arrest or asked a citizen to sign a complaint. Arrest activity was nearly twice as likely in crime as in noncrime incidents (13 and 7 percent, respectively). Even if police requests for signing a complaint are excluded from the arrest activity category, the percentages of crime and noncrime encounters producing arrests are still 8 and 4 percent, respectively (not shown in table). Arrest activity is by far most likely in violent crime incidents (33 percent), while the likelihood of arrest activity in nonviolent crimes and morals crimes is the same (14 percent). The relatively high proportion of disputes

TABLE 2.2   Police Activities in Encounters With Citizens

Incident Category	N	Type of Action[a]			
				Enforcement	
		Assistance	Coercion	Investigation	Arrest[b]
Crime (Total)	1657	49	15	43	13
Violent crime	171	66	26	75	33
Nonviolent crime	854	54	9	43	14
Morals crime	72	38	47	53	14
Suspicious circ.	560	37	17	33	7
Noncrime (Total)	4031	54	13	22	7
Traffic	1373	40	9	13	6
Disputes	491	71	30	42	16
Nuisances	609	57	23	38	9
Dependent persons	191	69	14	28	5
Medical	106	64	3	18	0
Information request	228	95	1	4	0
Information offer	160	48	1	31	3
General assistance	522	60	4	13	2
Miscellaneous	249	45	13	18	7
Gone on arrival	102	23	3	11	0

SOURCE: Police Services Study.

a. Figures represent the percentage of encounters for each incident category in which a particular action was taken. Figures are rounded to the nearest whole percent.
b. Does not include traffic citations.

producing arrest activity is consistent with Black's (1980: 130) finding that penalizing disputants is a common police response in interpersonal conflicts.

There are some clear patterns in the distribution of police activities among crime and noncrime encounters, but the diffusion of each type of police behavior is much wider than the current literature acknowledges. A citizen is nearly as likely to receive assistance in a crime incident as in a noncrime incident. There is about one chance in seven of being coerced in a crime encounter, and about one in eight in a noncrime encounter. Although enforcement activities are much more likely in crime encounters, noncrime encounters account for the majority of instances where such activity occurs. Unfortunately, traditional incident classification schemes obscure the nature of the police services that are actually provided.

RELATIONSHIP BETWEEN CRIME AND
NONCRIME POLICE WORK

Crime and noncrime aspects of patrol work are linked through their diffusion across a variety of public encounters, but they may be linked in more subtle ways as well. A thorough evaluation of any effort to alter the police role in noncrime services or to downgrade police response to these problems should be based on knowledge of the extent to which their success in crime fighting depends on the delivery of noncrime services. There are at least four models hypothesizing that police noncrime services improve their capacity to handle crime: the crime prophylactic model, the police knowledge model, the social work model, and the community cooperation model.

The crime prophylactic model posits that police intervention in many noncrime matters — particularly domestic feuds, neighbor quarrels, nuisance complaints, and dependent persons — defuses situations that might develop into full-blown criminal incidents if left untended by the police. Bard's (1970: 27) research on family crisis intervention led him to offer a tentative conclusion that police involvement in these problems may reduce the frequency and severity of assaults and homicides born of domestic quarrels; however, the limits of his design and measures make these conclusions highly speculative. Whether police should become involved in domestic crises seems moot today. According to a Police Services Study survey of patrol officers, the vast majority of patrol officers now believe that they should intervene when such disputes get out of hand.[9]

The principal question for evaluation researchers seems to be whether police precrisis intervention has any merit in reducing criminal violence. Research on domestic violence has grown rapidly in the last decade, but most studies select research subjects who have already escalated their interpersonal conflicts to crisis proportions. Consequently, we are unable to assess the possible effects of earlier police efforts (or the lack thereof), when the potential for domestic violence may have been brought to police attention through nuisance complaints, dependent person reports, and general assistance requests. Thus, whether police can make an effective contribution to the prevention of domestic criminal violence through their efforts (and the mobilization of their agencies) in noncrisis situations is a matter for further research. This type of study would be valuable in other areas besides domestic violence, such as the policing of skid-row vagrants, runaway juveniles, and other persons whose capacity to look after their own welfare is in question.

Wilson and Kelling (1982) propose a communitywide version of the individual crime prophylactic model described above. They argue that the spread of predatory crime into urban neighborhoods may be prevented or reduced by a police force that attends to the public order of the area. By showing little tolerance for disorderly behavior (drunks, addicts, beggars, noisy juveniles, loiterers, the deranged, and/or prostitutes), police reinforce the "natural" (that is, unofficial) control mechanisms in the community. This develops or sustains a willingness to assume responsibility for social control on the part of those who have a large stake in the neighborhood — its residents and business people. Because the neighborhood is orderly, these people will make greater use of public areas and reduce their vulnerability to crime. Maintaining an orderly neighborhood — and particularly one that *appears* orderly — signals potential law breakers that the official and unofficial forces of social control are active; crime is thus deterred.

This argument implies that police efforts to thwart crime should focus more on the prevention of public disorder (which is not necessarily illegal or best handled by enforcement activities) and less on response to reports of crimes that have already occurred. The authors suggest that the community version of the crime prophylactic model may have been operable in the Newark foot patrol experiment conducted by the Police Foundation (1981), but a systematic test of this model has yet to be conducted.

The police knowledge model assumes that officers' involvement in noncrime matters ensures a much broader exposure to the community than would occur if they dealt only with crime. This broader exposure facilitates their developing knowledge about community patterns, routines, and individuals, which is useful in anticipating crimes and solving cases. Opportunities for gaining crime intelligence are greatly restricted when police-community contacts are limited to crime incidents. The San Diego Community Profile study evaluated officers' self-reported knowledge of their beats. This project provided several organizational incentives for experimental patrol officers to develop beat knowledge through increasing the quantity and enhancing the quality of their noncrime encounters with the public. The project's evaluators found that "the Experimental Officers reported a slightly greater increase in knowledge about crime information sources than did the Control Officers" (Boydstun and Sherry, 1975: 67).

A recent analysis of officer knowledge of the beat conducted by the author examined the relationship between an officer's commitment to providing noncrime services and his or her ability to name one or more voluntary citizen groups active on his beat in volunteer patrol, crime prevention, or police-community relations (Mastrofski, 1982). Cross-sectional analysis of nearly 900 officers interviewed from the Police Services Study showed that officers with stronger commitments to the provision of noncrime services tended to be *less* knowledgeable, although the relationship was quite weak when other factors (department, officer, and beat characteristics) were controlled. Both this analysis and the San Diego study used measures of limited scope, so that neither can be regarded as producing conclusive evidence on the validity of the officer knowledge model.

The social work model supposes that police officers' capacities for coercion and assistance place them in a good position to encourage wayward individuals to internalize law abiding norms — in short, to rehabilitate them (Cumming et al., 1965; Muir, 1977). In fact, the notion that police can help rehabilitate wayward citizens is a relic of the Progressive era and finds little support among contemporary police (Walker, 1977: ch. 4). Nevertheless, police departments sponsor many programs justified by this model's hypothesis. The juvenile division (to a limited extent), the Police Athletic League, school programs, and the frequent (if scarcely visible) patrol officer counseling sessions all warrant closer assessment as potential influences on internalizing law-abiding norms.

The community cooperation model enjoys current favor among many national law enforcement figures and researchers (Davis, 1978;

Gay et al., 1977; Murphy and Plate, 1977; Reiss, 1971). They hypothesize that in delivering noncrime services to members of the public, police demonstrate that they can help as well as coerce, that they care about the wide array of human problems confronting people, and that they believe citizens to be worthy of civil treatment. Under these circumstances, the public may be more willing to volunteer information to police, report suspicious circumstances, file complaints, testify in court, and fulfill police requests related to crime-fighting efforts. When people see only the enforcement side of policing, they tend to be less responsive to police crime prevention programs and requests. This model encourages police to enlist the assistance of the public in fighting crime by showing a protective concern for the neighborhood. They recognize the important role that citizens play in "coproducing" arrests and convictions, and in deterring criminal activity (see Whitaker, 1980).

Police success in eliciting community support is determined in large part, so it is believed, by the extent to which police can convince members of the public that they are not there merely to make the "big pinch" or fill a citation quota, but rather to strengthen the entire fabric of community life by maintaining order and providing services. We lack adequate empirical tests of this model, although some evaluations of team policing experiments that apply these same principles touch on the question. Evaluations of team policing programs based on police officers' assessments of their impact tend to note a modest-to-substantial increase in police perceptions of citizen cooperation in crime fighting (Gay et al., 1977: 35; Fowler et al., 1979: 128-134). However, program evaluations based on citizens' assessments of their willingness to cooperate with police have not shown significant effects (Schwartz and Clarren, 1978: III-29-40, III-131; Fowler et al., 1979: 128-134).

The above-mentioned studies did not attempt to isolate the unique contribution of noncrime service delivery to the level of citizen cooperation. In contrast, the Police Services Study neighborhood surveys do supply evidence of the consequences of noncrime service delivery for citizen cooperation with police. Respondents reported about 6500 contacts with police (2612 crime and 3839 noncrime) for which they were willing to assess police performance and provide family income data. Figure 2.2 shows the percentage of crime and noncrime incidents in each family-income category that were rated satisfactory and unsatisfactory.[10] The figure shows a positive relationship between respondents' satisfaction with the police in these contacts and family income. Interestingly, within each income class, the proportion of satisfactory evaluations is consistently (and in most cases substantially) higher for noncrime that crime incidents, while the proportion of unsatisfactory evaluations in consistently lower for noncrime than for crime incidents.

Dean (1980) analyzed the impact of these evaluations of contact on citizens' general evaluations of police performance in the neighborhood. She found that having an unsatisfactory police contact relating to a criminal victimization tended to have the strongest negative impact on a respondent's general performance assessment, while a positive evaluation of the response to a general assistance problem showed the strongest positive effects. This suggests that police risk the largest reductions in general citizen evaluations if they respond to crime problems in an unsatisfactory manner, and that they may produce the largest improvements in overall evaluations if they respond satisfactorily to noncrime assistance calls.

Since Figure 2.2 shows that police responses to noncrime calls are more likely to be satisfactory and less likely to be unsatisfactory, the payoff of noncrime service delivery in community cooperation seems promising, although the extent to which these evaluations influence citizen behavior remains untested. It may be that the police are more effective with noncrime problems, that noncrime problems are more tractable, or that citizen expectations are more in line with police capabilities in noncrime cases. Regardless, the implications are clear: Cutting police response to noncrime incidents risks a substantial erosion of the public's perception of service quality, and this may be expected across income categories. Whether the increased police resources made available by such a change would produce a pronounced increase in the quality of service in crime incidents cannot be foretold by these data. Without additional evidence to justify confidence in such a result, cutting noncrime service would appear to place public support in unwarranted jeopardy.

THE DISTRIBUTION OF CRIME AND NONCRIME SERVICES

Reforms to alter the police role in noncrime service delivery are usually justified (and criticized) in terms of their impact on cost,

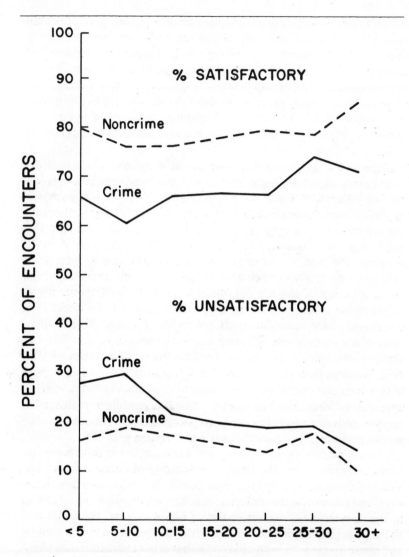

Figure 2.2 Percentage of Police Encounters Rated as Satisfactory and Unsatisfactory, by Family Income

NOTE: "Neutral" and "Don't Know" responses not shown.
SOURCE: Police Services Study neighborhood resident survey.

effectiveness, or efficiency. The question of who will suffer or benefit from these changes is rarely addressed explicitly because of the understandable desire of reformers to minimize the likelihood of political divisiveness that might damage a reform's chances. Performance evaluators, however, should be concerned about the distributional consequences of professional reform. The literature on the distrubition of urban services has produced a variety of hypotheses about how they are distributed. Those associated with social class are discussed below.

The underclass hypothesis proposes that the poor and minorities receive less than the welathy and whites, but most research on police service allocation does not support the underclass hypothesis. Studies of the distribution of police manpower report that neither race nor wealth are important factors in service allocation among urban neighborhoods (Lineberry, 1977; Weicher, 1971; Block, 1974). A study reporting the distribution of police expenditures among New York City community planning districts suggests that the major influence on distribution is the tax contribution per capita of the districts, although the extent of poverty in a district also shows a direct relationship to police expenditures (Boyle and Jacobs, 1982: 376). Evaluations of the distribution of police response times have also failed to demonstrate significant racial or wealth effects (Mladenka and Hill, 1978; Worden, 1981). These results have encouraged some researchers to conclude that police services are distributed in accordance with the unpatterned inequality hypothesis — that is according to professional service delivery rules that have no systematic relationship to the wealth or ethnicity of potential service recipients.

These studies do not distinguish between crime and noncrime service distributions. Maxfield's (1979) study of police calls for service in Chicago and San Francisco does make this distinction, however, and he found some differences in service distribution according to the demographic characteristics of patrol sectors. He found that the serious property crime workload was concentrated in low-income and minority areas in both cities, but that other characteristics peculiar to each district accounted for a larger share of the workload variation. For the distribution of less serious offenses, Maxwell found demographic features of the patrol sectors to have much less influence. The demography of patrol sectors showed no statistically significant relationship with the distribution of noncrime calls in San Francisco, but there was a pattern in Chicago: Disadvantaged areas produced a greater disturbance call workload. This suggests that the underclass hypothesis may apply to miscellaneous noncrime incidents, but that a compensatory model applies to disputes. In other words, the poor get less help with minor assistance problems, but they receive a relatively greater response with those problems that are threats to public order.

A limiation of the above analyses is that the distributional patterns are analyzed at an aggregate level (neighborhood and service district) rather than at individual and household levels, where most of these services are requested and delivered. In contrast, data from the Police Services Study survey of 12,022 neighborhood residents permit an examination of the distribution of the demand for crime and noncrime services to households. Neighborhood respondents were asked to indicate whether they or someone in their household had contacted police during the last year regarding criminal victimizations, requests for information, or requests for assistance. Descriptions of the nature of the problem were obtained for up to five victimizations, two requests for assistance, and two calls for information per respondent. Probes about some specific types of victimizations were conducted (robbery, assault, breaking and entering, burglary, theft from auto, auto theft, theft of personal item, and vandalism). No probes were conducted for information requests and assistance. Consequently, comparing absolute levels between these three categories would be misleading, but within each category it is possible to examine the distribution of requests across different groups of individuals. Only those incidents where there were some police-citizen contact (in person or by phone) are included in the analysis; unreported victimizations are excluded.

Respondents were grouped into seven family income categories,[11] and the ratio of requests to the number of households in each group was computed for each problem category listed in Table 2.1, except gone on arrival, information offer, and miscellaneous. The distribution of requests per thousand households was plotted for each type of problem. Some categories showing similar distributional patterns were combined for simplicity of presentation.

Figure 2.3 shows the distributions of the resulting five categories: violent crimes, less serious crimes (nonviolent crimes, morals crimes, and suspicious circumstances), serious order maintenance and assistance incidents (disputes, dependent persons, and medical), less serious order maintenance and assistance incidents (traffic, nuisances, general assistance), and telephone requests for information. The chart shows clear relationships between the rate of citizens' requests for service and their family income. Although not perfectly linear, there is a direct relationship between family income and requests involving less serious crime problems, less serious order maintenance and assistance problems, and telephone requests for information. Wealthier households request these services at a higher rate, but the pattern is reversed for violent crime and serious order maintenance problems.

The distribution of the various requests shows that wealthier households avail themselves of police service at a substantially greater rate than lower-income households for all categories except the most serious problems. The positive relationship between family income and request rates for most police services is consistent with a recent report by Sharp (1982), who found that in Wichita, citizen contacting of local public officials bore a strong positive relationship to socioeconomic status. That the less wealthy tend to seek most police services at a lower per-household rate than the welathier households does not mean that low-income groups account for an insignificant proportion of the demands placed on police. Of the Police Services Study households sampled, 41 percent were in the two lowest income brackets, and though their request rates were generally lower than other income groups, they still accounted for 37 percent of both crime and noncrime requests in this sample.

Unfortunately, the Police Services Study questionnaire did not inquire as to the nature of the police response to all request categories, so I am unable to report the distribution of police responses. Research on police telephone operator responses to calls for service indicates that 'dispatched units are promised in 60-80 percent of all request categories except general assistance, information requests, and in-

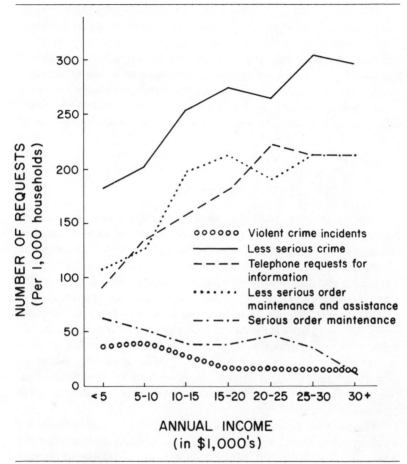

Figure 2.3 Distribution of Crime and Noncrime Requests by Family Income

SOURCE: Police Services Study neighborhood resident survey.

formation offers; hence some form of assistance is nearly always provided (Scott, 1981: 67). To what extent the police dispatch of officers is conditioned by household income is as yet unexplored. At this point, it seems likely that the people who stand to suffer the greatest loss if minor noncrime service cutback proposals are implemented, are those in middle- and upper-middle-income families. Low-income households are shown to call on police for severe crime and noncrime problems at a substantially higher rate than wealthier households, so a cutback in this area would be a proportionately greater loss for them. Of course, the importance of any household's loss of police service is probably greater as family income declines, since access to other alternatives is often constrained by the lack of funds.

SUMMARY

The debate over focusing American police work on crime or noncrime matters directed this chapter into three areas of inquiry: distinguishing between crime and noncrime police work, testing the relationship between noncrime police efforts and crime control, and examining the distribution of noncrime services in the community. The literature review and data analysis are briefly summarized below.

What police actually do in their encounters with the public is not easily predicted from the incident categories reflecting the traditional crime-noncrime distinction. Noncrime police activities (assistance) occur with nearly equal probability in crime incidents. Although crime incidents are about twice as likely to show arrest and investigative activity, noncrime incidents account for the majority of these actions.

Although the police occupational values clearly regard noncrime work as second rate, some research and reform literature raise the possibility that the quality of police crime control may be influenced by noncrime efforts. There have been few empirical assessments of the crime prophylactic, police knowledge, social work, and community cooperation models, although some support for the community cooperation model is found in the data presented here comparing citizen evaluations of the police response to both crime and noncrime requests for service. Citizens are more likely to be pleased and less likely to be displeased with the police response to noncrime — compared to crime — incidents, and other research shows that citizens' overall evaluations of police performance are most affected by poor performance in crime matters and good performance in noncrime matters.

Most research fails to find systematic police favoritism among social classes in the distribution of services, but measurement and aggregation problems may distort actual allocational patterns. The evidence presented here shows two distinct distributional patterns among households of different income groups. Lower-income groups request police assistance at a higher rate for serious crime, order maintenance, and assistance problems, but wealthier groups ask for police help at a higher rate for all other types of problems.

The above findings can neither confirm nor deny the wisdom of altering current police involvement in noncrime matters. The diffusion of different police behaviors across incident categories will make it difficult to reduce the noncrime workload simply by refusing to dispatch officers in response to certain incident categories. Our lack of knowledge about the influence of noncrime services on the police capacity to fight crime makes premature any wholesale attempt to reduce the noncrime efforts of police. The distributional pattern of demand for service displayed in the data suggests that cutting back the police response for less serious crimes, order maintenance, and assistance problems would inflict a disproportionately greater loss in service on middle- and upper-middle-income groups. The net effect of these findings, then, is to point to the need for further efforts in performance measurement.

IMPLICATIONS FOR PERFORMANCE MEASUREMENT

What limited efforts police departments make to measure their performance are virtually exhausted in crime, arrest, and clearance data. To the extent that noncrime services are measured, calls-for-service records are catalogued into incident categories and counted, with more dispatches presumably meaning better service. Slight changes in calls-for-service record-keeping could provide a wealth of information about the extent of assistance activity. Patrol officers could be provided with a set of response activity codes to be used in reporting the action(s) taken in an incident. Despite the limitations of self-reported activity data, such information could assist police managers in monitoring patterns of police discretion in rendering noncrime service. Furthermore, they could use these data to study the impact cf noncrime efforts on crime control and would thus have a more accurate picture of who is getting which noncrime services. Such data would also provide a useful check on the cost-effectiveness of the department's call-screening and dispatch system.

A major problem in measuring assistance responses is that they are so varied. Researchers tend to cope with this problem by focusing on a narrow, noncrime problem. While advantageous in some ways, this fragmented approach precludes a broader view of the noncrime aspects of police work. Although we need measures that reflect the unique features of assistance activities, we also need measures of shared characteristics.

One assistance dimension might be based on the level of officer effort entailed by a given type of response. Some forms of assistance are presumably "cheap," such as giving information, advice, and referral. Other forms are more costly: retrieval of lost property and people, escorts, personal transportation, physical assistance, and mediation. Time expended on a given activity may be one indicator of effort, but time is often difficult to parcel out among officer activities occurring simultaneously. Simply measuring the entire time expended on an incident dominated by assistance activity is another option, or different forms of assistance might be assigned magnitudes of effort according to police officers' perceptions of the amount of effort that each usually entails.

Improving measures of police assistance activity should help in developing models that predict police discretion in providing noncrime assistance. Sherman's (1980) review of research on police behavior suggests that it has been limited to explanations of police demeanor with citizens and of dispute-resolution strategies. Models for other forms of assistance might also be developed. McIver and Parks (1982) have begun to delineate a variety of assistance response patterns in disturbances, as well as disputes. Predicting patterns of assistance in other noncrime and crime incident categories would aid in developing a comprehensive model of police assistance. A variety of explanatory variables could be incorporated into such a model: situation-specific factors (characteristics and actions of participants in the incident, workload pressure); organizational factors (structural characteristics, supervision, incentive programs); and community characteristics. By explaining police discretion in providing noncrime services on an incident-by-incident basis, performance evaluators will be in a better position to regulate the supply of such services.

A final area for model development is in predicting demands for police noncrime services. Aggregate data might be used to associate fluctuations in the demography, economy, and politics of a jurisdiction with its demands for noncrime service. However, real advances could be made at the micro level as well. Victimization researchers have investigated the circumstances that predict whether a citizen will report a victimization to the police, but we have no similar research on how to predict a citizen's decision to bring noncrime problems to police attention. Bittner (1974) argues that it is the perception of an urgent need for decisive action where force may be required that impels citizens to call the police. However, citizens' views of the requisite thresholds of urgency, decisiveness, and force vary greatly. This variation is the basis for much of the initial police uncertainty about a situation.

While there is craft knowledge and folk wisdom about these matters, performance evaluators could improve departments' capacities to manage their noncrime workloads by providing more systematic evidence. For example, the urgency of the police response to a dispute is conditioned by the imminence and risk of physical injury, but at what point in the escalation or deescalation of disputes do people turn to police? Are there patterns associated with the personal characteristics of the disputants? What situational factors increase the frequency and severity of disputes that are brought to police attention (for example, blizzards, paydays)? When these elements are understood, police will be in a better position to anticipate demand and to assign accurate response priorities for noncrime services.

It is time for evaluators of police performance to give greater attention to the noncrime aspects of police work. Proposals to reduce police noncrime work cannot be adequately assessed until we know more about this work. Performance research should ultimately focus on the consequences of this work for the levels of crime, disorder, and personal welfare in communities. Until these relationships are well established, perhaps the police should temper their eagerness to divert more resources to the pursuit of criminals.

NOTES

1. These data were made available by Michael G. Maxfield of the School of Public and Environmental Affairs, Indiana University.

2. These data were made available by the Institute for Research in Social Science at the University of North Carolina and by the Workshop in Political Theory and Policy Analysis at Indiana University.

3. Neighborhood boundaries generally conformed to police beats, but boundaries were adjusted in some instances to increase socioeconomic homogeneity. In some of the smallest communities, the entire jurisdiction comprised the neighborhood. Seven neighborhoods were considered to be a poverty level ($4,000-$6,000 median family income) and were black (75 percent or more). Of the 33 neighborhoods in the next higher income range ($6,000-$14,000), seven were black, nine were racially mixed (25-75 percent black), and seventeen were white (less than 25 percent black). Eleven of the thirteen middle-income neighborhoods ($14,000-$18,000) were white, one was racially mixed, and one was black. All seven upper-middle-income neighborhoods ($18,000-$23,000) were white. In all, 36 of the neighborhoods were served by departments having more than 100 officers; eleven had departments of 50-99; and thirteen had departments of less than 50.

4. Most observations were made in single-officer units. See Caldwell (1978) for details on the patrol observation methodology.

5. Because of minor modifications in category makeup and coding conventions, this differs somewhat from the distribution reported by Whitaker (1982: 19) for the same data. Whitaker assigns an encounter to the crime category if *any* crime is involved, even if it is not the primary problem in the observer's judgment.

6. Asking someone to sign a complaint, while not technically an arrest, is a necessary first step in misdemeanors not personally observed by officers, and is therefore counted as an arrest activity.

7. These include the actual or threatening use of a weapon, using physical force by bodily contact, handcuffing, threats to arrest or place under surveillance, and other threats.

8. These include looking around the area, asking for a person's identification, and asking for information about the problem.

9. In-person interviews were conducted with 939 patrol officers assigned to the 60 study neighborhoods, of whom 91 percent felt that police should be involved in quieting family disputes that get out of hand.

10. "Neutral" and "Don't Know" responses are not shown in Figure 2.2. Neutral responses accounted for 11 percent of all responses and did not vary a great deal among income categories for crime and noncrime incidents.

11. There were 946 missing cases on the family income variable, leaving a sample of 11,076. The number of respondents per income group ranged from 456 ($25,000-$30,000) to 2,372 ($5,000-$10,000).

REFERENCES

BARD, M. (1970) Training Police as Specialists in Family Crisis Intervention. Washington, DC: Government Printing Office.

BITTNER, E. (1974) "Florence Nightingale in pursuit of Willie Sutton: a theory of the police," in H. Jacob (ed.) The Potential for Reform of Criminal Justice. Beverly Hills, CA: Sage.

BLACK, D. (1980) The Manners and Customs of the Police. New York: Academic Press.

BLOCH, P. B. (1974) Equality in the Distribution of Police Services: A Case Study of Washington, D.C. Washington, DC: Urban Institute.

BOYDSTUN, J. E. and M. E. SHERRY (1975) San Diego Community Profile: Final Report. Washington, DC: Police Foundation.

BOYLE, J. and D. JACOBS (1982) "The intracity distribution of services: a multivariate analysis." American Political Science Review 76: 371-379.

BROWN, M. K. (1981) Working the Street: Police Discretion and the Dilemmas of Reform. New York: Russell Sage Foundation.

CALDWELL, E (1978) "Patrol observation: the patrol encounter, patrol narrative, and general shift information forms." Police Services Study Methods Report MR-2. Bloomington: Workshop in Political Theory and Policy Analysis, Indiana University.

COLEMAN, C. A. and A. K. BOTTOMLEY (1976) "Police conception of crime and 'no crime'." Criminal Law Review (June): 344-360.

CUMMING, E., I CUMMING, and L. EDELL (1965) "Policeman as philosopher, guide and friend." Social Problems 12: 276-286.

DAVIS, E. M. (1978) Staff One: A Perspective on Effective Police Management. Englewood Cliffs, NJ: Prentice-Hall.

DEAN, D. (1980) "Citizen ratings of the police: the difference contact makes." Law and Policy Quarterly (October): 445-471.

FOGELSON, R. (1977) Big City Police. Cambridge, MA: Harvard University Press.

FOWLER, F., M. E. McCALLA, and T. W. MANGIONE (1979) "Reducing residential crime and fear: the Hartford Neighborhood Crime Prevention Program." Center for Survey Research, University of Massachusetts, and the Joint Center for Urban Studies of M. I. T. and Harvard University.

GAY, W. G., T. DAY, and J. P. WOODWARD (1977) Neighborhood Team Policing. Washington, DC: Government Printing Office.

GOLDSTEIN, H. (1977) Policing a Free Society. Cambridge, MA: Ballinger.

LINEBERRY, R. L. (1977) Equality and Urban Policy: The Distribution of Municipal Public Services. Beverly Hills, CA: Sage.

MANNING, P. K. (1977) Police Work: The Social Organization of Policing. Cambridge, MA: MIT Press.

MASTROFSKI, S. (1982) "Police knowledge of the patrol beat as a performance measure," pp. 53-76 in G. P. Whitaker (ed.) Modeling Police Agency Performance. Chapel Hill: University of North Carolina.

MAXFIELD, M. G. (1979) "Discretion and the delivery of police services: demand, client characteristics, and street-level bureaucrats in two cities." Ph. D. dissertation, Northwestern University.

McIVER, J. P. and R. B. PARKS (1982) "Effective and ineffective uses of patrol officer discretion." Workshop in Political Theory and Policy Analysis, Indiana University.

MENCKEN, H. L. (1942) Newspaper Days. New York: A. A. Knopf.

MLADENKA, K. R. and K. Q. HILL (1978) "The distribution of urban police services." Journal of Politics (February): 112-133.

MORRIS, N. and G. HAWKINS (1977) Letter to the President on Crime Control. Chicago: University of Chicago Press.

MUIR, W. K., Jr. (1977) Police: Streetcorner Politicians. Chicago: University of Chicago Press.

MURPHY, P. V. and T. PLATE (1977) Commissioner. New York: Simon & Schuster.

PEPINSKY, H. (1976) "Police patrolmen's offense-reporting behavior." Journal of Research in Crime and Delinquency (January): 33-47.

Police Foundation (1981) The Newark Foot Patrol Experiment. Washington, DC: Author.

PROTTAS, J. M. (1978) "The power of the street-level bureaucrat in public service bureaucracies." Urban Affairs Quarterly 13: 285-312.

REISS, A. J., Jr. (1971) The Police and the Public. New Haven, CT: Yale University Press.

RUBINSTEIN, J. (1973) City Police. New York: Garrar, Straus & Giroux.

SCHWARTZ, A. I. and S. N. CLARREN (1978) The Cincinnati Team Policing Experiment: A Technical Report. Washington, DC: Police Foundation.

SCOTT, E. J. (1981) Calls for Service: Citizen Demand and Initial Police Response. Washington, DC: National Institute of Justice.

SHARP, E. B. (1982) "Citizen-initiated contacting of government officials and socioeconomic status: determining the relationship and accounting for it." American Political Science Review 76: 109-115.

SHERMAN, L. W. (1980) "Causes of police behavior: the current state of quantitative research." Journal of Research in Crime and Delinquency (January): 69-100.

SILBERMAN, C. E. (1978) Criminal Violence, Criminal Justice. New York: Vintage Books.

SKOLNICK, J. H. (1975) Justice Without Trial: Law Enforcement in a Democratic Society. New York: John Wiley and Sons.

SMITH, D. A. and C. A. VISHER (1981) "Street-level justice: situational determinants of police arrest decisions." Social Problems (December).

SUMRALL, R. O., J. ROBERTS, and M. T. FARMER (1981) Differential Police Response Strategies. Washington, DC: Police Executive Research Forum.

VAN MAANEN, J. (1974) "Working the street: a developmental view of police behavior," in H. Jacob (ed.) The Potential for Reform in Criminal Justice. Beverly Hills, CA: Sage.

WALKER, S. (1977) A Critical History of Police Reform. Lexington, MA: Lexington Books.

WEICHER, J. C. (1971) "The allocation of police protection by income class." Urban Studies (October): 207-220.

WHITAKER, G. P. (1982) "What is patrol work?" Police Studies 4(4): 13-22.

——— (1980) "Coproduction: citizen participation in service delivery." Public Administration Review (May/June): 240-246.

WILSON, J. Q. (1975) Varieties of Police Behavior. New York: Atheneum.

——— and G. L. KELLING (1982) "The police and neighborhood safety: broken windows." Atlantic Monthly 249(3): 29-38.

WORDEN, R. E. (1981) "Street-level bureaucrats and the distribution of urban services: patrol officers and police services." Presented at the annual meetings of the Southwestern Political Science Association, Dallas.

Chapter 3

POLICE AGENCY CHARACTERISTICS
AND ARREST DECISIONS

DOUGLAS A. SMITH
JODY R. KLEIN

Police departments are people-processing agencies whose performance can be measured by a variety of outputs. Historically, meas-- ures of police performance have reflected the crime-control mandate of individual police departments. The development of Uniform Crime Report (UCR) data facilitated interorganizational comparisons of the effectiveness of police agencies in the control of crime. Over time, the reliability, validity, and comparability of UCR data have been increasingly questioned. Today the use of UCR data as a meaningful measure of police performance is shrouded in considerable doubt (see Whitaker et al., 1982).

Despite their limitations, UCR data have had a significant influence on performance measurement in police departments. One result of the historical tendency to evaluate police agencies with UCR data has been to increase the centrality of the crime-control function of police while subordinating their non-crime-control activities. Indeed, the institutional legitimation of police departments depends primarily

AUTHORS' NOTE: *A previous version of this chapter was presented at the 1982 meeting of the American Society of Criminology in Toronto. We would like to thank James R. Lincoln and Roger Parks for assisting us in the evolution of this research.*

on their image as crime-control agencies (see, for example, Manning, 1977).

In this chapter we examine the determinants of arrest decisions and the usefulness of arrests as a measure of police performance. We have chosen to study the arrest decision for three basic reasons: First, the recent "discovery" of police discretion in the arrest decision raises a number of issues concerning the administration of justice at the street level. Second, qualitative and quantitative evidence consistently indicates that police encounters with suspects that result in arrest are the exception rather than the rule. Finally, a significant body of research on arrest decisions has emerged over the last two decades allowing for cumulation of knowledge on this topic. We will briefly elaborate on these issues, highlighting what we believe to be the major concerns raised by these three facts and their implications for using arrest data as a measure of police performance.

In the sixties, systematic field research on police behavior "rediscovered" the discretionary nature of law enforcement (Rumbaut and Bittner, 1979). Both ethnographic (Banton, 1964; Bittner, 1967; Skolnick, 1966) and quantitative (Pilliavin and Briar, 1964; Black, 1968, 1970, 1971; Black and Reiss, 1967, 1970; Reiss, 1971) research shattered the myth of police acting as ministerial officers. In a comparative work of British and American police, Banton (1964) remarked: "The most striking thing about patrol work was the high proportion of cases where the police do not enforce the law." Subsequent studies echoed Banton's observation on the prevalence of non-enforcement.[1]

As a result of the consistency of research evidence on the prevalence of non-enforcement, most scholars today concur that policing is an inherently discretionary activity. Moreover, many police contacts with the public occur in low-visibility contexts, making it difficult for police organizations to regulate the outcomes of such interactions (Banton, 1964; Tifft, 1975). Additionally, the decentralized nature of police work makes direct supervision of police-citizen encounters problematic (Clark and Sykes, 1974; Tifft, 1975). Even if direct supervision of police-citizen encounters could be achieved, however, there is little reason to suspect that this would eliminate, or even greatly reduce, the discretionary latitude of police. Indeed, several scholars suggest that street-level discretion is an essential organizational survival strategy of contemporary police departments (see Manning, 1977; Brown, 1981; Lipsky, 1980).

Given that discretion is structurally embedded in the police role, patrol officers are more than simple enforcers of the law; they are its chief interpreters. By deciding to enforce or not to enforce the law in a given instance, police officers operationally define the limits of the law in society (Brown, 1981). Additionally, the police serve a gate-keeping function in the justice system. They provide prosecutors and courts with the majority of their criminal cases. Thus, department-level arrest rates reflect the cumulative exercise of officer discretion at the encounter level.

Most research on police decisions to arrest focuses on the influence of encounter-level factors such as suspect characteristics, offense type, and victim's disposition preferences. We believe that this tendency to examine the effects of encounter-level characteristics on the probability of arrest reflects two factors: First, the empirical study of police decisions to invoke the criminal process emerged against a background of theoretical turbulence in the study of social control. Specifically, the substantive claims of conflict theorists (for example, Turk, 1966, 1969) and labeling theorists (Erikson, 1962; Kitsuse, 1962; Becker, 1963) spoke directly to the issue of discretionary justice. Arguments that decisions to invoke the criminal process reflected extralegal as well as legal factors constituted the axis around which debates regarding the equality of justice revolved, and the study of police arrest decisions provided an ideal opportunity to examine the degree of bias on the front lines of legal control.

Second, we believe that the tendency of past research on police arrest decisions to focus on the influence of situational factors is symptomatic of what Reiss (1980) views as a general insensitivity among scholars to the influence of organizational structure and process on the functioning of justice system agencies (for example, police departments). To the extent that Reiss is correct, this is an unfortunate state of affairs, primarily because such fine-grained attention to encounter-level covariates of arrest leaves a number of questions unanswered.

Do the organizational characteristics of police agencies directly influence the arrest decisions of individual patrol officers? That is, are officers in "bureaucratic" police agencies more likely to arrest suspected offenders, while officers in professional departments are more conciliatory in their encounters with suspects, and hence less likely to arrest? Second, do the organizational properties of police agencies mediate the relationship between encounter-level characteristics and the probability of arrest? For example, does the influence of suspect characteristics on the probability of arrest vary across different types of police agencies? These and similar questions become even more critical when one considers the extent of interorganizational variability in police behavior that is revealed in some research.

Studies have shown that police behavior varies across police departments, as well as across situations and individuals (Friedrich, 1977; Wilson, 1967, 1968). Friedrich's (1977: 244) reanalysis of the Black-Reiss data revealed that the probability that police would arrest a suspect was .112 in Boston, .168 in Chicago, and .253 in Washington. Moreover, these differences in the probability of arrest are not attributable to varying levels of seriousness in crimes across the three cities (Friedrich, 1977: 246). In perhaps the best-known study of interorganizational variation in police behavior, Wilson (1968) found that arrest rates for larceny, juveniles, public intoxication, disorderly conduct, and assault varied markedly from one department to the next. To account for this variation, Wilson developed his now famous typology of police department styles (watchman, service, and legalistic).

A primary goal of this research is to examine the extent to which organizational properties influence the propensity of police officers to invoke the law of arrest. This approach may broaden our understanding of arrest decisions in a number of ways. Primarily, arrest decisions can be examined with respect to department-specific goals regarding the role and function of the police. To set the stage for subsequent analysis, we will briefly discuss the classification of police agencies into distinct types and then review the literature on the organizational context of policing.

ORGANIZATIONAL CHARACTERISTICS AND THE PROBABILITY OF ARREST

Police Agencies as Contexts

Our classification of police agencies is based on the pioneering work of Wilson (1967, 1968), whose classification of police agencies revolves around the concepts of bureaucratization and professionalism. Professional police agencies are divided into service and legalistic styles, depending on their degree of bureaucratization. However, all nonprofessional departments are considered by Wilson to operate under the watchman style, independent of their level of bureaucratization. In the current research, four types of police agencies are identified by cross-classifying bureaucratization with professionalism. Nonprofessional police agencies with shallow bureaucracies are labeled *fraternal,* while nonprofessional, bureaucratic police agencies are labeled *militaristic. Service* and *legalistic* agencies are, following Wilson, professional police agencies that vary in terms of bureaucratization. This classification of police agencies is shown in Figure 3.1.

Wilson argues that different styles of social control, specific to different types of police agencies, are reflected in and buttressed by the administrative ethos regarding the proper role and function of the police. In collecting the data analyzed in this chapter, police chiefs and other top administrative personnel were interviewed and asked to characterize their departments' style of operations. It is thus possible to determine whether top administrators in different types of police agencies (determined by cross-classifying bureaucratization with professionalism) hold different conceptions of the police role and have different expectations regarding appropriate officer behavior. If administrators in different types of police agencies were found to hold similar views about the proper police role, arguments for different styles of social control in different types of police agencies would appear problematic.

In fact, administrators in different types of police agencies, classified by location in a cell in Figure 3.1, did vary in their attitudes about what police departments should be doing. Administrators in five departments that are highly professional and nonbureaucratic emphasized service to the community as their primary mandate, while administrators in two other police agencies, both with shallow bureaucracies and high levels of professionalism, placed equal emphasis on service delivery and law enforcement. (Administrators in one department in this classification were not interviewed.) For departments that are nonbureaucratic and nonprofessional (labeled fraternal), administrators in two agencies emphasized service, one emphasized law enforcement, and administrators in four fraternal

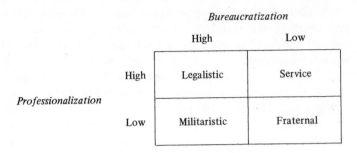

Figure 3.1   Classification of Police Departments by Degree of Bureaucratization and Professionalization

agencies placed equal emphasis on service delivery and law enforcement. Administrators in all four bureaucratic, nonprofessional agencies (labeled militaristic) emphasized law enforcement, while administrators in bureaucratic, professional agencies (labeled legalistic) were equally divided between a law enforcement emphasis and an orientation stressing both service delivery and law enforcement. Thus, distinguishing among police agencies by cross-classifying professionalism with bureaucratization does appear to capture differences in the operational philosophies of top administrators — a major indicator of different operational styles, according to Wilson.

For example, administrators in service-style agencies (low bureaucratization and high professionalism) are primarily concerned with police-community relations and service delivery. This orientation was summed up nicely by the chief of one service-style agency who considered his agency a "full service department." When asked to elaborate on the meaning of this, the chief replied that he saw his department as one in which

> if some problem can't be handled by itself the department can know where to direct the citizen, and will virtually lead the person by the hand and make sure the proper follow-up happens in such referrals.

This type of orientation toward the police role is characteristic of administrators in nonbureaucratic, professional police agencies. The implication of this style of social control is that law is not the principal determinant of police behavior.

Administrators in fraternal agencies (shallow bureaucracies with low levels of professionalism) are more likely to place an equal emphasis on service delivery and law enforcement than are their counterparts in service-style agencies. Even when service delivery is stressed in fraternal agencies, it is done so with only limited enthusiasm. For example, the chief of one fraternal agency characterized his department as a "very heavy service department. . . . Officers are asked to fix plumbing, chase pets, or do anything else that strikes the citizen's fancy." However, he went on to note that the policy of answering all calls for service was imposed on the department by City Hall, which he felt resulted in a "waste of taxpayers' money." Thus, even when service delivery is stressed in fraternal agencies, it often lacks the degree of support characteristic of nonbureaucratic, professional (service) police agencies.

The result of more emphasis on law enforcement in fraternal than in service agencies has implications for arrest decisions. Given the absence of professional norms in fraternal police agencies, the decision to invoke the law in encounters involving minor violations, such as vandalism and simple assaults, may be conditional on the characteristics of suspected violators. For example, blacks may be arrested for personal offenses by fraternal agencies, while whites may be less likely to be arrested for the same type of offense. In service-style agencies, stronger norms of professionalism tend to eliminate racial bias in the decision to arrest. Arrests for minor offenses should also be less likely in service-style than in fraternal agencies, independent of the race of the parties involved, because these problems are treated not as opportunities for law enforcement, but rather as instances where a therapeutic or conciliatory style of social control is mandated.

In highly bureaucratic, nonprofessional agencies (labeled militaristic), the emphasis of top administrators is clearly on law enforcement. As the chief of one such agency remarked: "The police officer's role is first and foremost to enforce the law." This sentiment was echoed in the remarks of another chief of a militaristic agency, who suggested that officers "can best spend their time by responding to crime calls, where their training and authority are useful." Accompanying the emphasis on law enforcement is a widespread lack of interest in service aspects of the police role. The chief of one militaristic agency remarked that officers should be relieved of "trivial service calls" and expressed the desire and the hope that civilian specialists would take an increasing responsibility for service calls in the future.

In bureaucratic police agencies that are also highly professional (labeled legalistic), administrators are more inclined to regard service as within the domain of legitimate police work; however, in no legalistic agency is law enforcement subordinated to service delivery. In instances where service delivery is stressed, it is usually intended to complement rather than replace an emphasis on law enforcement.

It appears, then, that bureaucratic police agencies operate under a mandate of law enforcement, while nonbureaucratic police agencies recognize service delivery as more central to the police role. However, in bureaucratic agencies that are nonprofessional, the concern with law enforcement seems almost obsessive, while in bureaucratic agencies with high levels of professionalism, service delivery is recognized as a necessary, though not dominant, component of the police role. In shallow police bureaucracies that are highly professional, the commitment to service delivery is clearly dominant, implying an almost therapeutic style of social control. In nonbureaucratic agencies lacking high levels of professionalism, the service orientation, while present, consistently competes with a law enforcement orientation toward the police role. Whether these contrasting orientations toward the police role result in a differential administration of justice across different types of police agencies is an empirical question and the focus of the subsequent analysis.

Direct Effects

Before proceeding to the analysis, a brief review of additional literature concerning the influence of organizational properties on police behavior is in order. Most discussions of organizational effects on police behavior focus on the degree of bureaucratization of police departments. There is consensus in the literature that the probability of arrest varies directly with the degree of bureaucratization of a given police agency. In large bureaucratic departments, arrest is more likely than in smaller, fraternal police agencies.

A number of explanations for this difference exist. Several scholars argue that institutional autonomy varies directly with bureaucratization (Silver, 1967; Fogelson, 1977; Miller, 1977; Brown, 1981). Large police agencies are more independent from the communities in which they operate, while smaller police departments are more dependent on the communities they serve. This implies different sources of legitimation for police agencies of varying degrees of bureaucratization. The mandate of large, bureaucratic police departments rests on their image as dispassionate servants of the law. Conversely, small police agencies depend more on community support to legitimize their position. One possible result of this situation might be that small police agencies exchange leniency for public support (Brown, 1981). Thus, in smaller police agencies, external community pressure may constrain the degree to which strict and aggressive law enforcement becomes the dominant operating ethic of the police.

Wilson (1967, 1968) also advances the thesis that the probability of arrest varies directly with the bureaucratization of a police department. Briefly, Wilson's argument is that certain organizational properties of police departments (such as the degree of bureaucratization) result in a specific ethos — a particular set of shared values and beliefs about the administration of justice — which in turn influences the behavior of officers in the field.

Consider Wilson's legalistic department. Legalistic police agencies are generally large, and are characterized by centralized decision making, a number of special squads, and a pronounced rank hierarchy. This organizational structure creates a number of promotional opportunities that can be used as incentives to reward certain types of officer performance. Wilson (1968: 172) is clear on the type of behavior expected of individual patrol officers in legalistic police agencies:

> Whenever he acts on his own initiative or to the extent he can influence the outcome of disorderly situations in which he acts on the initiative of the citizen, the patrolman is expected to take a law enforcement view of his role.

In the aggregate, the operational norm of strict and aggressive law enforcement will result in a greater probability of arrest in legalistic departments. Wilson (1968: 173) argues the position clearly:

> The legalistic style does mean that, on the whole, the department will produce many arrests and citations. . . . When police

are called by the public to intervene, they are likely to intervene formally, by making an arrest or urging the signing of a
complaint, rather than informally, as through conciliation or by
delaying an arrest in hopes that the situation will take care of
itself.

Thus, one potential consequence of the bureaucratization of police
agencies is to increase the likelihood of arrest in police-suspect
encounters.

In contrast to the legalistic department, watchman and service-
style police agencies operate under a mandate of order maintenance
rather than law enforcement. In smaller police agencies, several
factors converge to lessen the probability of arrest. First, smaller
police agencies have fewer specialized units to which patrol officers
can aspire. This lack of specialization has important implications for
officer behavior. According to Wilson (1968: 155), in small police
agencies "there will be few places to which one can be transferred in
the department and few incentives to seek transfer there." The behavioral implication of relatively little organizational specialization is
clear: "If there are few rewards outside of the patrol force there is little
incentive to work hard to get out" (Wilson, 1968: 155). Thus, in
smaller police agencies, production norms (often measured by the
number of arrests) are less significant than in larger, more bureaucratic police departments.

Additionally, in smaller agencies, police work is more of a craft
than an occupation, and authority is vested more in the individual
officers than in the roles that they occupy. These two factors imply
somewhat different definitions of appropriate police conduct. It is
possible that status within the organization would accrue to individual
officers who demonstrate they can control situations using a number
of interpersonal mechanisms rather than arrest (see, for example,
Muir, 1977). Thus, in small police agencies, it may be the officer who
mediates disputes who is rewarded, while making arrests may indicate an officer's inability to handle such matters.

In the data on which our analysis was conducted, bureaucratization of police agencies was measured as the sum of four standardized
variables representing four components of bureaucratization. The

four variables are (1) specialization, or the degree of horizontal differentiation (measured by the number of occupational divisions within a department), (2) authority structure, or the degree of vertical differentiation (measured by the number of ranks in the department), (3) agency size (measured as the number of sworn and civilian employees), and (4) the percentage of civilian employees in the department. The mean interitem correlation among these four measures was .731.

Arrest probabilities were also hypothesized to covary with other characteristics of police departments. Chief among these was professionalism, usually measured by aggregate education measures. Greater professionalism was hypothesized to decrease the probability of arrest. Cited as support for this position is the tendency of more educated officers to report that they would be less likely to arrest suspected offenders, suggesting that peer support for arrest as a means of handling encounters might be weaker in departments composed of more educated officers (see Finckenauer, 1975). This might be especially true if, as some research suggests, patrol officers rely heavily on peers and colleagues for definitions of appropriate behavior (Skolnick, 1966; Bittner, 1970). Thus, the expectation was that the professionalization/education of police agencies should, with all else held constant, have a negative effect on the probability of arrest in police-suspect encounters.[2]

While the majority of attention devoted to organizational effects on officer behavior has emphasized bureaucratization and professionalization, other organizational traits are occasionally cited as potential determinants of officer behavior. One additional organizational characteristic occasionally mentioned is the degree to which decision making is centralized in the hands of supervisory personnel. The general argument is that increasing the centralization of decision making in police agencies will increase the probability of arrest. This relationship is expected because patrol supervisors are believed to adopt a more formal, legalistic orientation toward the police role than patrol officers, who operate with a more pragmatic orientation toward the law (Manning, 1977). In the analysis that follows, centralization is measured as the proportion of police-suspect encounters that involve patrol supervisor contact with the patrol office.

Some scholars also argue that the behavior of individual police officers is influenced by the tenure composition of the police department (Wilson, 1968). The general contention in the literature is that in more tenured police agencies, officers are less predisposed to the norms of aggressive law enforcement. Indeed, one characteristic of Wilson's fraternal police agency is a more experienced collective of officers. According to Wilson, this organizational feature is partly responsible for the low probability of arrest in these departments. Thus, with all else held constant, police officers in longer-tenured departments might be less likely to invoke the law.

Data and Variables

The data used in the present analysis were collected as part of a larger evaluation of police services conducted in 1977.[3] The data are comparable to previous observational data on police behavior (for example, Reiss, 1971; Sykes and Clark, 1975), in that 5688 police-citizen contacts were observed and recorded by trained civilians riding on 900 patrol shifts. The observational data were collected in the jurisdictions of 24 police departments operating in three metropolitan areas: Rochester, New York; St. Louis, Missouri; and Tampa-St. Petersberg, Florida. In addition to the observational data, patrol officers in each of the 24 departments were interviewed. These interviews were conducted with virtually all the officers who were observed in the field, making it possible to match the responses of individual officers with their observed field behavior. Also, by interviewing officers directly, we were not forced to rely on departmental records for items (for example, average educational levels) that quickly become outdated. In addition to the officers observed in the field, interview data on such items as years of education and experience were collected from additional random samples of patrol officers. Finally, data on many global properties of the police departments were collected (for example, size, number of ranks, and data on organizational structure). One advantage of these data is the considerable variation that exists in the organizational structures of the departments studied. For example, the departments range in size from 13 to over 2000 sworn officers.

Our dependent variable was whether a patrol officer made an arrest, given a contact with a suspect. Previous empirical research on the relationship between organizational properties of police departments and officer behavior has relied on arrest rates as the dependent variable (for example, Wilson, 1967, 1968; Reppetto, 1975; Swanson, 1978), but this means that only that portion of the variance in arrest that lies *between* police departments was examined. By focusing on the individual police-citizen encounter as our ultimate dependent variable, we were able to partition the total variation in arrest decisions into within- and between-department components. This integration of multilevel data helped to determine the relative influence of situational factors and organizational properties on the probability of arrest.

Of the 5688 police-citizen encounters observed, 950 involved police contact with suspected violators. These 950 encounters were the subject of our analysis. At the encounter level, we included a number of variables that previous research has identified as important to the arrest decision. Specifically, we included measures of the seriousness of the offense; the sex, race, and age of the suspect; the dispositional preferences of victims (if the encounter involved a victim); the relational distance between the suspect and victim; the demeanor of the suspect; and whether or not a supervisor was involved in the decision to invoke the law. (For recent reviews of previous research using these variables, see Black, 1980; Sherman, 1980; Smith and Visher, 1981.) Additionally, we considered such officer characteristics as experience, level of education, race, and degree of job satisfaction.[4] A detailed description of the coding of these variables and their respective means and standard deviations is presented in Table 3.1.

Interorganizational Variation in the Decision to Arrest

We began our analysis by examining the total effect of police departments on arrest decisions. Table 3.2 lists the unadjusted probabilities of arrest for each of the 24 police departments. The number of cases (encounters) on which these probabilities are based is given in

TABLE 3.1   Description of Variables in Analysis (N = 950)

Variable Name	Description	M	s.d.
Arrest	1 = suspect arrested; 0 = suspect released	.182	.386
Offense	Offense seriousness scale using the following categories: (1) public order offenses (e.g., disorderly conduct, vagrancy); (2) vice offenses; (3) minor property crime (e.g., vandalism); (4) moderate property crime (e.g., shoplifting); (5) serious property crime (e.g., burglary); (6) minor violent (e.g., simple assault); (7) serious violent (e.g., aggravated assault, armed robbery)	3.414	1.929
Black suspect	Dummy variable for black suspect	.478	.499
Male suspect	Dummy variable for male suspect	.797	.402
Suspect age	Three-category indicator of suspect age: (1) under 18; (2) 19-35; (3) over 35	1.928	.737
Victim informal	Victim requests that officer handle matter informally (e.g., just warn offending party)	.201	.401
Victim formal	Victim requests that an arrest be made	.097	.296
Victim/Suspect known	Dummy variable indicating that the victim and suspect are friends, neighbors, or otherwise acquainted	.352	.478
Victim Suspect strangers	Dummy variable indicating that the victim and suspect are strangers	.096	.294
Suspect Antagonistic	Three-category indicator of the demeanor of the suspect: (0) cooperative, (1) verbally hostile, (2) physically hostile	.227	.656
Supervisor	Dummy variable indicating whether a supervisor was contacted during the encounter for instructions or advice or came to the encounter while it was in progress	.201	.401
Officer experience	Officer experience in years	5.691	3.740
Officer job satisfaction	Likert-type item assessing the officer's perception of working conditions: range 0 (low) to 8 (high)	2.410	2.530
Black	Dummy variable coded 1 if black officer	.160	.367

(continued)

TABLE 3.1 (Continued)

Variable Name	Description	M	s.d.
Officer education	Officer education in years	13.960	1.518
Bureaucratization	Sum of standardized variables consisting of (1) the log of the number of employees (M = 5.880, s.d. = 1.604); (2) the number of ranks in the department (M = 6.110, s.d. = 1.751); (3) the number of specific divisions in the department—e.g., juvenile, public relations, SWAT (M = 8.294, s.d. = 3.682); (4) the percentage of civilian employees in the department (M = .228, s.d. = .088)	.000	3.269

parentheses. The data indicate that the probability of arrest does indeed vary across police departments, but a number of interesting questions may not be addressed based on the data presented in this form. For example, do the differences in the probability of arrest between departments reflect the influence of department structure per se, or do they indicate the differential composition of encounter-level covariates across the 24 departments? Hauser (1970) has argued that any claim of organizational effects must demonstrate that relevant individual variables have been controlled for. Officers in Department 20 invoked the law relatively infrequently (probability of arrest, .057), but it may simply be the case that the offenses that the officers encountered were of such a minor nature that a formal response (arrest) was not likely in the first place. Data addressing these types of issues are presented in Table 3.3

This table reports a series of OLS regression models that collectively address the hypothesis that organizational differences contribute uniquely to the probability of arrest. The columns in group I regress arrests on fourteen encounter-level covariates. The results show that 26.1 percent of the variance in arrest can be accounted for by situational factors. Specifically, arrest is more likely: (1) as the offense becomes more serious, (2) if a victim requests that an arrest be made, (3) if the suspect is antagonistic, or (4) if a supervisor is involved in the encounter either in person or by radio. Conversely, the probability of arrest is significantly decreased if a victim requests an informal resolution of the problem.[5]

TABLE 3.2   Unadjusted Probability of Arrest for 24
             Police Departments

Department Code	Probability of Arrest
10	.176 (170)
20	.057 (35)
25	.100 (20)
30	.333 (6)
40	.220 (91)
50	.265 (49)
55	.140 (50)
60	.140 (43)
62	.162 (37)
64	.150 (20)
66	.056 (18)
68	.182 (22)
70	.251 (179)
80	.120 (50)
81	.095 (21)
82	.320 (25)
83	0 (7)
84	.333 (6)
85	.056 (18)
86	.222 (18)
87	.125 (8)
88	.235 (17)
89	.231 (13)
90	.037 (27)
Grand Mean	.182
Total N	(950)

Group II presents a different set of regression estimates for the probability of arrest. Here we regress arrests on a set of 23 dummy variables representing the 24 police departments. To identify this equation, we omitted a large metropolitan police agency in the state of New York. The intercept from this equation (.176) represents the average probability of arrest for encounters observed in the omitted department (Department 10). The slope estimates are deviations in the mean probability of arrest for each department from the probability of arrest in the missing department. This model indicates that arrest is significantly more likely to occur in three departments (50, 70, and 82) and significantly less likely in five departments (20, 66, 83, 85, and 90) relative to the omitted department.[6]

The most interesting feature of group II is the relatively small R^2 (.035). This means that only 3.5 percent of the total variance in arrest lies between the 24 police departments studied. It is important to note that this figure represents an upper bound to the proportion of variance in arrest that can be explained directly by any or all police department characteristics (Alexander and Griffin, 1976). This fact is even more interesting when we consider the substantial organizational variability between these police agencies on a number of organizational structure measures such as size, percentage of civilians, specialization, and number of ranks.

In group III we combine the variables in the two previous data groups into a single equation. This equation permits a direct test of the hypothesis that police agencies influence the probability of arrest in a fashion that is independent of individual-level covariates. Specifically, the net influence of police departments, controlling for the fourteen encounter-level variables, is reflected in the difference in the R^2s between group III and group I (.293 − .261 = .032). Thus, police agencies contribute slightly more than a 3 percent increment to the explained variance. While this difference is statistically significant (F = 1.79; d.f. = 23,912), it is relatively small and would hardly substantiate any claim that a major portion of the variance in police arrest decisions is uniquely attributable to the influence of police organizations per se.

Note also that there are several changes in the significance of the slope coefficients between groups II and III for the departments dummies. The reason for this is that the slopes for the departments in group III represent deviations of the *adjusted* departmental means on the dependent variable (arrest) from the *adjusted* mean of arrest for the omitted department.[7]

We are now in a position to answer the question of whether the observed differences in the probability of arrest across police agencies represent the impact of organizations per se. Recall that the probabil-

TABLE 3.3 Regression of Arrest on Encounter-Level Covariates and Police Department Dummies

	I			II			III		
Variable	*b*	*S.E.*	*B***	*b*	*S.E.*	*B*	*b*	*S.E.*	*B*
Offense	.043*	.006	.214				.044*	.006	.217
Black suspect	.035	.025	.046				.037	.027	.047
Male suspect	.014	.030	.015				.011	.031	.001
Suspect age	-.009	.016	-.017				-.019	.017	-.036
Victim informal	-.091*	.036	-.094				-.104*	.036	-.107
Victim formal	.281*	.044	.216				.278*	.044	.213
Victim/Suspect known	-.057	.032	-.071				-.061	.032	-.076
Victim/Suspect strangers	.061	.046	.046				.041	.047	.301
Suspect antagonistic	.148*	.019	.252				.154*	.019	.262
Supervisor	.150*	.031	.156				.164*	.032	.170
Officer experience	.002	.003	.021				.001	.003	.018
Officer job satisfaction	-.000	.002	-.005				.000	.002	.003
Black officer	.003	.038	.002				.001	.039	.001
Officer education	.000	.008	.001				.001	.008	.003
Dept 20				-.119*	.071		-.064	.069	
Dept 25				-.076	.091		-.019	.088	
Dept 30				.157	.160		-.090	.154	
Dept 40				.043	.050		.096*	.048	
Dept 50				.089*	.062		.173*	.060	
Dept 55				-.036	.061		.027	.061	

	b	S.E.	b	S.E.
Dept 60	−.037	.066	.027	.062
Dept 62	−.014	.069	.077*	.068
Dept 64	−.026	.091	.114*	.090
Dept 66	−.121*	.095	.031	.092
Dept 68	.005	.087	.106*	.086
Dept 70	.075*	.041	.107*	.040
Dept 80	−.056	.062	−.025	.062
Dept 81	−.081	.089	.067	.087
Dept 82	.144*	.083	.150*	.080
Dept 83	−.176*	.148	−.056	.141
Dept 84	.157	.160	.144	.153
Dept 85	−.121*	.095	−.148*	.092
Dept 86	.046	.095	.028	.093
Dept 87	−.051	.138	.036	.134
Dept 88	.059	.097	.047	.099
Dept 89	.054	.111	.075	.107
Dept 90	−.139*	.079	−.075	.077
Intercept	−.041		.176		−.082
R^2	.261		.035		.293

*Significant at less than .05 except for department dummies, where significance indicates that the metric coefficient exceeds its standard error.

**b = metric coefficient; S.E. = standard error of b; B = standardized beta.

ity of arrest in Department 20 was low (.057, Table 3.2). The slope for this department (−.119) from group II in Table 3.3 indicates that this difference was significant relative to the probability of arrest in our omitted department (Department 10, p = .176). But when individual level determinants of arrest are controlled for (group III) the slope for Department 20 is no longer significant (b = .064, S.E. = .071). This indicates that the difference between the unadjusted probabilities of arrest in Departments 10 and 20 (−.119) is the result of differences in individual-level variables between these two departments, and not that officers in Department 20 are less likely to invoke the law relative to their counterparts in Department 10 (the omitted category). We would add that group III does indicate that officers in Department 85 are significantly less likely to invoke the law, while officers in Departments 40, 50, 62, 64, 68, 70, and 82 are significantly more likely to make arrests after controlling for the influence of situational factors.

Thus, at this point we can note that police departments do have a statistically significant, but relatively small, impact on the probability of arrest after controlling for a number of encounter-level determinants of arrest. In the following section, we examine the influence of specific organizational properties of police departments on the probability of arrest.

Organizational Properties and the Decision to Arrest

Table 3.4 reports a series of equations that regress arrest on a number of measures of organizational properties and individual-level determinants of arrest. Group I examines the effect of six organizational characteristics on the probability of arrest, with controls for encounter-level covariates. The organizational properties examined are: (1) the level of bureaucratization, (2) the average educational level of police officers in a given department, (3) the proportion of black officers on the force, (4) the average level of officer job satisfaction, (5) the mean number of years of officer experience, and (6) the proportion of encounters involving a supervisor.

TABLE 3.4 Regression of Arrest on Encounter-Level Covariates and Organizational Variables

Variable	I b	I S.E.	I B#	II b	II S.E.	II B
Offense	.042**	.007	.211	.044**	.007	.220
Black suspect	.042	.026	.055	.036	.024	.047
Male suspect	.012	.030	.012	.013	.029	.014
Suspect age	−.014	.017	−.026	−.014	.016	−.027
Victim informal	−.099**	.036	−.103	−.100**	.036	−.104
Victim formal	.275**	.044	.211	.269**	.044	.206
Victim/Suspect known	−.060*	.033	−.075	−.058*	.033	−.071
Victim/Suspect strangers	.057	.046	.044	.056	.046	.043
Suspect antagonistic	.146**	.019	.249	.155**	.019	.263
Supervisor	.167**	.033	.173	.159**	.032	.165
Officer experience	.002	.004	.023	.003	.003	.034
Officer job satisfaction	−.000	.002	−.002	−.001	.002	−.013
Black officer	.000	.039	.000	.013	.038	.012
Officer education	.000	.008	.001	.000	.008	.001
Organizational Properties						
M Supervisor	−.029	.129	−.009			
M Officer experience	−.016*	.008	−.073			
M Officer job satisfaction	−.020	.023	−.040			
M Black officers	.002	.109	.001			
M Officer education	−.066*	.035	−.066			
Bureaucratization	.008*	.004	.071			
Department Groupings						
High bureaucratization and high education				.107**	.034	.139
High bureaucratization and low education				−.005	.039	−.005
Low bureaucratization and low education				.065*	.040	.060
Intercept	1.141			−.104		
R^2	.272			.277		

#b = metric coefficient; S.E. = standard error of b; B = standardized beta.
*Significant at less than .10 level.
**Significant at less than .05 level.

It was found that the probability of arrest varies directly with the level of departmental bureaucratization. Officers in more bureaucratic departments are somewhat more likely to arrest suspected violators after controlling for other organizational properties and encounter-level covariates. Thus, to the extent that Wilson's departmental styles are conceptualized as reflecting differences along a continuum of bureaucratization, these results support Wilson's thesis.

Additional support for Wilson's argument is reflected in the negative effect of mean officer experience on the likelihood of arrest. Wilson noted that a major component of the watchman police department was a tendency for officers to be older, with more years of tenure. Our analysis shows that officers in departments characterized by higher average levels of experience are less likely to invoke the law. We would stress the fact that the experience level of an individual officer involved in an encounter had no effect on the probability of arrest (b = .002). This implies that patrol officers' propensity to arrest is influenced instead by the tenure composition of the department.

Several scholars have characterized police departments as punishment-centered bureaucracies in which officers develop individual survival strategies to help cope with the uncertainties of their occupational milieu (Manning, 1977; Brown, 1981). One of the best survival strategies is a policy that revolves around the avoidance of risk. Making an arrest can involve occupational risk. In addition, the arrest could be defined by the organization as a bad arrest, and complaints against the arresting officer could be filed, potentially prompting the department to take action against the officer. We suspect that more experienced officers are more committed, in the aggregate, to an operational ethic dedicated to minimizing occupational risk, and that this orientation to law enforcement is more intricately woven into the operating style of longer-tenured departments.

Officers in more professional departments (those with higher average levels of officer education) are less likely to make arrests. We would note that individual officer's educational level had no effect on the probability of arrest (b = .000). Our finding of no relationship between individual officer education and the probability of arrest is contrary to the research of Bozza (1973), who did find a positive relationship. It should be noted, however, that this difference may reflect both the limited nature of Bozza's sample (24 police officers in a California department) and our use of additional multivariate controls. An additional test of the effect of officer education on arrest decisions appears in Finckenauer's (1975) study of 98 police recruits in New Jersey. Based on responses to vignettes, Finckenauer found that college-educated officers were less likely to invoke the criminal process.

In the current data there is a negative effect of departmental educational levels on the probability of arrest in individual encounters. The propensity of patrol officers to arrest was determined instead by the educational composition of the police department as a whole. Finckenauer's results also indicate that support for arrest as a means of dispute settlement is weaker among more educated officers. If this is the case, it is plausible that in departments with higher average educational levels, the decision to arrest may lack strong informal-group support. Although the specific structural mechanism that facilitates this process is unclear, our results indicate that officers in more educated departments are significantly less likely to invoke the law. At the same time, however, we should stress that it is only when education is treated as an *organizational* property of police departments that it influences officer behavior.

To this point, we have examined the influence of six specific organizational properties on the probability of arrest. We are now in a position to determine what proportion of the variance in arrest that is uniquely attributable to the influence of police departments can be accounted for by the six organizational properties included in group I of Table 3.4. Recall that the difference between the R^2s of groups III and I in Table 3.3 represented the total proportion of arrest variance that can be ascribed to the influence of organizational characteristics $(.293 - .261 = .032)$. In contrast, the difference in R^2s between group I of Table 3.4 and group I of Table 3.3 represents the increase in arrest variance due to six specific organizational traits $(.272 - .261 = .011)$. Thus, our six measured organizational properties account for 34.4 percent of the total variation in arrest that is due to the influence of police departments (.011/.032 = .344). We stress that the proportion of variance in arrest decisions that is attributable to the influence of police organizations per se is relatively small (.032); however, the tenure and educational composition of the department, as well as the level of departmental bureaucratization, directly influence the probability of arrest independent of the specific features of police-citizen encounters.[8]

Finally, group II in Table 3.4 addresses the question of whether there is any direct effect on the probability of arrest when departments are cross-classified according to bureaucratization and professionalism. To identify this equation, service-style departments (low bureaucratization and high professionalism) was the omitted category. The slope coefficients for department types in group II indicate differences in the adjusted mean of arrest relative to the category left out. They indicate that the adjusted probability of arrest in legalistic departments is .107 higher than the adjusted probability of arrest in service-style departments. Moreover, this difference is significant at less than the .05 level. Interestingly, the adjusted probability of arrest was highest in departments that are both highly bureaucratic and highly professional, whereas bureaucratization alone does not increase the probability of arrest, as evidenced by the nonsignificant negative coefficient for militaristic departments (highly bureaucratic, but with low levels of professionalism). These results are generally congruent with expectations derived from Wilson's thesis, although the coefficient for militaristic departments was unexpected. (We anticipated that militaristic departments would have *higher* probabilities of arrest than service-style or fraternal departments.)

Correlates of Arrest:
A Within-Department Analysis

From the analysis presented thus far, it is clear that situational aspects of police-citizen encounters (such as the dispositional preferences of victims or the seriousness of an offense) are far more powerful determinants of arrest than are the properties of police organizations. But it would be premature at this point to discount totally the influence of police organizations on officer behavior. Much of Wilson's theoretical work suggests that the organizational properties of police departments condition the effects of individual-level determinants of arrest. For example, he argues that racial disparity in the probability of arrest is greatest in fraternal police agencies, becoming less pronounced as departments become more bureaucratic. Technically, this is an issue of interaction between encounter-level covariates of arrest and the type of police agency in which the encounter occurs. The thesis can be examined by estimating a separate model of arrest for each of our four types of police departments (legalistic, militaristic, service-style, and fraternal). Data from such an analysis are presented in Table 3.5.

This table lists the results of a regression of arrests on our fourteen encounter-level covariates within each departmental grouping. Of the 950 total encounters with suspects, 362 were observed in legalistic departments, 205 in militaristic departments, 241 in service-style departments, and 142 in fraternal police agencies.

Seriousness of offense had a positive affect on the probability of arrest across all departmental contexts. Thus, we did not find support for Wilson's thesis that the seriousness of an offense is a stronger predictor of arrest in legalistic departments. Instead, officers operating in diverse organizational contexts weigh the nature of an offense equally in their decisions to invoke the law, causing the probability of arrest to vary directly with offense severity in a manner that is independent of organizational context.

In addition, there is relatively little interorganizational variation in the influence of suspect characteristics on the probability of arrest. Independent of other aspects of an encounter, black suspects are somewhat more likely to be arrested by militaristic police departments (high bureaucratization and low professionalization), but the magnitude of this disadvantage is not statistically significant (b = .095, S.E. = .050). In these data, the probability of arrest was also not directly affected by the sex of the suspect. Males are slightly more likely than females to be arrested in legalistic and militaristic depart-

TABLE 3.5 Regression of Arrest on Encounter-Level Covariates Within Organizational Groupings Based on Bureaucratization and Education

Variable	Legalistic			Militaristic			Service			Fraternal		
	b	S.E.	B**	b	S.E.	B	b	S.E.	B	b	S.E.	B
Offense	.047*	.011	.219	.031*	.013	.174	.051*	.012	.274	.057*	.020	.257
Black suspect	.042	.042	.050	.095	.050	.130	-.000	.051	-.000	-.016	.069	-.021
Male suspect	.053	.050	.051	.073	.066	.075	-.050	.056	-.058	-.006	.075	-.006
Suspect age	-.118*	.027	-.010	.022	.034	.045	-.001	.032	-.002	-.006	.046	-.222
Victim informal	-.121*	.056	-.126	-.059	.078	-.062	-.055	.077	-.059	-.039	.109	-.036
Victim formal	.342*	.067	.277	.186	.095	.145	.192	.100	.133	.131	.136	.091
Victim/Suspect known	-.050	.055	-.057	-.041	.064	-.054	-.174*	.068	-.222	.077	.089	.097
Victim/Suspect strangers	.032	.074	.025	.000	.107	.000	-.050	.106	-.035	.206*	.098	.167
Suspect antagonistic	.167*	.034	.236	.149*	.031	.376	.100*	.044	.151	.228*	.066	.256
Supervisor	.274*	.059	.230	.190*	.071	.195	.144*	.054	.188	.050	.085	.058
Officer experience	-.001	.005	-.012	.005	.008	.073	.001	.008	.006	-.002	.018	-.009
Officer job satisfaction	-.000	.004	-.004	-.002	.003	-.054	.001	.004	.024	-.003	.007	-.034
Black officer	.040	.061	.033	-.036	.087	-.040	.089	.081	.093	-.078	.101	-.069
Officer education	.004	.014	.014	-.010	.018	-.055	.042*	.019	.147	-.018	.023	-.072
Intercept	-.107			-.068			-.602			.405		
R^2	.351			.331			.235			.274		
N	362			205			241			142		

*Significant effect at less than .05 level.
**b = metric coefficient; S.E. = standard error of b; B = standardized beta.

ments, but the magnitude of this disadvantage was not significant. Thus, the race and sex of suspected violators do not directly influence the probability of arrest in these four departmental contexts.

A suspect's age, however, was found to have a significant negative effect on the probability of arrest in legalistic police agencies (highly bureaucratic and highly professional). Closer examination of the data indicates that this effect is attributable to the propensity of police in legalistic agencies to respond more punitively to youthful offenders. In the legalistic police agencies studied, police officers arrested 22.1 percent of suspects under the age of eighteen, compared to 12.5, 12.7, and 7.5 percent in fraternal, service-style, and militaristic departments, respectively. Thus, there is some support in these data for the notion that police officers in legalistic departments treat the infractions of youthful offenders more seriously than do officers in other types of police agencies. We should note, however, that neither the bureaucratization nor the professionalism of a social control agency increases by itself the probability of arrest of youthful offenders. Thus, in highly bureaucratic, nonprofessional (militaristic) agencies, youthful offenders are no more likely to be arrested. Also, in non-bureaucratic, professional (service-style) agencies, juveniles are no more likely to be arrested. It is only in agencies that are both bureaucratic and professional that the law is more likely to be invoked against youthful offenders.

The dispositional preferences of victims have a strong effect on the probability of arrest, but only in legalistic departments (high bureaucratization and high professionalism). Given the assumed emphasis on the interpersonal aspects of dispensing justice in service and fraternal police agencies, one could argue that it is in these contexts that the dispositional preferences of victims should have a stronger impact on the behavior of police officers, but such an expectation overlooks an important legal dimension of the dispositional preferences of victims. By requesting that an arrest be made, the victim is indicating that he or she is more likely to cooperate in the subsequent adjudication of the case. Conversely, by requesting that the matter be handled informally, without an arrest, the victim is announcing that future cooperation in the adjudication process may be problematic. Thus, the finding that police officers in legalistic departments are more responsive to the dispositional preferences of victims is consistent with the thesis that officers in legalistic departments attach more weight to variables with legal implications.

In service and fraternal police agencies, the probability of arrest reflects the relational distance between the suspect and the victim (see Black, 1971). Controlling for all other variables in the model, the probability that officers in service-style departments will invoke the law is reduced by 17.4 percent if the victim and suspect are related or acquainted. Conversely, the probability of arrest by fraternal police agencies is increased by 20.6 percent if the victim and suspect are strangers. In both legalistic and militaristic police departments, the probability of arrest is not directly influenced by the relational distance between suspect and victim. Collectively, these findings reflect the informal nature of dispute settlement in service-style and fraternal police agencies.

In all types of police departments, antagonistic suspects are more likely to be arrested than are their nonantagonistic counterparts. This finding is consistent with numerous studies documenting the liabilities of disrespectful behavior toward police officers (Piliavin and Briar, 1964; Black and Reiss, 1970; Lundman, 1974; Sykes and Clark, 1975; Smith and Visher, 1981). What is interesting about the current analysis is that while antagonistic behavior increases the probability of arrest across all departmental contexts, it has its most profound effect in the context of fraternal police agencies. In legalistic and militaristic police departments, officers are seen as instruments of the law to a greater degree, while in service-style and fraternal police agencies, authority rests more in the person. Thus, antagonistic behavior may present more of a challenge to the authority of the individual officer in service-style and fraternal departments than in legalistic and militaristic departments. The fact that officers in service-style departments to do not react as punitively to antagonistic suspects as do officers in fraternal departments may reflect the influence of greater professionalism (education) in service-style departments.

Finally, the influence of a supervisor on the probability of arrest is conditional on departmental context. Manning (1977) has argued that a police officer's orientation to his or her occupational role varies across the rank hierarchy. Officers in lower ranks (patrol officers) tend to see their role as primarily peace keeping, although there may be considerable within-department variation on this point. Given their frequent contact with the public, patrol officers develop a pragmatic orientation toward the law. In this view, the law is seen as only one resource available to police officers to facilitate their peacekeeping function. As one moves up the rank hierarchy (for example, to patrol supervisor), conceptions of the police role change. Abstract ideals of justice replace pragmatic orientations to the law. Additionally, occupants of higher ranks may subscribe more to the institutionalized mythology of police work as primarily law enforcement.

If Manning's insights are correct, we would expect that in more bureaucratic departments, patrol supervisors might bring to encounters a distinctive set of expectations regarding appropriate police action. In highly bureaucratic departments, patrol supervisors are more clearly field commanders, while in fraternal or service-style police agencies they are more likely to participate in encounters as equals, providing backup and other assistance rather than issuing directives or commands. We found in both bureaucratic types of police departments (legalistic and militaristic) that if a patrol supervisor was involved in an encounter, the probability of arrest was significantly increased ($b = .274$ in legalistic departments, $b = .190$ in militaristic departments). In service-style departments, the influence of a supervisor was also significant ($b = .144$), though smaller in magnitude. Only in fraternal police agencies did the involvement of a supervisor have no significant effect on the probability of arrest.

CONCLUSIONS

Our analysis has shown that police decisions to invoke the law are influenced by the demands of the immediate situation, certain organizational properties of police departments, and the organizational context in which police-citizen encounters occur. By far the most important factors influencing the arrest decisions of police officers are certain aspects of the police-citizen encounter itself, such as the dispositional preferences of complainants, the seriousness of the offense, the relational distance between suspect and victim, and the involvement of a supervisor in the encounter. Three properties of police agencies (mean officer education, mean officer experience, and the degree of bureaucratization) directly influence the probability of arrest, but the strength of these effects is uniformly small. While organizational properties have little direct influence on the probability of arrest, the present analysis has also shown that the influence of several situational variables on the decision to arrest is conditional on the organizational context in which the police-citizen encounter occurs (see Table 3.5).

What are the implications of these findings for using arrests as a measure of police performance? First, any measure of performance must be relative to some set of objectives or goals. Also, objectives and goals must be specific to a particular unit of analysis (for example, officers or police agencies). Evidence emerged from interviews with organizational elites (police chiefs and heads of patrol operations) indicating that considerable variation exists across police agencies in the amount of emphasis that police administrators place on service-delivery versus crime-control aspects of patrol work. Wilson argued that such variations in the organizational ethos are manifested and reflected in the attitudes of organizational elites. Moreover, differences in the elites' attitudes regarding the police role systematically vary by the classification of department types presented in Figure 3.1. Thus, on one dimension there appears to be support for the thesis that differences in organizational ethos covary with the structural characteristics of police agencies (that is, bureaucratization and professionalism).

Differences in organizational ethos regarding the administration of justice result in two distinct empirical observations: First, the direct influence of organizational properties on the probability of arrest, while statistically significant, is very slight at best. Indeed, organizational properties or styles only account for approximately 3 percent of the variance in arrest after encounter-level covariates of arrest have been controlled for.

This suggests that differences between departments in the volume of arrests reflect factors other than differences in the propensity of officers to make an arrest given an encounter with a suspect. Since the volume of arrests is a function of the number and type of police-suspect encounters weighted by the propensity to arrest in any given encounter, we would argue that the primary source of interorganizational variations in the volume of arrests are the differences in the types of encounters that police officers have in different types of police agencies.

The stronger discriminating influence of situational factors relative to organizational properties on the decision to arrest is not surprising. Police work involves controlling people and situations, and officers must often make quick decisions without the luxury of extended deliberation. The need to act quickly in potentially volatile situations forces police officers to rely on aspects of the encounter itself for clues as to whether or not an arrest would be an appropriate action to take. While the encounter itself provides some information on which officers can act, the police organization determines the relative weight that officers attach to various aspects of police-citizen encounters. Thus, for example, the dispositional preferences of victims are important determinants of police behavior in legalistic police departments (highly bureaucratic and highly professional) but exert no influence on officers' decisions to arrest in fraternal police agencies (shallow bureaucracies with low levels of professionalism).

In all cases, the use of arrest data for comparative purposes across police agencies must consider the centrality of the crime-control function (and hence the emphasis is placed on arrest) across the departments being compared. Current results indicate that to understand the determinants of arrest, one must consider the type of police agency responsible for the decision to arrest. Police in different types of police agencies *do* behave differently, and to deny this fact is to deny one important aspect of the reality of police work.

NOTES

1. Several studies based on observational data of police-citizen encounters have found that the probability of arrest in any given encounter is quite low. In a study of police-juvenile contacts, Black and Reiss (1970) found that only 15 percent of the encounters that could have ended in arrest actually did so. A replication of the Black and Reiss study by Lundman et al. (1978) found a similarly low proportion of encounters ending in arrest (16 percent). Moreover, this low probability of arrest does

not apply only to juveniles. In a study of arrest decisions for both juveniles and adults, Smith and Visher (1981) report that arrest occurred in only 18 percent of police contacts with suspected violators.

2. The correlation between our indicator of bureaucratization and the average educational level of officers in our sample of 24 departments is .271 which, while significantly different from zero, is far short of the often assumed one-to-one correspondence between these two variables.

3. The Police Services Study was conducted under the auspices of the Workshop in Political Theory and Policy Analysis at Indiana University and the Center for Urban and Regional Studies at the University of North Carolina at Chapel Hill. Funding was made possible from National Science Foundation grant GI43949 and from grant 78NIAX0020 from the National Institute of Justice.

4. We have selected these officer characteristics for analysis on the basis of arguments in the extant literature that they are related to the decision to arrest (see generally, Sherman, 1980). Past research suggests that more educated (Bozza, 1973), less experienced (Friedrich, 1977), and more occupationally satisfied officers (Friedrich, 1977) make more arrests, but the majority of these "officer effects" are inferred from simple bivariate relationships. Additionally, these officer traits, when aggregated across police departments, become indicators of meaningful organizational properties that are substantively different from the individual-level measures. Consider officer education levels: The aggregate level of officer education (the average years of education for each officer) in a specific department is an indicator of departmental professionalism, which has potentially different implications from the education level of a specific officer. This distinction is especially acute when one considers the high degree of occupational solidarity among police officers. We suspect that, as a result, police officers are especially sensitive to the influence of colleagues and that their work behavior is potentially shaped by their expectations of how other officers will (or at least might) respond to their actions. Thus, these officer traits were selected because they have received attention from previous researchers and, when aggregated, are indicators of meaningful organizational traits.

5. Because we used a binary dependent variable, our estimated slopes represent shifts in the marginal probability of arrest. For example, the slope coefficient for a victim requesting that an arrest be made (.281) implies that on the average, holding all other variables in the equation constant, a request for an arrest by a victim increases the probability of arrest by 28.1 percent.

6. Because of the small number of observations in most departments, we employed a less stringent criterion of statistical significance for the slopes of departmental dummies. Specifically, if the metric coefficient for a department dummy exceeded its standard error, we identified this effect as significant. We have chosen this criterion because variables whose slopes exceed their standard errors result in increments to the adjusted R^2, while variables that fail to meet this criterion impair prediction and produce decrements to the adjusted R^2 (see Rao and Miller, 1971: 37).

7. Specifically, these deviations are from the mean probability of arrest in the omitted department after the fourteen individual-level covariates have been controlled for.

8. If we ran an aggregate regression model using 24 cases (the number of departments) where we regressed the adjusted mean of arrest on our six organizational properties, the R^2 from that equation would also be .344. While this would give the impression of better explanatory power of our six measured organizational properties, we would have to emphasize the fact that this would only refer to the variance in arrest that lies between departments. Thus, while these six organizational traits account for 34.4 percent of the between-department variance in arrest, they only account for 3.2 percent of the total variance in arrest.

REFERENCES

ALEXANDER, K.L. and L.J. GRIFFIN (1976) "School district effects on academic achievement: a reconsideration." American Sociological Review 41: 144-151.

BANTON, M. (1964) The Policeman in the Community. New York: Basic Books.

BECKER, H. (1963) Outsiders. New York: Free Press.

BITTNER, E. (1970) The Function of Police in Modern Society. Washington, DC: National Institute of Mental Health.

—— (1967) "The police on skid row: a study of peace keeping." American Sociological Review 32: 699-715.

BLACK, D. (1980) The Manner and Customs of the Police. New York: Academic Press.

—— (1971) "The social organization of arrest." Stanford Law Review 23: 63-77.

—— (1970) "The production of crime rates." American Sociological Review 35: 733-748.

—— (1968) "Police encounters and social organization: an observational study." Ph.D. dissertation, University of Michigan.

—— and A.J. REISS, Jr. (1970) "Police control of juveniles." American Sociological Review 35: 63-77.

—— (1967) "Patterns of behavior in police and citizen transactions," pp. 1-139 in Studies in Crime and Law Enforcement in Major Metropolitan Areas, Vol. 2. Washington, DC: Government Printing Office.

BOZZA, C.M. (1973) "Motivations guiding policemen in the arrest process." Journal of Police Science and Administration 1: 468-476.

BROWN, M.K. (1981) Working the Street. New York: Russell Sage Foundation.

CLARK, J.P. and R. SYKES (1974) "Some determinants of police organization and practice in a modern industrial democracy," pp. 455-494 in D. Glaser (ed.) Handbook of Criminology. Beverly Hills, CA: Sage.

ERIKSON, K. (1962) "Notes on the sociology of deviance." Social Problems 9: 307-314.

FINCKENAUER, J. (1975) "Higher education and police discretion." Journal of Police Science and Administration 3: 450-457.

FOGELSON, R. (1977) Big City Police. Cambridge, MA: Harvard University Press.

FRIEDRICH, R.J. (1977) "The impact of organization, individual and situational factors on police behavior," Ph. D. dissertation, University of Michigan.

HAUSER, R. M. (1970) "Context and consex: a cautionary tale." American Journal of Sociology 75: 645-664.

KITSUSE, J. I. (1962) "Societal reaction to deviant behavior." Social Problems 9: 247-256.

LIPSKY, M. (1980) Street-Level Bureaucracy. New York: Russell Sage Foundation.

LUNDMAN, R. (1974) "Routine arrest practices: a commonweal perspective." Social Problems 22: 127-141.

——— R. SYKES, and J. P. clark (1978) "Police control of juveniles." Journal of Research in Crime and Delinquency 15: 74-91.

MANNING, P. K. (1977) Police Work: The Social Organization of Policing. Cambridge, MA: MIT Press.

MILLER, W. (1977) Cops and Bobbies. Chicago: University of Chicago Press.

MUIR, W. K. (1977) Police: Streetcorner Politicians. Chicago: University of Chicago Press.

PILIAVIN, I. and S. BRIAR (1964) "Police encounters with juveniles." American Journal of Sociology 70: 206-214.

RAO, P. and R. L. MILLER (1971) Applied Econometrics. Belmont, CA: Wadsworth Press.

REISS, A.J. (1980) "Variation in criminal justice research," pp. 357-379 in M. Klein and K. Teilman (eds.) Handbook of Criminal Justice Evaluation. Beverly Hills, CA: Sage.

——— (1971) The Police and the Public. New Haven, CT: Yale University Press.

REMBAUT, R. G. and E. BITTNER (1979) "Changing conceptions of the police role," pp. 239-289 in N. Morris and M. Tonry (eds.) Crime and Justice: An Annual Review of Research. Chicago: University of Chicago Press.

REPPETTO, R. (1975) "The influence of police organizational style on crime control effectiveness." Journal of Police Science and Administration 3: 274-279.

SHERMAN, L. W. (1980) "Causes of police behavior: the current state of quantitative research." Journal of Research in Crime and Delinquency 17: 69-100.

SILVER, A. (1967) "The demand for order in civil society: a review of some themes in the history of urban crime, police and riot," in D. Bordua (ed.) The Police: Six Sociological Essays. New York: John Wiley.

SKOLNICK, J. (1966) Justice Without Trial. New York: John Wiley.

SMITH, D. A. and C. A. VISHER (1981) "Street-level justice: situational determinants of police arrest decisions." Social Problems 29: 167-177.

SWANSON, C. (1978) "The influence of organization and environment on arrest practices in major U.S. cities." Policy Studies Journal 7: 390-398.

SYKES, R. and J. P. CLARK (1975) "A theory of deference exchange in police-civilian encounters." American Journal of Sociology 81: 584-600.

TIFFT, L. (1975) "Control systems, social basis of power and power exercise in police organizations." Journal of Police Science and Administration 3: 66-76.

TURK, A. T. (1969) Criminality and the Legal Order. Chicago: Rand McNally.

——— (1966) "Conflict and criminality." American Sociological Review 31: 338-352.

WHITAKER, G. P., S. MASTROFSKI, E. OSTROM, R. B. PARKS, and S. PERCY (1982) Basic Issues in Police Performance. Washington, DC: National Institute of Justice.

WILSON, J. Q. (1968) Varieties of Police Behavior. Cambridge, MA: Harvard University Press.

——— (1967) "The police and the delinquent in two cities," in S. Wheeler and H. M. Hughes (eds.) Controlling Delinquents. New York: John Wiley.

Chapter 4

EQUITY IN POLICE SERVICES

ELINOR OSTROM

In a recent discussion of research on equity in urban service delivery, Rich (1982: 4) comments that he was "struck by the fact that research in this area is even less cumulative than in most other areas of social-science inquiry." Rich identifies normative and methodological problems that contribute to this lack of cumulation. Disagreement about the meaning of equity is the first problem. Because alternative definitions of equity derive from different normative positions, efforts to arrive at a single definition for use in research on urban service distribution cannot be expected to succeed. However, many disagreements among researchers result from their implicit, unconscious use of different definitions of equity. Clarifying the components of those different definitions can help those seeking to measure equity become more precise about the values that their measurements involve.

Rich identifies two methodological problems that adversely affect cumulation in research on equity. The first problem involves the issue

AUTHOR'S NOTE: *The author is appreciative of the support of National Science Foundation grants NSF SES 79-13397 and APR 74-14059 A03. The findings and opinions expressed herein, however, are solely those of the author and do not necessarily reflect those of the foundation. This paper has benefited greatly from the critical review given it by John McIver, Vincent Ostrom, Roger B. Parks, and Gordon P. Whitaker, and the capable typing and editing done by Patty Smith and Teresa Therrien.*

of what should be measured when one is interested in the distribution of urban services. In studies of local policing, for example, scholars measure the tax base, police expenditures and personnel allocation, police activities, crime or victimization rates, and/or citizen attitudes toward and evaluations of the police. All of these are potentially legitimate indicators of police resources, of various stages in the process of police service delivery, or of the final outcomes of that process. Yet little agreement exists on where to take measures of equity in the process of service production and delivery. Rich (1982: 8) argues strongly that "only with outcome measures can we address the questions of equity in service delivery directly." In the same volume, however, Jones (1982) strongly recommends that scholars examine the distribution of resources and efforts in the intermediate stages of production and distribution, arguing that each stage in the process has its own associated costs and benefits.

The second methodological issue identified by Rich relates to problems in defining the appropriate units of analysis for asking questions about equity. All too often, scholars have used census tracts to examine patterns of service distribution. But these units have no intrinsic interest; they are simply used as surrogates for potentially interesting differences among areas such as income or racial composition. Rich urges scholars to use more meaningful, intracity units of analysis, such as the neighborhood boundaries defined by neighborhood associations. For some urban goods and services, no geographical unit is appropriate — for example, if they are not distributed to a particular geographical territory. Further, Rich urges scholars to examine interjurisdictional differences in service delivery patterns, as well as the intrajurisdictional patterns that have so far dominated the research agenda.

In this chapter, I will examine two of the problems identified by Rich as adversely affecting the cumulation of research efforts on the equity of service delivery. The specific service examined will be policing. First, I will discuss a general principle of equity, originally defined by Selten (1978), that may help to illuminate the relationship among different concepts of equity used in recent research. Second, I will examine how the most common indicators of police service are used in research on equity and discuss the problems they generate in interpreting the meaning of different observed distribution patterns.

The third issue — the unit-of-analysis problem — has been examined in a recent study (Ostrom, 1983).

THE CONCEPT OF EQUITY

As Rich points out, in the literature on urban service distribution, the terms "inequality" and "inequity" are frequently used and yet rarely defined. The literature on equality and equity is both vast and contentious (see, for example, Jencks et al., 1972; Miller, 1977, 1981a, 1981b; Okun, 1974; Shoup, 1964; Thurow, 1970). While many different equity criteria have been identified (see Whitaker and Mastrofski, 1976, for a good review), the important work of Levy and his colleagues (1974) on the distribution of urban services to neighborhoods within a large urban jurisdiction has focused the attention of urban scholars on the following three standards for evaluating the equity of service distribution:

(1) *Market Equity* — whether a public agency distributes services to citizens in proportion to the amount of taxes they pay. (Example: more patrol units assigned and/or faster response time to neighborhoods that contribute higher taxes.)

(2) *Equal Opportunity* — whether a public agency distributes services to all citizens equally, regardless of what the citizen contributes in taxes. (Example: patrol units assigned to neighborhoods according to a per capita formula, and response time equal to all calls for service.)

(3) *Equal Results* — whether a public agency distributes services so as to produce equal outcomes for each citizen. (Example: equal crime rates in all neighborhoods, or equal levels of satisfaction with police.)

In addition to these three criteria, a fourth criterion is frequently employed:

(4) *Need* — whether a public agency distributes more services to citizens facing conditions over which they may have little control and with which they need assistance. (Example: faster response time for calls for service involving potential physical harm or higher levels of patrol in "high crime" neighborhoods.)

A General Principle

Selten (1978) points out that almost all specific equity criteria can be understood as special cases of a more general equity principle that applies to many situations in which rewards or costs are allocated to individuals within a group. He defines this general principle in terms of a specific set of rewards allocated over a given set of elements. In order to apply this general concept of equity to the problem of urban service delivery, I will define Selten's reward as a service distributed to individuals living within a defined territory or to groups of people in a set of neighborhoods.

To define Selten's general equity principle, one needs to conceptualize a group of individuals (n) who are allocated a service (s) according to some *standard of distribution*. This standard defines how a measurable service (s_i) will be allocated to every group member (i). The general equity principle also requires a *standard of comparison,* which assigns a positive weight (w_i) to each group member (i).[1] An egalitarian standard of comparison (such as those used in both the equal opportunity and equal results criteria defined above) is simply the case in which $w_i = 1$ for i, . . . n. Although the standard of comparison is the same for equal opportunity and equal results, these two criteria differ in terms of the standard of distribution. The standard of distribution for equal opportunity is based on resources or service activities, while the standard of distribution for equal results utilizes service outcomes. Market equity involves a different standard of comparison. In market equity, $w_i \neq 1$. Rather, each w_i is assigned a weight equal to the amount of taxes paid by the ith citizen. Finally, an equity criterion based on need assigns w_i a weight that measures the problems that an individual faces.

An equitable distribution is defined, then, as a service distribution (s_i, . . . s_n) that satisfies the following condition:

$$\frac{s_1}{w_1} = \frac{s_2}{w_2} = \ldots = \frac{s_n}{w_n}$$

Equitable service distributions allocate the same ratio of service units to weight units for all observations in the set. This definition may be applied to all the equity criteria discussed above. Selten (1978: 293) points out that the definition of an equitable service combination "crucially depends on the standard of distribution and on the standard of comparison which is applied to the situation." This general formulation of the concept of equity provides a way to sort out the various meanings of equity and to overcome the confusion and lack of cumulation described by Rich.

Multiple Indicators of W and S

Three schemes for weighting w are implicit in the equity criteria used for evaluating police service distribution: (1) equal weight to each element in the set (for example, each household or neighborhood), (2) weight proportionate to resources contributed, and (3) weight proportionate to need. Each of these represents a fundamentally different conception of what an equitable distribution should be, and yet all three types of weighting may be used validly in the analysis of equity in service distribution. The choice among them is a normative one involving theories about what government should do for its citizens, but that is not the topic of this chapter.

While standards of comparison (w) are relatively few in number, with each reflecting a distinct normative view, standards of distribution are far more numerous, though often methodologically flawed. For example, some urban scholars have used public resources (tax base, tax rate, or public expenditures) as an indicator for s in their analyses of equity (see, for example, Hill, 1974; Neiman, 1982). When such financial input variables are used as measures of service, it is presumed that public expenditures are directly related to the services actually received by citizens. The notion that expenditures are directly related to activities or output has not been empirically demonstrated, however, and has long been criticized. Schuman and Greenberg (1972: 369), for example, argue:

> The adequacy of the services a city provides its citizens cannot be judged accurately by the amount of money expended or the number of persons paid to provide the services. High levels of either may simply indicate inefficiency, excessive patronage, or some other feature of urban life irrelevant to satisfactory services.

In a more recent analysis, Lewis (1982: 204) asserts that in "no case are expenditures validly employed as proxy measures of government services (outputs)" (see also Merget and Berger, 1982; Rich, 1982).

A major factor affecting expenditures for urban services is the success of unions in winning higher wages and in negotiating production strategies that use more personnel. Municipal expenditures are thus relatively high in northeastern metropolitan areas, where municipal employees are more unionized than in other regions.

> Local political acquiescence to union demands in the Northeast has resulted in municipal work forces that are often far above average in size and in wages. In the early 1970's, in the New York region, there were approximately 40 percent more municipal workers per capita than the national average, and these workers received wages 10-15 percent higher than private sector workers in similar occupations [Schneider, 1980: 551].

Police union contracts frequently specify the use of two officers in each patrol car.[2] Unfortunately, doubling the personnel required to carry out routine patrol duties does not necessarily double the amount of service received by local communities. Higher expenditures for police can represent expenditures made primarily for the comfort and ease of police officers rather than for higher levels of service for citizens.

While most scholars agree that expenditure data are not valid measures of service, finding adequate measures of s for police services is extremely difficult. Thus, many scholars continue to use expenditure data, even while acknowledging the inadequacy of this proxy measure. In reality, the final output of urban policing is reflected in the general state of affairs in a community, such as the level of safety, perceived feelings of safety, and various perceptions of the quality of police services received in a neighborhood (Ostrom, 1973). As Bahl and Burkhead (1977: 261) express it:

> Police protection is probably at the low end of the measurability spectrum. The final output is a social state measured perceptually by citizen attitudes as to whether streets are safe.

While the final output is difficult to measure, resource and personnel data are relatively easy. These represent different stages in a series of phenomena that include:

(1) the allocation of public funds to a police department budget;

(2) the allocation of funds within a police department to different divisions (such as the Patrol Division, the Detective Bureau, the Traffic Bureau, and so forth);

(3) the use of budgeted positions to hire and allocate personnel within the Patrol Division to specific neighborhoods;

(4) the deployment of police personnel to respond to demands placed on them from different neighborhoods within a city;

(5) the activities that police undertake and their attitudes and demeanor toward citizens;

(6) the effects of police activities on threats to safety and security; and

(7) the cumulative effects of threats to safety and security on citizens' perceptions, fears, and evaluations.

Major conceptual and methodological problems exist in attempting to use data from observations made early in this series of phenomena as proxy measures for effects occurring later in the series. For example, data about the allocation of police to different neighborhoods provide a poor measure of services distributed to citizens. Because "production functions" for policing are so poorly understood (Lineberry, 1977; Schoup and Mehay, 1971; Merget and Berger, 1982), efforts to determine the relationship between levels of police manpower and crime rates have been notoriously unsuccessful (Chaiken and Larson, 1971; Kelling et al., 1974; Larson, 1972). The availability of resources does not have a known and determinate relationship to police activities, much less to crime rates or to citizen feelings of safety or evaluations of police services.

Some scholars, recognizing that the relationship of inputs to services is poorly understood, interpret the distribution of inputs or activities primarily as an indicator of intermediate processes, and *not* as a proxy measure for the final output. Mladenka (1974: 4), for example, interprets response-time measures in this fashion:

> If response time can be shown to have a direct, immediate effect upon arrest probabilities and a long term impact upon crime rates, then it can be inferred that inequality in the distribution of response time among neighborhoods may have some relationship to the level of crime in those neighborhoods. Even in the absence of a demonstrated association between police response time and arrests, however, all citizens are entitled to an equitable response in regard to their calls for police assistance.

Resource or activity measures may be instructive, of course, if they are recognized for what they are and are understood in the context of our lack of knowledge of police production functions. Since so little is known about the production function for police, and since researchers have relied on such different indicators as proxy measures of service, considerable disagreement exists about the equity of police service delivery. Scholars who have examined the distribution of police services to neighborhoods within and across large central cities have come to different conclusions about the equity of police services, depending on: (1) which cities they have studied, (2) which steps in this series of transformations they observed and measured, and (3) how they interpret the meaning of the indicators they used.

Most of the studies that have attempted to develop a quantitative measure of service in regard to policing have examined one or more of the following: (1) the distribution of police personnel throughout the different districts within a jurisdiction, (2) police response time to calls for service originating in different districts of a jurisdiction, (3) comparative crime or victimization rates, and (4) citizen feelings of safety and evaluations of police performance. None of these measures is fully satisfactory when used alone. Serious problems of interpretation for each are discussed in the following review of research on the distribution of police service.

STANDARDS OF DISTRIBUTION USED IN ASSESSING
POLICE SERVICE EQUITY

Police Personnel Allocation

Studies of the equity of police service distribution have relied heavily on measures of the allocation of police personnel to different neighborhoods. In an early study, Weicher (1971) concluded that patrol units in Chicago during 1959 were allocated in a manner that favored lower-income districts; that is, they received more officers.

In connection with a legal suit over the equality of police service delivery to a relatively affluent neighborhood, as contrasted to a relatively poor district in Washington, D.C., Bloch (1974) concluded that police personnel were distributed to the two neighborhoods in an equitable manner. Bloch used a need criterion to evaluate the distribution of personnel, but he was conscious that the actual allocation of personnel to specific neighborhoods is an input measure and not a measure of output. In his report, he reflects:

> Unequal distribution of inputs does not necessarily result in poorer service. For example, a small number of police who are highly motivated and well trained may provide better emergency services and better crime protection in one district than a larger number provide in other districts. However, since fully satisfactory measures of quality of service are difficult to obtain, input measures may be used as one indication of equal treatment [Bloch, 1974: 2-3].

Bloch uses several additional measures to supplement his data on the distribution of police personnel to the two neighborhoods studied. Given the consistent pattern in his findings, Bloch expresses confidence in his assessment that police services are allocated in an equitable manner between the two neighborhoods.

A careful and detailed analysis of personnel distribution at both the district and beat level in the city of Houston was conducted by

Mladenka (1974: 34), who argues: "Equity in the distribution of police manpower requires that resources be allocated on the basis of crime and call for service rates." Crime rates and calls for service are the standards of comparison being used to assign weights under a need criterion. The number of calls for service in a district accounted for most of the variance in personnel allocation at both the beat and district levels. Since higher levels of crime occur in minority and poor neighborhoods, this allocation formula assigns more officers to these neighborhoods. Therefore, Mladenka concluded that there was no evidence of inequity in the distribution of police personnel in the city of Houston (see also Mladenka and Hill, 1978).

In an influential study of urban service delivery, Lineberry (1977) used measures of the allocation of police personnel to nine large population sectors in San Antonio. This was his only indicator of police service. He found a relatively equal distribution of personnel across all sectors, standardized by population, crime rates, and radio calls for service — the three standards for comparison (w) that he used. Somewhat more personnel were assigned to sectors with high proportions of minority residents. In general, these were also the high crime areas of the city. Using a need criterion, Lineberry concluded that police services were distributed equitably in San Antonio.

Interpreting Allocation Patterns

The conclusion reached by most scholars examining the allocation of police personnel to different neighborhoods within a single jurisdiction is that these patterns are equitable. Personnel are allocated primarily to those neighborhoods that have the highest levels of crime or calls for service (need). When the need criterion is utilized, the researcher is implicitly assuming that the assignment of more police to predominantly high-crime and minority neighborhoods is primarily for the benefit of the residents of those areas. Lineberry, for example, relies on simple personnel allocation patterns to reject an "underclass" hypothesis that racial minorities and poor families are being discriminated against in the delivery of urban services. He rejects this hypothesis based on police personnel data and on data relating the location of fixed facilities, such as parks, to neighborhood characteristics.

Mladenka also assumes that the assignment of more police to minority neighborhoods is an indicator of higher levels of assistance being provided to those with special needs. However, after finding both police personnel and response time (discussed below) to be allocated equitably, he speculates as to why this should be so. Mladenka presumes that police are most likely maximizing their self-interest by means of the production strategies they adopt. As he argues, the practices of the Houston Police Department are scrutinized daily in both the local press and on TV:

> The reported incidence of a string of robberies and murders or a series of rapes in a predominantly black neighborhood is likely to have an immediate impact upon the citizens of a wealthy, low crime area located miles across town. A police decision to allocate additional manpower in the violent crime district will probably be perceived by individuals in the wealthy neighborhood as a measure designed to enhance their own security [Mladenka, 1974: 46].

While Mladenka interprets the heavier allocation of personnel to minority and poor neighborhoods as equitable given a "need" criterion, he also recognizes that this pattern of allocation tends to enhance the security of residents in wealthy neighborhoods within the same city. This theme — that the allocation of more police personnel to black neighborhoods may be as much or more to protect wealthy, white citizens living in other neighborhoods — has been articulated repeatedly by black activists concerned with what the police do, as well as with how many officers are assigned to their neighborhoods.

In discussing this problem of interpretation, Altshuler (1970: 149) notes that few black leaders accept as valid the notion that more police personnel mean better police service for the residents of black neighborhoods. "Many black leaders," Altshuler (1970: 149) summarized, "argue . . . that the apparent redistribution which now occurs within cities is of little value to the supposed beneficiaries," while more militant leaders insist:

> White police should be viewed as an army of occupation, concentrated in ghetto areas mainly to protect white-owned property, to impose white middle class mores on the black community, and to let the blacks know clearly who is boss [Altshuler, 1970: 149].

A prominent, black, law enforcement official points to the fact that the property in many black ghettos is owned primarily by white businessmen or white absentee owners. The service rendered in the ghetto in many instances is "not a service for the black community, but a service for a businessman that [sic] leaves the community each night" (Brown, 1977).

The concerns raised by black leaders should alert urban researchers to the fact that patterns of police personnel allocation cannot simply be accepted at face value as an indicator of services delivered. One needs to inquire much deeper into the process of urban service delivery in order to make a reasoned judgment about the level of services received by citizens.

The point of this discussion is not to question findings that most large police departments allocate personnel according to formulas based on crime rates and the volume of calls for service, nor is it questioned that this policy usually results in more police officers being assigned per capita to poor neighborhoods than to wealthy neighborhoods in the same jurisdiction. The problem is in how these findings should be interpreted. The dominant interpretation has been that such findings demonstrate that service delivery is equitable, based on a need criterion. Without knowing how police respond, what activities they undertake, and how these activities are related to the needs of those living in poor and minority neighborhoods, however, we should not presume that manpower distribution figures are sufficient evidence on which to base judgments about equity. The difference between an occupying army and a service-oriented police force cannot be determined solely by examining personnel allocation. The riots in Miami reminded us once again that it is what police do, rather than how many there are, that affects the sense of justice and equity among blacks living in central cities.

Residents of wealthier neighborhoods in central cities frequently hire private patrols to supplement the efforts of local police departments. Police administrators in Houston told Mladenka (1974: 45) that they felt that this additional private investment policing "allowed the department to concentrate more of its resources in high crime/low income areas." Unfortunately, these additional services are not taken into account in the service distribution figures included in scholarly analyses.

Response Time

In analyzing response-time distributions, most scholars use the racial and income characteristics of a neighborhood as weighting factors. Furstenberg and Wellford (1973) conducted one of the earliest studies on citizen-reported response time within a single city — Baltimore. When questioned by independent, civilian black interviewers, black respondents reported a longer response time than white respondents (Furstenberg and Wellford, 1973: 401): "Within this sample, twice as many blacks as whites had to wait at least 15 minutes for the police to arrive (23 percent compared to 12 percent)."

A contradictory finding was reported by Mladenka (1974) in his study of response times to different neighborhoods by the Houston Police Department. For administrative purposes, Houston is divided into 20 districts and 103 beats. Mladenka aggregated socioeconomic characteristics from block census track data to the beat and district level. After examining systematic samples of calls for service to the Houston Police Department, he found that an average of 38 minutes elapsed from the initiation of a call to the time of arrival of the first patrol unit. (It should be noted that the jurisdiction of the Houston Police Department covers an extremely large area.) Response time tended to be lowest for a prowler or a serious disturbance and highest for a theft or burglary. There was no evidence that police responded less quickly to calls for assistance from black and/or low-income neighborhoods. Indeed, Mladenka was unable to discern *any* variation in police response based on demographic variables. The only variation in response he could discern related to the type of call involved. Using need as his criterion, Mladenka concluded that in terms of the problems citizens faced, response time was distributed equitably within the city of Houston.

Interpreting Response-Time Patterns

The problems involved in interpreting response-time patterns are discussed by Nardulli and Stonecash (1981) in their study of the distribution of police services in Champaign, Illinois. They found that the average response time in the Northend, a predominantly black neighborhood, was almost twice as far as that in the Southwest, the "country-club" district of Champaign. Nevertheless, Nardulli and Stonecash (1981: 96) do not accept these response-time patterns (or similar personnel distribution patterns) as "indicators of real distributional patterns," pointing out that a low average response time in a particular neighborhood may simply reflect the preponderance of serious crimes and other emergency needs in that neighborhood. They note further that calls for service related to alleged assaults were disproportionately high in the Northend and that routine, nonemergency calls were disproportionately high in the Southwest. Thus, controlling for type of problem, one might conclude that the pattern of findings changes.

Nardulli and Stonecash's criticism of reliance on average response-time measures aggregated to neighborhoods as evidence of the equity of urban police distribution patterns goes even deeper and is addressed to the acceptance of a prevailing paradigm in most recent empirical studies of urban service distribution patterns. "The paradigm directs researchers to select various indicators of a given service and then to compare them across neighborhoods or census tracts that vary in their social, political, and/or economic makeup" (Nardulli and Stonecash, 1981: 96). They argue that this approach does not provide much information about the delivery of urban services. If proper controls are introduced, one may get a reasonably accurate overview of the distribution of intermediate, or even final, services, but even then, questions concerning the structure of service delivery are often left unanswered. For example, discrimination — which has long been viewed almost entirely as an additive factor, as a result of which race or poverty will have a direct linear effect on response time or other indicators — is very likely a much more complex process:

> If, for example, professional-rational criteria dominate the procedures for disbursing a service, it might be that race or class affects the implementation of those criteria — that is, that an interactive relationship exists between professional-rational criteria and sociopolitical criteria. Consider . . . the amount of effort expended on an investigation of a burglary case. The primary criterion for expending effort might be the amount of evidence available. However, for a given amount of evidence, more effort might be expended in cases where the victim is white or middle class than where the victim is black or lower class [Nardulli and Stonecash, 1981: 98].

Nardulli and Stonecash also point out that statistical suppression effects may obscure relationships unless care is used to understand processes and to control for relevant variables.

When examining several different sources of influence on the way police handle assault, traffic, and minor property crimes, Nardulli and Stonecash argue that bureaucratic rules will have the most influence on those aspects of police service delivery that are undertaken within or under the close supervision of police headquarters. Thus, in allocating cars to service, dispatchers are expected to follow the particular allocational rules devised within any particular police department. In Champaign, for example, dispatchers did follow the rule of "first come, first served, except in emergencies" (Nardulli and Stonecash, 1981: 167). Response time was determined almost entirely by the amount of time from initial call to dispatching and was not affected by factors other than the simple bureaucratic rule.

As the action shifts from headquarters to the field, however, discretion by individual officers increases. Once an officer arrives on the scene, he or she may be able to exercise much discretion, particularly in those cases that are less serious, where it is unlikely that either the courts or supervisors at headquarters will scrutinize the actions taken. Nardulli and Stonecash found that individual police officers varied significantly in the probability that they would arrest black suspects. In analyzing the response to calls for service involving violence, one of the strongest explanatory factors for the decision to arrest was the interaction of the presence of a black suspect *and* an officer with a high propensity to arrest black suspects. Similarly, they found that officers varied in their propensity to issue tickets, and that owners of older cars or cars registered outside the Champaign-Urbana area were much more likely to be ticketed than were residents of the area or the more affluent owners of new cars.

Among the responses that police can offer when called into service, Nardulli and Stonecash found that the speed of response was under the greatest bureaucratic control and was most likely to be allocated primarily according to established rules. In regard to those actions occurring in distant locations, however, many sociopolitical and specific, incident-related factors affected police responses to citizen demands. Thus, in light of the Nardulli and Stonecash critique, scholars should be hesitant to rely entirely on response times when conducting inquiries concerning the equity of police service delivery. One needs to go beyond the mere speed of response to examine this rate as it is affected by both the problems involved and the relevant neighborhood demographic variables. Where possible, other types of police response data should also be included.

Crime and Victimization Rates

Two of the most cited theoretical discussions of equity in police services (Shoup, 1964, and Thurow, 1970) use crime rates as their indicators of s. Shoup (1964: 384) states:

> Equality of crime rates per capita among residential districts is taken to signify equal probability, for any person in one district compared with any person in any other district, that he will be the victim of a crime in a given time period. Such probability is taken as a measure of the product, police protection: the lower the probability, the greater the product. If every person faces the same probability, the service, police protection, is said to be distributed evenly, or equally.

Empirical studies of equity have not, however, used crime or victimization rates as extensively as they have used personnel allocation and measures of response time.

In several studies by researchers associated with the Workshop in Political Theory and Policy Analysis, victimization data were collected to ascertain whether victimization rates in similar neighborhoods (controlling primarily for income and race) served by small- or medium-sized suburban police departments were higher than victimization rates for neighborhoods within large cities (Ostrom et al., 1973; Ostrom and Whitaker, 1973; Ostrom and Parks, 1973; Rogers and Lipsey, 1975). A consistent finding was that neighborhoods served by small- to medium-sized municipal departments had equal or lower victimization rates than comparable neighborhoods inside central cities. Given that the problems faced by the different types of police departments were relatively similar, and that other performance data were consistent with the equal or lower victimization rates, it was concluded that the small- to medium-sized police departments were more effective in delivering police services than were the very large departments. Further, in several of the studies, the small- or medium-sized deparmtents were also more efficient. Their costs were lower, while their output was equal or better. An additional analysis of distributional equity using victimization rates and other indicators has recently been completed (Ostrom, 1983).

Interpreting Crime and Victimization Rates

The problems in interpreting FBI crime statistics are well known. A vast literature has criticized the use of the FBI Uniform Crime Reports as a simple indicator of police output. Some of the difficulties involved in using FBI data include:

(1) many categories of "serious crimes" are not included in the list;

(2) all crimes included are weighted equally;

(3) a large but variable proportion of crimes are not reported to police; and

(4) police departments have substantial control over whether a crime reported to them is recorded accurately.

Given that an extensive literature has been devoted to questions of the validity and reliability of crime statistics, I will not present a further review here.[3]

Because of the general dissatisfaction with officially recorded data, experiments were started in the mid-1960s with methods to collect data reflecting the level of crime in major cities through the use of survey techniques (see Skogan, 1976, for a review). These have been used primarily to generate information on jurisdictionwide rates of victimization. Consequently, the data collected by the Bureau of the Census for the U.S. Department of Justice cannot be used to examine patterns of victimization across neighborhoods within large cities, or even to compare suburban rates in a metropolitan area to rates within the central city. It is possible, though costly, to collect victimization data for particular neighborhoods within and across cities, and such data are generally thought to be a more valid and reliable source of crime rates than the FBI Uniform Crime Reports, but puzzles still remain in interpreting crime data of either kind.

Given that police are only marginally able to affect the level of crime in an area, how should one appropriately interpret a lower crime rate in one neighborhood as contrasted with another? Since citizens are "co-producers" of the safety of a neighborhood, should

crime rates of any kind be used to evaluate the equity (or effectiveness) of public police forces (Parks et al., 1981)? Are police services
distributed inequitably if there is more service in neighborhoods
where crime rates are higher than they are in similar neighborhoods
where citizens are less willing to cooperate with the police in reporting
crimes and suspicious circumstances, locking their cars and homes,
and in helping to keep watch over the neighborhood? These are
perplexing questions that need much attention when using indicators
of service affected by many factors besides the actions of the public
agency that is expected to "produce" the service.

Citizen Attitudes Toward and Evaluations of Police

Measures of citizen attitudes toward police have been collected
through random samples of urban populations and used as service
measures in a variety of studies evaluating the equity and effectiveness of local police. The major question in many of these studies is
whether black and white residents living in the same jurisdiction
evaluate police services similarly. Thus, race of the respondent has
been the standard of comparison (w) used in most analyses. Across
most cities in the United States, citizens of all racial and income
groupings are relatively positive in their evaluations of local police.
However, a consistent finding is that black respondents are less
satisfied with the services they receive from local police and less
positive in their orientation to local police than are white respondents.

One of the earliest studies was that of Bayley and Mendelsohn
(1969), who explored the difference in citizen evaluations of police
made by black, white, and Hispanic respondents living in Denver.
They report that minority members of the community, especially
those with Spanish surnames, were consistently less positive in their
evaluation of performance by the Denver police in their neighborhoods than were white respondents:

Twenty-seven percent of the Dominants said that the police
did an excellent job in their neighborhood; only 2% dissented.
Among Negroes, 12% said police did an excellent job and 7%
said they did a bad job. Among the Spanish-named, 11% said
the job done was excellent and 13% said it was bad. As one can
see, the unfavorable judgments of police performance were

twice as common among Spanish-named as among Negroes, which in turn were three times as common as among Dominants [Bayley and Mendelsohn, 1969: 111].

They also point out that the amount of contact between minority residents and police was greater than that between whites and police. A higher percentage of minority respondents indicated that they or someone in their family had been badly treated by a police officer, and a lower proportion of minority respondents indicated that they were satisfied with what the police did for them when called help (Bayley and Mendelsohn, 1969: 117). Bayley and Mendelsohn (1969: 119) concluded that "it will take actions and not just words to regenerate relations between police and minorities." In 1972, the Denver Urban Observatory asked similar questions in a general random sample of the residential population. In a comparison of those data with the data collected by Bayley and Mendelsohn several years previously, Lovrich and Taylor (1975) found little improvement in the evaluations of police by minorities as compared to those by white respondents.

Durand (1976) also conducted a dynamic analysis of the distribution of police services (as well as three other services) in a single city — St. Louis. Blacks were less positive in their evaluations of police services than whites, although satisfaction rates of both blacks and whites had declined. Durand (1976: 705) argues that these declines did not result from generational or migrational changes in the population, but rather from "sharp divergences between expectations and perceived performance among long-time residents."

In addition to the studies focusing on single cities, a number of studies have compared evaluations of police made by black and white respondents in several cities. The general finding that blacks are less positive in their evaluations persists in the studies that include multiple cities. Not surprisingly, differences among residents living in separate cities are generally greater than differences among residents living within the same city.

Schuman and Gruenberg (1972) analyzed data on a large sample of blacks and whites from 15 cities collected for the National Advisory Commission on Civil Disorders. In all, 51 percent of the black respondents and 71 percent of the whites reported themselves "generally satisfied" with the quality of police protection in their neighborhood (Schuman and Gruenberg, 1972: 370). Similar ethnic differences in satisfaction have been reported for public schools, parks and playgrounds, and garbage collection, although the level of satisfaction varies by service area.[4] Further, an analysis of these data on a city-by-city basis revealed considerable variation across cities, although the difference in satisfaction between whites and blacks remained. Schuman and Gruenberg (1972: 375) concluded:

> City and race produce independent variation in dissatisfaction. . . . While blacks are almost always less satisfied than whites when city is held constant, blacks in one city are often more satisfied than whites in another city.

Perhaps the most interesting finding reported by Schuman and Gruenberg is that racial variations in service satisfaction could be explained not by the race of individual respondents, but by the racial and social class composition of the neighborhood in which respondents lived.

The Urban Observatory conducted a citizen survey in ten cities, including Denver, as mentioned above. A series of questions designed to measure different aspects of citizen evaluations of police services were included. One important question asks: "In general, how would you rate the job the police do of protecting people in this neighborhood — very good, good enough, not so good, or not good at all?" (Fowler, 1974: 237). In each of the ten cities, the majority of the citizens rated police protection of their neighborhood "very good" or "good enough," but this varied by city, ranging from a low of 57 percent in Boston to a high of 87 percent in San Diego. In all cities, blacks were less positive than whites, but only in Boston did the proportion of black respondents favorably evaluating police protection in their neighborhoods fall below 50 percent.[5] In general, although there are some nonmonotonic relationships in a few cities, citizen ratings of police protection in the neighborhood vary monotonically with income, with ratings of the police improving as the income of respondents increases.

It is the consistency of the difference in black and white attitudes toward and evaluations of urban police and other services that led Lineberry and his colleagues to address the underclass hypothesis. It seemed reasonable to presume that blacks, poor families, and minorities in general received "the short end" of most distribution policies. The rejection of the underclass hypothesis, then, based on data about facility location, personnel allocation, and response time, leaves unanswered the question of why blacks are consistently less positive in their evaluations of policing.

Interpreting Citizen Attitudes and Evaluations of Police

A perplexing problem in measuring the output of police is the somewhat fragile set of relationships between what police do and how they are evaluated. Some general relationships are relatively well established. For example, citizen evaluations are negatively related to the amount of time it takes police to respond (Furstenberg and Wellford, 1973; Percy, 1980; Dean, 1980), although when police state that they will be somewhat delayed in responding to a call, citizens are less likely to evaluate them negatively than when they are late and do not offer a prior explanation (Pate et al., 1976). Further, when police take the time to explain what they are doing in terms of follow-up, respondents are generally more satisfied than when police do not explain their actions (Furstenberg and Wellford, 1973). Regardless of the particular action, however, black respondents remained more dissatisfied with police performance than whites. Furstenberg and Wellford (1973: 402) have proposed that the persistent difference between blacks and whites occurs primarily among those least satisfied with the services they receive:

> Specifically, blacks who report poor service (a delay in response time or no follow up) are much more likely to react negatively than whites who had similar complaints. Conversely, whites are somewhat more inclined than blacks to discount those instances of poor service in their overall estimation of satisfaction with police performance. Thus, it is not the quality of service as such that accounts for racial difference — blacks and whites generally received the same treatment — but the way that service is defined by the racial groups.

This interpretation raises serious issues about the role of racial differences in the assessment of respondents' evaluations of policing, some of which are examined below.

One possible explanation is that blacks' dissatisfaction with urban policing reflects their level of dissatisfaction with the treatment of blacks in society more generally. The police are viewed as a symbol of a dominant white society. Thus, criticism of policing can be seen as one way of articulating a more general criticism of how authority has been used to discriminate against blacks in many circumstances (Stipak, 1979).

A second explanation regards the types of neighborhoods that are predominantly black. Because of discrimination in the housing market, blacks are more likely to live in older, more densely settled neighborhoods in which a high proportion of the other residents are also black. Blacks' criticism of urban police may thus reflect a general unhappiness with the high levels of crime and personal violence in the neighborhoods in which they live.

A third explanation is that blacks' criticisms of urban police forces may relate directly to the current behavior of those forces (Parks, 1982). While Furstenberg and Wellford's (1973) study raises questions about this explanation, other studies have found discriminatory behavior toward blacks and other minority groups on the part of police (Rossi et al., 1974; Groves and Rossi, 1970; Nardulli and Stonecash, 1981; but see also Reiss, 1971).

A fourth explanation — strongly related to the second and third — is that since many blacks live in neighborhoods characterized by high levels of crime, they make more demands on police. The alleged slow response time by police may thus result from their inability to keep up with the increased volume of calls.

A fifth explanation is that almost all major studies examining the differences between black and white attitudes toward and evaluations of police have been conducted in large cities. In this setting, problems may exist due to both the lack of communication of poor and minority residents' needs to public officials, and to the size of the bureaucratic apparatus within large municipal police forces (Ostrom and Whitaker, 1973; Parks, forthcoming; Parks and Ostrom, 1981). In contrast, blacks living in small, suburban communities may be able to articulate their preferences more effectively and be served by a more responsive police department. Analysis presented elsewhere (Ostrom, 1983) demonstrates that low-income black residents served by small, separately incorporated cities evaluate police more positively than do low-income black residents living in central cities. All of these explanations must be given some initial credibility, at least until more systematic and penetrating analyses can be made of the reasons for persistent differences between black and white citizens' evaluations of police.

Like the standards for distribution discussed earlier, citizen evaluations of police services are not entirely satisfactory measures of s, either. Without a considerable context of data about related service delivery processes, citizen evaluation measures can be as difficult to interpret as any of the other measures discussed.

CONCLUSION

Empirical analysis of the equity of urban police service delivery is an extremely difficult task. The lack of cumulation that Rich (1982) bemoans is not surprising when one looks carefully at the problems involved in using any of the current measures. Scholars must dig deeper than surface appearance before they can assess with any validity whether police services are distributed equitably within or across city boundaries. Reliance on any single indicator of service is fraught with the possibility of misinterpretation. The need for multiple measures of service (standards of distribution) and an examination of how those indicators are related is as great for equity analysis as it is for the evaluation of effectiveness or efficiency (Ostrom, 1977).

In addition to the methodological problems addressed in this chapter, deep normative issues remain unresolved by this focus on the interpretation of indicators. Decisions concerning which standards of comparison should be used in computing proportional equality cannot and should not be made on the basis of the present examination of different indicators of distribution and their meaning. The normative and methodological problems involved in the evaluation of urban service delivery arrangements are substantial and ever present, and it is only by recognizing the extent of these problems that we can hope to gain a better understanding of the equity of police service delivery. By improving our indicators of distribution, we can then proceed in the development of valid and articulate statistics (Miller, 1981a) based on different normative conceptions and embodied in different standards of comparison. This strategy would not yield a single measure of equity. Instead, multiple measures based on valid data and well-defined, but different, normative goals should be used consciously by social scientists in their evaluations of the equity of many existing or proposed institutional arrangements.

NOTES

1. Selten's work was influenced by Homans' (1961) concept of distributive justice. Since Aristotle, proportional equality has been one of the conceptual foundations for the concept of equity. Recent works that also base their definition of equity on proportional equality include: Bell (1974), Oppenheim (1968), Patchen (1961), and Adams (1965). See also Berkowitz and Walster (1976).

2. Two-officer patrol cars are frequently justified on the grounds of increasing the safety of police officers. Given the practice of sending back-up patrol units for any potentially dangerous calls for service, however, no evidence exists that assigning two officers to a patrol unit actually increases their safety (see Boydstun et al., 1977).

3. See Ostrom (1971) for a discussion of the major criticisms of the FBI crime reports as measures of output (see also Biderman, 1966; Black, 1970; Skogan, 1977).

4. Respondents were most pleased with garbage collection in their neighborhoods, and least pleased about the quality of parks and playgrounds for children.

5. In Boston, only about 30 percent of the black respondents were positive in their evaluations of neighborhood police protection. Three cities (Albuquerque, Denver, and San Diego) did not have a large enough black population to allow for analysis in the sample of racial variations in opinion (Fowler, 1974: 163).

REFERENCES

ADAMS, J. S. (1965) "Inequity in social exchange," pp. 267-299 in L. Berkowitz (ed.) Advances in Experimental Social Psychology, Vol. II. New York: Academic.

ALTSHULER, A. (1970) Community Control. New York: Pegasus.

BAHL, R. W. and J. BURKHEAD (1977) "Productivity and the measurement of public output," pp. 253-270 in C. H. Levine (ed.) Managing Human Resources: A Challenge to Urban Governments. Beverly Hills, CA: Sage.

BAYLEY, D. H. and H. MENDELSOHN (1969) Minorities and the Police. New York: Free Press.

BELL, W. (1974) "A conceptual analysis of equality and equity in evolutionary perspective." American Behavioral Scientist 18 (September): 8-35.

BERKOWITZ, L. and E. WALSTER (1976) Equity Theory: Toward a General Theory of Social Interaction. New York: Academic Press.

BIDERMAN, A. D. (1966) "Social indicators and goals," pp. 68-153 in R. A. Bauer (ed.) Social Indicators. Cambridge, MA: MIT Press.

BLACK, D. J. (1970) "Production of crime rates." American Sociological Review 35: 733-748.

BLOCH, P. B. (1974) Equality of Distribution of Police Services: A Case Study of Washington, D. C. Washington, DC: Urban Institute.

BOYDSTUN, J. E., M. E. SHERRY, and N. P. MOELTER (1977) Patrol Staffing in San Diego. Washington, DC: Police Foundation.

BROWN, L. P. (1977) "Bridges over troubled waters: a perspective on policing in the black community," pp. 79-106 in R. L. Woodson (ed.) Black Perspectives on Crime and the Criminal Justice System: A Symposium. Boston: G. K. Hall.

CHAIKEN, J. M. and R. C. LARSON (1971) Methods for Allocating Urban Emergency Units. New York: Rand Institute.

DEAN, D. (1980) "Citizen ratings of the police: the difference contact makes." Law and Policy Quarterly 2 (October): 445-471.

DURAND, R. (1976) "Some dynamics of urban service evaluations among blacks and whites." Social Science Quarterly 56 (March): 698-706.

FOWLER, F. J. (1974) Citizen Attitudes Toward Local Government, Services, and Taxes. Cambridge, MA: Ballinger.

FURSTENBERG, F. F. and C. F. WELLFORD (1973) "Calling the police: the evaluation of police services." Law and Society Review 7 (Spring): 393-406.

GROVES, W. E. and P. H. ROSSI (1970) "Police perceptions of a hostile ghetto." American Behavioral Scientist 13: 727-743.

HILL, R. C. (1974) "Separate and unequal: governmental inequality in the metropolis." American Political Science Review 68 (December): 1557-1568.

HOMANS, G. C. (1961) Social Behavior: Its Elementary Forms. New York: Harcourt Brace Jovanovich.

JENCKS, C. et al. (1972) Inequality: A Reassessment of the Effect of Family and Schooling in America. New York: Basic Books.

JONES, B. D. (1982) "Assessing the products of government," pp. 155-170 in R. Rich (ed.) Analyzing Urban-Service Distributions. Lexington, MA: Lexington Books.

KELLING, G. L. et al. (1974) The Kansas City Preventive Patrol Experiment: A Summary Report. Washington, DC: Police Foundation.

LARSON, R. C. (1972) Urban Police Patrol Analysis. Cambridge, MA: Massachusetts Institute of Technology Operations Research Center.

LEVY, F. S., A. J. MELTSNER, and A. WILDAVSKY (1974) Urban Outcomes. Berkeley: University of California Press.

LEWIS, C. W. (1982) "Interpreting municipal expenditures," pp. 203-218 in R. C. Rich (ed.) Analyzing Urban-Service Distributions. Lexington, MA: Lexington Books.

LINEBERRY, R. L. (1977) Equality and Urban Policy: The Distribution of Municipal Public Services. Beverly Hills, CA: Sage.

LOVRICH, N. P. and G. T. TAYLOR (1975) "Police-community relations, LEAA funds, and the development of community attitudes." Presented at the annual meetings of the American Society for Public Administration, Chicago.

MERGET, A. E. and R. A. BERGER (1982) "Equity as a decision rule in local services," pp. 21-45 in R. C. Rich (ed.) Analyzing Urban-Service Distributions. Lexington, MA: Lexington Books.

MILLER, T. C. (1981a) "Political and mathematical perspectives on educational equity." American Political Science Review 75 (June): 319-333.

────── (1981b) "Articulate statistics and educational equity." Policy Sciences 13 (April): 205-226.

────── (1977) "Conceptualizing inequality," pp. 335-350 in M. Guttentag (ed.) Evaluation Studies Review Annual, Vol. 2. Beverly Hills, CA: Sage.

MLADENKA, K. (1974) "Serving the public: the provision of municipal goods and services." Ph.D. dissertation, Rice University.

────── and K. Q. HILL (1978) "The distribution of urban police services." Journal of Politics 40 (February): 112-133.

NARDULLI, P. F. and J. M. STONECASH (1981) Politics, Professionalism, and Urban Services: The Police. Cambridge, MA: Oelgeschlager, Gunn & Hain.

NEIMAN, M. (1982) "An exploration into class clustering and local-government inequality," pp. 219-234 in R. C. Rich (ed.) Analyzing Urban-Service Distributions. Lexington, MA: Lexington Books.

OKUN, A. M. (1974) Equality and Efficiency: The Big Tradeoff. Washington, DC: The Brookings Institution.

OPPENHEIM, F. E. (1968) "The concept of equality," pp. 102-108 in D. L. Sills (ed.) International Encyclopedia of the Social Sciences, Vol. 5. New York: Macmillan.

OSTROM, E. (1983) "The distribution of police services to suburban and center city neighborhoods within metropolitan areas." Presented at the Midwest Political Science Meeting, Chicago.

────── (1977) "Why do we need multiple indicators of public service outputs?" National Conference on Nonmetropolitan Community Services Research. Washington, DC: Government Printing Office.

────── (1973) "On the measurement and meaning of output and efficiency in the provision of urban police services." Journal of Criminal Justice 1 (Summer): 93-112.

────── (1971) "Institutional arrangements and the measurement of policy consequences: applications to evaluating police performance." Urban Affairs Quarterly 6 (June): 447-475.

────── and R. B. PARKS (1973) "Suburban police departments: too many and too small?" pp. 368-402 in L. H. Masotti and J. K. Hadden (eds.) The Urbanization of the Suburbs. Beverly Hills, CA: Sage.

────── and G. P. WHITAKER (1973) "Do we really want to consolidate urban police forces? A reappraisal of some old assertions." Public Administration Review 33 (September/October): 423-433.

OSTROM, E. and G. P. WHITAKER (1973) "Does local community control of police make a difference? Some preliminary findings." American Journal of Political Science 17 (February): 48-76.

PARKS, R. B. (forthcoming) "Linking objective and subjective measures of performance." Public Administration Review.

────── (1982) "Citizen surveys for police performance assessments: some issues in their use." Urban Interest 4 (Spring): 17-26.

────── and E. OSTROM (1981) "Developing and testing complex models of urban service systems," pp. 177-199 in T. N. Clark (ed.) Urban Policy Analysis: Directions for Future Research. Beverly Hills, CA: Sage.

——— P. BAKER, L. KISER, R.J. OAKERSON, E. OSTROM, V. OSTROM, S.L. PERCY, M. VANDIVORT, G.P. WHITAKER, and R. WILSON (1981) "Consumers as coproducers of public services: some economic and institutional considerations." Policy Studies Journal 9 (Summer): 1001-1011.

PATCHEN, M. (1961) "A conceptual framework and some empirical data regarding comparisons of social rewards." Sociometry 24 (June): 136-157.

PATE, T., A. FERRARA, R.A. BOWERS, and J. LORENCE (1976) Police Response Time: Its Determinants and Effects. Washington, DC: Police Foundation.

PERCY, S.L. (1980) "Response time and citizen evaluation of police." Journal of Police Science and Administration 8 (March): 75-86.

REISS, A.J. (1971) The Police and the Public. New Haven, CT: Yale University Press.

RICH, R.C. [ed.] (1982) Analyzing Urban-Service Distributions. Lexington, MA: Lexington Books.

ROGERS, B.D. and C.M. LIPSEY (1975) "Metropolitan reform: citizen evaluations of performances in Nashville-Davidson County, Tennessee." Publius 4 (Fall): 19-34.

ROSSI, P., R. BERK, and B. EIDSON (1974) The Roots of Urban Discontent. New York: John Wiley and Sons.

SCHNEIDER, M. (1980) "Resource reallocation, population movement and the fiscal condition of metropolitan communities." Social Science Quarterly 61 (December): 545-566.

SCHOUP, D.C. and S.L. MEHAY (1971) Program Budgeting for Urban Police Services. Los Angeles: University of California Institute of Government and Public Affairs.

SCHUMAN, H. and B. GRUENBERG (1972) "Dissatisfaction with city services: is race an important factor?" pp. 369-392 in H. Hahn (ed.) People and Politics in Urban Society. Beverly Hills, CA: Sage.

SELTEN, R. (1978) "The equity principle in economic behavior," pp. 289-301 in H.W. Gottinger and W. Leinfellner (eds.) Decision Theory and Social Ethics. Dordrecht, Holland: D. Reidel.

SHOUP, C.S. (1964) "Standards for distributing a free government service: crime prevention." Public Finance 19: 383-392.

SKOGAN, W.G. (1977) "Dimensions of the dark figure of unreported crime." Crime and Delinquency 23 (January): 41-50.

——— (1976) "Victimization surveys and criminal justice planning." University of Cincinnati Law Review 45: 167-206.

STIPAK, B. (1979) "Citizen satisfaction with urban services: potential misuse as a performance indicator." Public Administration Review 39 (January/February): 46-52.

THUROW, L.C. (1970) "Equity versus efficiency in law enforcement." Public Policy 18 (Summer): 451-462.

WEICHER, J.C. (1971) "The allocation of police protection by income class." Urban Studies 8 (October): 207-220.

WHITAKER, G.P. and S. MASTROFSKI (1976) "Equity in the delivery of police services." Presented at the annual meetings of the Southern Political Science Association, Atlanta.

II

COURTS AND PERFORMANCE

Chapter 5

SANCTION SEVERITY, FEEDBACK, AND DETERRENCE

SHELDON EKLAND-OLSON
WILLIAM R. KELLY
MICHAEL SUPANCIC

The core concern for deterrence research has been the link between criminal behavior and the certainty, severity, and (less frequently) celerity of sanctions imposed by the criminal justice system. Most often this link is assumed to operate through psychological mechanisms of fear and rational choice. While this seems like a relatively straightforward problem for study, experience has shown otherwise.

Gibbs (1975: 1) begins his comprehensive review of deterrence studies by stating: "This book is a continuous denial of immediate prospects for satisfactory answers to questions about crime, punishment, and deterrence." After more than a decade of research, Tittle (1980) has restated his earlier conclusion (Tittle and Logan, 1973: 385) that deterrence studies suggest "only that sanctions apparently have some deterrent effect under some circumstances." Nettler (1982: 111) asserts: "The question of general deterrence is one of the most difficult questions, perhaps *the* most difficult one, put to criminologists." In reality, the question for deterrence research is not

AUTHORS' NOTE: *An earlier version of this chapter was presented at the 1982 annual convention of the American Society of Criminology in Toronto.*

whether punishment shapes behavior. There is ample evidence from laboratory experiments that it does (for example, Newman, 1978: 223-249). Rather, the question is when and under what circumstances the experimentally demonstrated influences of punishment apply to the operations of the criminal justice system in the community.

The list of unresolved issues is impressive: What is the most useful typology of punishment properties and deterrent effects (Gibbs, 1975: 29-40; Beyleveld, 1980: xx-xxiii)? Do the qualities of punishment operate in a continuous fashion or through a series of successive thresholds (Brown, 1978; Tittle, 1980; 9, 223-224)? How do certainty, severity, and celerity interact (Grasmick and Green, 1981)? Is there an identifiable lag structure defining the period between changes in sanctions and changes in behavior rates (Loftin and McDowall, 1982)? What is the relative importance of deterrence when compared to the influence of normative culture and interpersonal relationships (Erickson et al., 1977; Meier and Johnson, 1977; Akers et al. 1979)? What are the mechanisms through which formal sanctions and individual actions are linked (Anderson et al., 1977; Tittle, 1980; Ekland-Olson, 1981)?

Each of these questions presents impressive methodological difficulties and empirical complexities. For the purposes of this discussion, we will concentrate on the methodological issues that arise when one attempts to assess the deterrent impact of sanction severity. We first note the shift in measurement strategies from the use of statutory provisions to the use of official records. Next, since it is just as reasonable to assert that the criminal justice system adjusts to changes in the crime rate as it is to suggest that the crime rate is influenced by criminal sanctions, we focus on longitudinal studies of deterrence, attempting to refine the conclusions drawn from cross-sectional research. Because cross-sectional and longitudinal analyses, as well as the conceptual underpinnings of the deterrence doctrine, point to the importance of data on individuals' perceptions of sanction severity, we review several strategies for gathering perceptual data on sanction severity. Finally, we consider the utility of extended field research for studying an issue that has largely evaded other research techniques. The mechanisms through which perceptions of sanction severity translate into individual action are examined.

VARIABLE NATURE OF SENTENCE SEVERITY

Since the severity of punishment is such an important aspect of the deterrence doctrine, it is crucial that we have valid and reliable measures of severity. In one sense, the measurement of sentence severity is straightforward: One year in prison is less severe than three; three years is less severe than ten. Beyond the ranking of similar sanctions (that is, sanctions measured with the same unit), however, the issue becomes complicated: Five years in prison are not necessarily only half as severe as ten years; a year in prison may be quite severe for some persons but less severe for others. Likewise, a $1000 fine may represent a substantial penalty for some but no more than pocket change for others. What is more, the severity of certain sanctions (for example, commitment to a mental institution) may change over time. In addition, it is difficult even to compare some sanctions. Which is more severe — public flogging, ten years probation, an indeterminate commitment to a mental institution, or three years in prison?

What is needed is a means for standardizing sanction severity across sentence types, individuals, and circumstances. The proposal made here is that standardization be carried out in terms of the impact that a sanction will have on an individual's life circumstances. Before we discuss this proposal in detail, it is useful to review alternative measurement strategies.

MEASUREMENT STRATEGIES USING OFFICIAL STATISTICS

Since the mid-1960s, noticeable and sensible refinements have been made in deterrence studies by distinguishing between the *prescribed, actual,* and *perceived* severity of sanctions. These refinements began with attempts to study more carefully the impact of criminal sanctions on homicide rates. Among sociologists, Gibbs's (1968) ground-breaking article on deterrence was in part an attempt to move beyond evidence based on statutory provisions for capital punishment. Instead of comparing homicide rates among states with and without provisions for capital punishment (see Sellin, 1959), Gibbs estimated the actual severity of sanctions by scoring states according to the median months served on a homicide sentence by persons in state prisons on December 31, 1960. Although this measure is not equivalent to the actual median length of sentences served, it is clearly a closer approximation to actual sentence severity than were the measures used in previous studies.

Similarly, Tittle (1969) published an article in which three measures of severity were reported and linked to a wide array of offenses. The first measure was the mean time served by prisoners released in 1960 who had been convicted of a specified offense. The second measure reported the median sentence given felony offenders imprisoned in 1960, while the third reported the number of crimes punishable by death. Of the three, the first comes closest to measuring actual sanction severity, since it reflects the time served by a cohort of persons, all convicted of a felony. The reference point of Tittle's second measure is less clear. In one sense it measures actual sentences imposed; in another, it is simply a version of prescribed sentences. Court sentences, by their very nature, are prescriptive. Like statutory prescriptions, however, they may be implemented in a number of ways. For example, "good time" can be substracted from "flat time" for prison administrative reasons, and a sentence of five years on probation can be more or less constraining, depending on the discretion of one's probation officer. Tittle's third measure continued the tradition of tapping statutory prescriptions rather than actual practices.

The sociological analyses of Gibbs and Tittle were contemporary with Becker's (1968) suggestion that the deterrence question is closely linked to existing economic theory, in which rational actors weigh costs and benefits in making decisions. The substantial econometric and sociological literatures growing out of these beginnings are closely linked. In each case, measurement strategies have focused on actual practices as reflected in official statistics. Some examples of the severity measures used in this type of research are presented in Table 5.1. The general conclusion has been that the certainty of punishment appears to be a better predictor of aggregate crime rates than the severity of punishment. This conclusion has remained quite tentative, however, in part because analyses of official statistics have failed to resolve a critical feedback issue (that crime affects punishment), and because these analyses have failed to incorporate perceptual data.

TABLE 5.1   Severity Measures Based on Official Statistics

Author	Publication Date	Severity Measure
Gibbs	1968	Median number of months served on homicide sentence by all persons in prison on December 31, 1960
Becker	1968	Average time served before first release
Tittle	1969	Mean length of time served by felony prisoners released from state prison in 1960; median sentence for state felony offenders imprisoned in 1960; and number of crimes punishable by death
Gray and Martin	1969	Median number of months served on homicide sentence by all persons in prison on December 31, 1960
Chiricos and Waldo	1970	1960 severity: Median length of sentence served by state prisoners released in 1960 1964 severity: Median length of sentence served by state prisoners released in 1964 % change in severity: $$\frac{(1964 \text{ severity}) - (1960 \text{ severity})}{(1960 \text{ severity})}$$
Bailey et al.	1971	Same as Chiricos and Waldo (1970)
Bean and Cushing	1971	Median number of months served on homicide sentence by all persons in prison on December 31, 1960
Logan	1972	Mean length of time served by felony prisoners released from state prisons in 1960
Antunes and Hunt	1973	Median length of sentence served by persons in prison on December 31, 1960
Ehrlich	1973	Average time served by offenders in state prisons for a specific crime before their first release

(continued)

TABLE 5.1 Continued

Author	Publication Date	Severity Measure
Sjoquist	1973	Average length of sentence served by inmates released from state and federal institutions who had been charged with either robbery, burglary, or larceny over $50
Carr-Hill and Stern	1973	Proportion of persons convicted of a given crime who received a particular punishment, based on total number of recorded offenses
Erickson and Gibbs	1975	Median months served in state prisons by individuals released in 1960
Kau and Rubin	1975	Average time served by inmates in state prison for personal crime (murder, forcible rape, or aggravated assault) and property crime (burglary, larceny, or auto theft).
Passell	1975	Mean (1960) or median (1951) number of months spent in prison by convicted murderers released that year
Ehrlich	1975a	Severity based on possible outcomes for murder: execution, imprisonment, other punishment, or no punishment
Forst	1977	Mean time served by homicide prisoners released from prison (including parolees)
Black and Orsagh	1978	Mean time served in state prisons for homicide and non-negligent man-slaughter

Longitudinal Analysis and the Feedback Issue

The limitations of cross-sectional research for assessing the deterrence doctrine have been widely acknowledged (see, for example, Carr-Hill and Stern, 1973; Geerken and Gove, 1975; Logan, 1975). These problems become particularly acute when we try to assess the relative importance of "system strain" versus deterrence for explaining an observed inverse relationship between sanction features and crime rates. Whereas the deterrence doctrine suggests that the crime rate decreases as the severity and certainty of punishment increase, the system strain hypothesis (Logan, 1975) suggests that increases in the crime rate place a burden on the limited resources of the criminal justice system, and that through various mechanisms (for example, plea bargaining, probation, and parole), the system then reduces the severity of its sentencing practices (Henshel and Silverman, 1975). Of course, both the deterrent and the system strain processes may operate at the same time; the point is that cross-sectional studies are weak to the point of inappropriateness when it comes to dealing with the issue of system dynamics.

In this regard, Fox (1979: 42), focusing on the relation between crime rates and changes in police expenditures, notes:

> The cross-sectional data employed in these studies (e.g., Greenwood and Wadycki, 1973; McPheters and Stronge, 1974; Swimmer, 1974a, 1974b) are, however, inappropriate . . . [as] the cross-sectional approach does not measure the impact of crime trends on expenditures for police. More specifically the comparison of between-city variation in expenditure with between-city variation in the crime rate, lagged two years, does not assess the influence of *changes* in the crime rate on *changes* in expenditures.

Greenberg and his associates (1979: 844) also argue that cross-sectional data are inappropriate for estimating the effects of crime on punishment and vice versa. They note that in most cases, estimates of these reciprocal effects are biased.

A more logical and methodologically sound strategy, one that addresses the issue of system dynamics and avoids statistical bias, involves the use of longitudinal data. This approach includes regression/structural-equation estimations of annual time series of crime rates, law enforcement, and other control variables (for example, Ehrlich, 1975a; Land and Felson, 1976; Kleck, 1979); two-wave and multi-wave panel models (for example, Tittle and Rowe, 1974; Logan, 1975; Greenberg et al., 1979); estimations of lagged and instantaneous effects of crime rates and law enforcement strategies; and interrupted time-series analyses of crime rates before and after specified intervention strategies (for example, Ross et al., 1982).

The purpose of this section is to review the longitudinal research on the deterrence question. Special emphasis will be given to the determination and estimation of lag structures since, as other analysts have noted, deterrence research provides little information regarding the length of time required for changes in sanction features to influence crime rates (Loftin and McDowall, 1982; Land and Felson, 1976) — information that is useful, both for policymaking and theoretical reasons.

Much of the time-series research concentrates on crime as a predictor of sanction features (for example, Fox, 1979; McDowall and Loftin, 1982). This research is also relevant to our present concern, however, in that we envision a process model that posits an effect of sanction severity on crime, and a consequent effect of crime on sanction severity at some later point.

$$\text{Severity}_{t-k} \longrightarrow \text{Crime}_{t-i} \longrightarrow \text{Severity}_t \longrightarrow \text{and so forth}$$
$$\text{where } k > i$$

Although we will focus on the $Severity_{t-k} \longrightarrow Crime_{t-i}$ portion of the sequence, as well as the nature of the time lags involved, no model of deterrence can afford to ignore the subsequent effect of crime on severity (Greenberg and Kessler, 1982; Greenberg et al., 1979). In addition, much of the time-series research on deterrence uses indirect measures for the severity and certainty of punishment — typically, arrest clearance rates (Greenberg et al., 1979), police expenditures (Land and Felson, 1976) and police employee data (Loftin and McDowall, 1982). Thus, additional longitudinal research using measures more directly related to sentence severity is obviously needed.

Structural equation models. Perhaps the most sophisticated multivariate structural-equation modeling of annual time series of sanctions and crime rates is provided by Land and Felson (1976), and by Kleck (1979). Building on the work of Biderman (1966), Land and Felson estimated equations for the determinants of annual changes in crime rates (violent and property offenses) and police expenditures. Their predictor variables included the proportion of males aged 15-24; the consumer price index; the gross national product; and federal, state, and local police expenditures per 100,000 population. All effects in the equations were instantaneous (zero lag assumed), except for the lagged dependent variable or autoregressive effect. Although the specifications of the violent- and property-crime equations differed slightly, one of the most consistent effects noted was the significant *negative* impact of per capita police expenditures on crime rates.

Kleck (1979) formulated structural-equation models of homicide rates using annual data for the period from 1947 to 1973 (for example, arrests, convictions, capital punishment, gun ownership, and other factors). Of primary interest here are the effects of arrests, convictions, and capital punishment on homicide rates. These variables were measured as follows: the percentage of murders and cases of non-negligent manslaughter that were cleared by arrest, the percentage of persons charged with murder or non-negligent manslaughter who were convicted, and two indicators of capital punishment — an execution rate and a simple count of executions. Similar to the findings of Land and Felson (1976), all deterrence variables were assumed to have instantaneous (zero-lag) effects on the homicide rate. Kleck (1979) reported statistically significant negative effects of clearance and conviction rates on homicides, while neither measure of capital punishment had a statistically significant effect.

Linear panel models. After noting that the regression- and/or structural-equation modeling of annual time series of crime rates and sanction features has clear advantages over cross-sectional analysis, Greenberg and his colleagues (1979: 844) go on to point out that some methodological problems remain: "Since it is still necessary to make use of instrumental variables to obtain a unique solution, parameter estimates are subject to the same possible source[es] of bias as estimates derived from cross-sectional analyses." To disentangle any reciprocal effects that crime rates and sanction features may exhibit, a slightly more complex estimation procedure is required. Greenberg et al. (1979: 844-846) advocate linear-panel models. Despite the utility of this approach, however, it is important to note that the estimation of (instantaneous) reciprocal effects is only part of the question; the issue of lag structure remains. Unfortunately, both Greenberg et al. (1979) and Greenberg and Kessler (1982) make rather simplistic assumptions regarding the nature of the temporal lag.

As mentioned above, Greenberg and his colleagues employed linear-panel models in their analyses. Greenberg and Kessler (1982) used a two-wave (1960 and 1962) panel of the violent crime rate (VCR) and police spending (PS) to estimate the effects of both the VCR on PS, and vice versa, in 130 American cities. The authors also included several control variables, primarily sociodemographic and political in nature. The empirical results from several different specifications (see Greenberg and Kessler, 1982, for details) cast strong doubts on the plausibility of a stronger deterrent effect on violent crime by increased police spending. In short, Greenberg and Kessler (1982) found no instantaneous nor lag (two years) effects of police spending on crime. It is important to note, however, that their linear-panel model only spans two years, and that both police spending and violent crime were very stable over that period. The stability of these variables — particularly that of the VCR — indicates that its best predictor may be its lag value, since the latter decreases the likelihood that any other independent variable — especially police spending — will have a statistically significant effect on the VCR.

In a separate analysis Greenberg et al. (1979) used a multiwave-panel model of the per capita crime rates and the arrest clearance rates from 1964 to 1970 in 98 American cities. As in Greenberg and Kessler (1982), the authors intended to estimate both instantaneous and lag (reciprocal) effects of law enforcement on crime, and vice versa, with the crime rate broken down by felony type. Using a four-wave panel to assess changes in the crime and arrest rates in 1964-1966, 1966-1968, and 1968-1970, the authors found no statistically significant instantaneous or lag (ranging from one to three years) effects for the arrest clearance rate on that of various felony crimes. Some plausible explanations for the null effect of deterrence are offered: For example, criminals were probably not informed regarding changes in arrest practices or policy, thus leaving them ignorant of any change in the probability of arrest.

Interrupted time series. Whereas Greenberg et al. (1979) and Greenberg and Kessler (1982) provide a statistically tractable methodology for estimating the impact of sanction features on crime, they only marginally address the issue of lag structure. One of the more interesting approaches to this aspect of the deterrence effect is an analytic strategy referred to as an "interrupted time series" (McDowall et al., 1980; Ross, 1982). Essentially, this method attempts to detect major changes (structural shifts) in a time series and to link them with the intervention of some policy or practice. Much of the deterrence research using this strategy focuses on changes in the drinking-and-driving laws and how these affect highway accidents (for example, Ross, 1973, 1975, 1977, 1982; Ross et al. 1982).

The empirical evidence on the deterrent effect of more severe drinking-and-driving legislation is mixed. Statistics on traffic-related mortality in Sweden and Norway show little relationship to the passage of stiffer drinking-and-driving laws, while other studies in France and Britain do suggest some deterrent effect (Ross et al., 1982). Less convincing are results from analyses of auto accidents and blood-alcohol distributions in the Netherlands (Noorduzij, 1977), Canada (Carr et al., 1974), and in New Zealand and Australia (Hurst, 1978). Some support for the deterrence hypothesis comes from interrupted time-series analyses of auto crashes before and after major drinking-and-driving law enforcement campaigns (Ross, 1982). For example, substantial drops in auto accidents followed significant enforcement campaigns in England, New Zealand, Australia, and the United States (Ross et al., 1982).

These data indicate that law enforcement campaigns, with their attendant publicity, are a critical factor — perhaps even a necessary condition — for the appearance of a deterrent effect. Thus, the analysis of publicized enforcement efforts, rather than the passage of legislation or the use of unpublicized enforcement practices, may represent a more reliable test of the deterrence doctrine. From this evidence, as well as the conceptual nature of the deterrence doctrine, it is clear that perceptions play a central role in determining the general impact of sanctions.

These interrupted time-series studies are quite informative with regard to the role of lag structure in defining the relation between sanctions and behavior rates that proved so elusive in the work of Greenberg et al. (1979) and others. The analysis of monthly data suggests that, at least in some situations, short-term lags (less than a year) are appropriate. Ross (1982) provides considerable evidence supporting the contention that after a law enforcement campaign, rates of behavior will return to or approach preintervention levels after a relatively short period of time. The actual length of time is probably a function of the duration and intensity of the campaign. Whatever the lag, it is clear that when the deterrent effects of an intervention variable decay in a relatively short period, a deterrent effect is likely to be missed using annual data. Unfortunately, existing research on this subject has been guided more by the availability of annual data than by compelling theoretical or empirical issues.

Assessing Lag Structures. Clearly, methodological advances in the area of longitudinal deterrence research have been achieved. Land and Felson (1976) and Kleck (1979) have formulated rather sophisticated structural-equation models, while Greenberg et al. (1979) and Greenberg and Kessler (1982) have presented models that may avoid particular forms of statistical bias when estimating the effects of crime rates and sanction features. In addition, Ross (1982) has demonstrated the utility of the interrupted time series for assessing the impact of intervention variables.

One nagging concern, however, involves lag structure. Since deterrence implies a causal relation, model estimation must pay particular attention to the amount of time between changes in policy or practice and consequent impacts on the crime rate. As Loftin and McDowall (1982: 394) note:

> In essentially exploratory research, such temporal (i.e. lag) specifications are bound to be arbitrary, resting on little more than crude appeals to common sense. If investigators do not know *a priori* whether crime rates and . . . [sanction features] . . . are associated at all, they can hardly know *a priori* the temporal patterning of the association.

We suggest two methods for assessing lag structures. Neither is new, but given the lack of theoretical guidance on the issue of lags in the deterrence literature, we feel that further consideration of these methods is warranted.

Loftin and McDowall (1982) and McDowall and Loftin (1982) rely on the pioneering work of Granger (1968) and Box and Jenkins (1970) for identifying temporal causality and estimating the strength of various lag effects. Briefly, Granger (1968) argues that if X causes Y at some lag (say six months), then knowledge of the lagged X variable will give a better prediction of Y than would knowledge of the previous Y value. That is, X is a better predictor of Y than are past values of Y.

The cross-correlation function (CCF) is an exploratory statistic that permits the estimation of lag and instantaneous effects of X on Y and Y on X. However, before estimation of the CCF, autocorrelations or trends must be eliminated from the time series, since the presence of a time-related trend tends to bias the interpretation of the CCF. The influential work of Box and Jenkins (1970) provides a method for detrending autocorrelated time-series data. First, using an autoregressive integrated moving average (ARIMA) model, the nature of the trend is identified. Next, the parameters of the model are estimated. Finally, the residuals from the detrended model are calculated. ARIMA modeling is more successful than some other methods of detrending, such as differencing, since it allows the exact determination of the trend structure (see Box and Jenkins, 1970; Granger and Newbold, 1977). For relevant substantive examples of this methodology, see Loftin and McDowall (1982) and McDowall and Loftin (1982).

While estimation of the cross-correlation function on detrended time series is useful for determining the presence of lagged and/or instantaneous effects, this approach is limited in that the estimated effects are zero-order correlations. This poses no problem as long as it is reasonable to assume that the full impact of a deterrent effect is contained in a single year, whether sanction properties are lagged one, two, three, or more time periods behind the crime rate.

As in economic theory, where capital appropriations in quarter t may result in capital expenditures in several subsequent quarters (Johnston, 1972), a law enforcement campaign at time t may have a major effect on crime at time $t+1$, $t+2$, $t+3$, or later (see Fox, 1979). The distributed-lag technique is useful for handling this continuing-effect model of deterrence.

Estimation of the distributed lag (in terms of ordinary least squares regression) can be expressed as a function of current (instantaneous) and k lagged values of X:

$$Y_t = a + b_1X_t + b_2X_{t-1} + b_3X_{t-2} + \ldots + b_kX_{t-(k-1)} \quad [5.1]$$

The major difference between the distributed-lag technique and the cross-correlation function is that in the former, lag effects are *partial* coefficients; one is able to estimate the distribution of the partial lag effects. Each b_i in equation 5.1 represents the unique partial impact of each lagged X, whereas the cross-correlation function only estimates the distribution of zero-order lag effects. Of course, the problem of autocorrelation must be addressed once again when using the distributed-lag technique. As with the cross-correlation function, ARIMA models are appropriate. The specifics of estimating distributed lags are detailed in Johnston (1972), among other econometric texts.

MEASURING PERCEIVED SANCTION SEVERITY

The statistical techniques in the research reviewed to this point have been aimed at assessing more accurately the link between sanction features and crime rates. All of this research, however, has depended on available published statistics (for example, police expenditures, manpower, clearance rates, and sentencing patterns). As these cross-sectional and longitudinal studies accumulated, it became apparent that the measurement of actual sanction severity (as reflected in official statistics) was an improvement over the measurement of prescribed severity (as reflected in statutory provisions), but there was still the problem of individual differences in how sanctions were perceived.

Suspects may or may not know about actual sentencing practices. Even if sanctioning practices are known, different individuals may perceive the severity of sentences in very different ways. Given that the deterrence doctrine depends on a rational-man model, such perceptual variations are important. Erickson and his colleagues (1977) go so far as to assert that the deterrence doctrine reduces

> to the assertion that when a criminal act is contemplated, the *perception* of a high risk of a swift and severe reaction by legal officials is *sufficient* condition for omitting that act.

Although this summarization captures a core idea, certain complexities should be noted. For example, Cook (1980) notes that individuals differ according to their "willingness to accept risks," their "honesty preference," their evaluation of profits, and that they may adopt different "standing decisions" for or against criminal activities. One challenge for deterrence research thus becomes how to uncover the circumstances under which such perceptual differences occur, and thus the circumstances in which the threat of criminal sanctions has more (or less) impact.

Once the perceptual side of sanction severity is introduced, index construction becomes much more complicated. Some examples of self-report measurement strategies are included in Table 5.2. Three

TABLE 5.2   Severity Measures Based on Perceptual Data

Author	Publication Date	Severity Measure
Salem and Bowers	1970	Responses from deans and student body presidents concerning sanctions imposed for drinking and library offenses, and for cheating
Bailey and Lott	1976	Respondents asked to anticipate: What do you think would happen to you if you were caught by the police committing one of the following crimes: marijuana use, sale of marijuana, petty theft (stealing something worth $60), grand theft (stealing something worth over $60), or shoplifting?
		(a) release by police without arrest, (b) arrest but no conviction, (c) conviction with probation and/or fine only, (d) conviction and a jail sentence, (e) conviction and a prison sentence
		Also asked: If your parents (guardian) found out that you had committed one of the crimes listed below, how do you think they would feel about you?
		(a) very displeased, (b) displeased, (c) neutral—no feelings one way or the other, (d) pleased, (e) very pleased
		If your close friends found out that you had committed one of the crimes listed below, how do you think they would feel about you?
		(Same responses as with parents.)
Kraut	1976	Respondents' estimated likelihood of 11 possible consequences if they were caught for shoplifting; combined into index by weighting respondents' estimates of likelihood for each consequence by its median seriousness rank

(continued)

TABLE 5.2 Continued

Author	Publication Date	Severity Measure
Silberman	1976	Respondents' ratings of 11 offenses according to whether they would be very likely, likely, unlikely, or very unlikely to get the maximum penalty if convicted of committing each offense
Meier and Johnson	1977	Respondents asked: How severe are the courts in this community for this offense? (a) not strict enough, (b) about right, (c) too strict
Anderson et al.	1977	Respondents asked to estimate the maximum prison penalty in Florida for illegal possession of marijuana, first offense; responses categorized: 0-2 years, low severity; 2.5-5 years, medium severity; more than 5 years, high severity
Jensen and Erickson	1978	Discussed in text
Erickson and Gibbs	1979	Discussed in text
Buchner	1979	Discussed in text
Tittle	1980	Discussed in text
Grasmick and Bryjak	1980	Discussed in text
Grasmick and Green	1981	Discussed in text

related approaches are apparent: (1) procedures based on Thurstone's Law of Comparative Judgment; (2) procedures grounded in magnitude estimation as developed by Stevens and others; and (3) procedures that concentrate on specifying the reference point of sanctions.

Thurstone's Law of Comparative Judgment

Thurstone's Law of Comparative Judgment (1927) is illustrated in Buchner's (1979) research. The sanctions that Buchner considers are listed in Table 5.3. To ease the respondent's task, sanctions were divided into three groups. Respondents were asked to make paired comparisons of sanction severity within each group and then between the less severe sanctions in the higher group and the more severe sanctions in the adjacent lower group. In this way, a continuous ranking of sanction severity was achieved. Analysis of the patterns of these comparisons yielded severity scale values for all of the sanctions. These scale values were then analyzed to obtain weights for the various components of each one (for example, medical probation, jail, or prison). Viewed as a general procedure, the absolute values of the scores obtained by the paired-comparison procedure are arbitrary, since both the zero point and the scale factor are arbitrarily set.

A variation of the logic underlying the law of comparative judgments has been applied to the seriousness of crimes, and there is no reason why the same procedures could not be applied to the perceived severity of sanctions. In this version, based on what Torgeson (1954) refers to as the "law of categorical judgments," respondents are asked to place a number of stimuli into categories arranged along a continuum.

Sellin and Wolfgang (1964) had respondents place various crimes along an eleven-category continuum, from least serious to most serious. A similar procedure was followed by Rossi and his colleagues (1974), where respondents were asked to categorize short descriptions of offenses into nine levels of seriousness. These levels were treated as an interval scale, and the average score was assigned to each offense. Although these procedures were designed to present equally spaced categories, this may or may not be accurate. More important, since this scale is constrained by a specified number of categories, it may not always allow enough discrimination by respondents. This latter possibility seems to have been a problem in the study by Rossi et al. (1974), in that many offenses clustered at the upper end of the continuum, indicating that if higher scores had been possible, some offenses would have been so categorized. To handle such problems (constrained scale range and category spacing), magnitude estimation procedures have been utilized.

MAGNITUDE ESTIMATION OF COMMUNITY PERCEPTIONS

In the mid-1970s, a number of field surveys, designed in part to assess public perceptions of sanction severity, were conducted by a

TABLE 5.3   Comparison of Sanctions

Group I	3½ years probation
	3 years medical probation
	4 years probation
	9 years probation*
	10 years probation*
	1-2 months county prison*
Group II	6-12 months county prison
	3-23 months county prison*
	3-20 months state correctional institution
	3-23 months state correctional institution**
	4-22 months state correctional institution
Group III	1-10 years state correctional institution**
	2-4 years state correctional institution**
	2-10 years state correctional institution
	3-9 years state correctional institution
	4-8 years state correctional institution

SOURCE: Buchner, 1979.

*Compared to all other sentences in their group, as well as with the sentences marked with the same number of asterisks in the adjacent group.

group of sociologists at the University of Arizona. In an article reporting some of these data, Erickson and Gibbs (1979) suggest that the perceived severity of different sanctions be assessed through magnitude estimation procedures.

These procedures are grounded in the psychophysical experiments of Stevens (1957, 1962), where the goal was to measure subjective responses to physical stimuli. They have been used to estimate crime seriousness (Sellin and Wolfgang, 1964), and to scale attitudes in general (Stevens, 1966; Hamblin, 1974). The procedures provide respondents with a standard against which subsequent judgments are compared. For this reason, it should be somewhere near the middle of the continuum of interest. A value is assigned to this standard, either by the researcher or the respondent. This value should be one that can be easily multiplied or divided (for example, 100). Respondents are then given an assortment of judgment situations and asked to compare the stimuli against the standard. For example, if the standard were given the value of 100 and a comparison stimulus were judged to be twice as much on the continuum of interest (for example, loud, bright, or severe), a value of 200 would be assigned. If the stimulus were thought ot be half as loud, severe, hot, or whatever, a value of 50 would be assigned. The resulting distribution of scale scores is likely to be highly skewed, since the scale is unbounded on the high end and bottoms out at zero. Hence, either the median or the geometric mean should be used as the measure of central tendency.

In the Arizona surveys, respondents were instructed to think of one year in jail as the standard and to assign a value of 100 to this punishment. They were then given a list of other penalties and asked to assign a value to each reflecting its perceived severity as compared to one year in jail. Thus, if respondents thought that two years in prison was more than twice as severe as one year in jail, they might assign the two-year prison sentence a value of 250. On the other hand, one year of probation might be assigned a value of 75.

Using these data, Erickson and Gibbs (1979) compared the perceived severity of the punishments listed in Table 5.4. This comparison took two forms. First, respondents were asked how much of each punishment (jail time, prison time, probation, and fine) it would take to reach a specified severity score (for example, 200). A severity score of approximately 200 corresponded to 1.34 years in prison, 3.25 years in jail, 25 years on probation, and approximately a $10,000 fine. Since each of these punishments corresponded to the same severity score, their perceived severity was said to be the same. Second, the relative severity of similar amounts of various punishments were compared. The data suggest that five years in prison, jail, and probation corresponded to perceived severity scores of approximately 564, 277, and 76, respectively.

One advantage of these comparisons is that the relative perceived severity of a wide range of sanctions becomes available. Comparable data on such diverse sanctions as flogging, probation, prison, and commitment to a mental institution could be similarly generated. Since all scores relate to a single standard and a zero point is assumed, a score of 200 on the perceived severity scale can be interpreted as twice as severe as a score of 100 and one-third as severe as a score of 600, even when the punishments are quite different. From the Arizona data, it was concluded that five years in prison is almost

TABLE 5.4   Penalties Used in Magnitude Estimation Procedures

Prison	1 year or 365 days
	5 years or 1825 days
	10 years or 3650 days
	15 years or 5475 days
Jail	1 month or 30 days
	2 months or 60 days
	6 months or 180 days
	1 year or 365 days
Probation	1 year or 365 days
	5 years or 1825 days
	10 years or 3650 days
	15 years or 5475 days
Fines	$100
	$300
	$1000
	$2000
	$10,000

SOURCE: Erickson and Gibbs, 1979.

seven and a half times (564 divided by 76) as severe as five years on probation.

Comparing across different levels of sanctions, Erickson and Gibbs (1979) found that the relative perceived severity of different sanctions changed. For example, as the penalty moved from 1.34 years in prison (severity score of 200) through 40 years in prison (severity score 2800), the ratio of a year in prison time to a year in jail time increased from 2.43 to 3.39. The ratio of one year in prison to one year on probation went from 18.66 to 42.24, and the ratio of one year in prison to dollar amount increased from $7,463 to $15,768.

There are a number of applicants for these data. Through transformation rules it would be possible to translate perscribed and actual sentences into perceived severity scores. Comparisons could then be made across time, states, and communities, thereby allowing a more direct test of the general deterrence doctrine. One could also compare differences in the level of relative severity assigned to one type of punishment (for example, prison time) across groups (for example, marital status). Similarly, one could compare sensitivity to different levels of the same punishment (for example, a $100 to a $10,000 fine) across social-class categories in order to assess the influence of life circumstances on perceptions of sentence severity. Responses could be examined through factor analysis to identify perceived types of sanctions and how these types might differ from one group of respondents to another (see, for example, McClelland and Alpert, 1982).

Such analyses have one important limitation: Magnitude estimation procedures yield a measure of perceived severity relative to a specified standard. In the Arizona studies, all sanctions were compared to one year in jail. Thus, punishments were perceived to be X times more severe than one year in jail. Similarly, quite different sanctions were perceived to be equal in severity, compared to one year in jail. Unfortunately, we have no information on perceived severity in absolute terms, when for a wide range of questions that is exactly what we need. For example, various theoretical issues presented by the deterrence doctrine call for perceived absolute levels of severity, as do tests of the hypothesized calculations of the rational person (Palmer, 1977). Similarly, if we think of the severity of sanctions as operating according to a threshold model (for example, Tittle, 1980: 223-236), we are again required to provide data, not on sanctions compared to a standard, but on severity in absolute terms. It has also been suggested (for example, Grasmick and Green, 1981) that the importance of sanction severity may be contingent on the level of certainty and, alternatively, that the impact of sanction certainty may be conditioned by the level of severity. In either case, data on the perceived absolute level of severity are required.

Absolute levels of perceived severity could be obtained if we knew the perceived severity of the standard (one year in jail) in absolute terms. In the Arizona studies, this was arbitrarily assigned the value of 100, even though going to jail might be quite different for persons in different marital, occupational, economic, and criminal record categories. Suppose instead that we were able to construct an independent scale, based on how disruptive one year in jail was perceived to be for the respondents themselves. Given this value, relative perceived severity scores could be adjusted accordingly. Of course, life disruption is only one possibility; others are provided in the perceptual research concentrating on the personal reference point of perceived severity.

PERSONAL REFERENCE POINTS AND
DETERRENCE MECHANISMS

Although not inherent in the procedures themselves, the reference point has been left quite general in both paired-comparison and magnitude-estimation procedures. In Buchner's (1979) research, 58 judges in a large metropolitan city were asked to rank the sentences listed in Table 5.3. There was no attempt to specify the types of actors to which sentences would be applied (young, old, married, single, and so forth), nor the settings in which the sanctions would be imposed. In this sense, the perceived general severity of various sanctions was assessed.

For Erickson and Gibbs (1979), perception of general severity was also the central issue. Data were collected from random samples of residents in four Arizona cities at two points in time (1974 and 1975). Both sets of surveys included responses from policemen, as well as adults drawn randomly from households in each city. The recipient of the punishment was specified as either an adult or a juvenile. With this additional specification and variation in respondents, it was possible to assess how perceptions varied among categories of respondents (police and citizens), as well as across the characteristics of those punished (juvenile or adult).

Although Erickson and Gibbs (1979) found few differences, other data suggest that comparisons may be quite important. When asked which was more severe, imprisonment for two weeks or revocation of their driver's license for six months, half the respondents in a Swedish study (cited in Grasmick and Bryjak, 1980: 476) viewed the jail sentence as more severe, while the other half felt the six-month revocation of their driver's license to be more severe. Not surprisingly, this variation was related to the respondents' dependence on their automobiles, suggesting more generally that the perceived severity of a sentence varies across life circumstances and may depend in large measure on how disruptive the sentence is perceived to be.

While useful for the questions posed, Buchner's (1979) index, as well as those generated by Erickson and Gibbs (1979), are of limited value for many claims of the deterrence doctrine. Most important, the perceptions included in these severity scales do not refer to the respondents themselves, although a core figure in deterrence doctrine is the person making judgments about *personal* risks and payoffs on the basis of his or her own life circumstances, not those of some hypothetical general public. In some cases, this personal reference point has been included (see, for example, Grasmick and Green, 1981; Grasmick and Bryjak, 1980; Jensen and Erickson, 1978; Tittle, 1977, 1980).

Grasmick and his associates constructed their measure of perceived severity by asking respondents to "imagine you had been arrested and found guilty and the court had decided what your punishment would be." Respondents were then instructed to "think about what that punishment probably would be for *you*." Finally, they were asked to "indicate how big a problem that punishment would create for your life." Response options included: (1) No problem at all, (2) hardly any problem, (3) a little problem, (4) a big problem, and (5) a very big problem. In this way, not only was the personal reference point specified, but the dimension of comparison was also determined — that is, how problematic a penalty might be.

Sanctions can be problematic in various ways — physical discomfort or deprivation, material loss, self-concept damage, and/or disrupted interpersonal relations. If we are to explore the mechanisms through which sanctions operate, and thereby the conditions under which they become more or less of a deterrent force, it would be useful to have information on which kinds of sanction-induced problems are most important.

Jensen and Erickson (1978) provide some relevant data on this point. Questionnaires were administered to high school students at two points in time. Students were instructed to imagine that they had been caught and taken to juvenile court. They were then asked how much they would worry about the police hurting them, a judge sending them to a reformatory, a judge putting them on probation, how their parents might react, a delinquent record keeping them out of college, a record keeping them from getting a good job, other teenagers thinking badly of them, their teachers thinking badly of them, and thinking badly of themselves. In this way, three types of problems were considered — formal punishments, reactions of significant others, and restricted opportunities to realize common success goals.

Given this multidimensional approach to sanction severity, these data offer the possibility of exploring, albeit somewhat tentatively, how various sanction dimensions are related to one another, and thereby the mechanisms through which sanction severity operates. Unfortunately, this analysis was not reported. Instead, we must turn to the wo⌐k of Tittle (1980) for relevant data on sanction mechanisms.

In Tittle's research, an estimate of sanction severity was obtained by asking respondents how upset they would be if (1) arrested and (2) put in jail for punishment. In addition, respondents were asked to estimate the amount of respect they would lose "among people you know personally if they found out about it." The respect items were combined with various certainty estimates to construct a general scale of sanction fear, as well as subscales for interpersonal, community, and formal sanction fear and severity. Thus it was possible to estimate the relative importance of interpersonal disruption, community reaction, and formal sanctions.

Comparing the relative deterrent potency of informal and formal sanctions, Tittle (1980: 240-242) concluded: (1) persons are likely to be deterred by the possibility of informal sanctions; (2) the apparent effects of formal sanctions are dependent on the perception of informal reactions; (3) the perceived severity of informal sanctions is "far more potent" than perceptions of certainty and operates independently of the level of certainty (indicating that the neglect of sanction severity growing from studies of official statistics should be reconsidered); (4) the deterrent impact of the perceived certainty of informal sanctions "appears to be totally dependent upon perceived severity"; and (5) social control as a general process appears to be rooted almost completely in informal sanctioning.

Among the dimensions of sanctions that Tittle (1980) compares, the disruption of one dimension of interpersonal relationships (loss of interpersonal respect) appeared to be the most potent predictor of self-estimated future behavior. One important implication of these findings is that they provide a link between psychological perceptions of sanction severity and the structural considerations of interpersonal networks. Close attention should thus be given to conceptualizing and measuring the strength of interpersonal relations, as well as to relational responses to the disruptive impact of punishment. This issue will be taken up later in the chapter.

Tittle's (1980: 240) data also suggest little relationship between the objective properties of sanctions and individual perceptions: "Hence an important challenge for future research is to identify the processes involved in the formation of individual perceptions of sanctions and to specify the role of objective sanction characteristics in those processes." Once again, longitudinal data are called for.

Perceptual deterrence research has also suffered from the cross-sectional problems considered previously. In addition to gathering data at one point in time, many perceptual deterrence data incorporate a troublesome quirk. While aimed at testing the deterrence model, which assumes that perceptions precede behavior, some questionnaires have asked respondents to report current perceptions of potential sanctions along with past behavior, thus reversing the hypothesized order. Although there have been some exceptions to this general tendency (for example, Teevan, 1976; Erickson, 1976; Tittle, 1980), this reversal, along with the cross-sectional nature of the self-report surveys, has precluded any firm conclusion regarding the experiential (criminal behavior leading to perceptions of sanctions) and deterrence (perceptions of sanctions leading to criminal behavior) models (for example, Saltzman et al., 1982). It is possible, of course, that both processes might be operating. Unfortunately, cross-sectional studies with a reverse-question format leave us where we began; we think something is operating, but we are not exactly sure what it is.

Self-report studies with a reverse-question format rely on an assumption of perceptual stability. If perceptions are stable across time, responses should provide information about the state of mind when the behavior is reported to have taken place. Although plausible, this assumption confronts important theoretical and empirical contradictions. For behavior in general, and criminal behavior in particular, there is reason to assume that perceptions reflect substantial instability (Briar and Piliavin, 1965; Collins, 1981; Saltzman et al., 1982).

Saltzman et al. (1982: 177-180) provide longitudinal data correlating perceptions of arrest risk for both a generalized "other" and for oneself at two points in time (approximately one year apart):

For all but one of the perceptual measures . . . the estimate of sanction risk significantly differs from Time 1 to Time 2. . . . At the very least, the data presented here suggest that the assumption of perceptual stability, crucial for the proper causal interpretation of these findings from prior deterrence studies, is not strongly supported.

Although there are limitations imposed by the sample (respondents were freshmen at a major state university), these data, coupled with more general arguments (for example, Collins, 1981), put the burden of proof on those who would assume perceptual stability when conducting deterrence research.

Further analysis of the data by Saltzman et al. (1982) suggests that perceptions of personal risk have a stronger deterrent influence than perceptions of aggregate risk. Similar results have been reported and argued by Tittle (1980) and by Grasmick and Bryjak (1980), among others. While hardly surprising, these results offer further support for a more general point: "Sociological concepts can be made fully empirical only by grounding them in a sample of [the] typical micro-events that make them up" (Collins, 1981: 988). Hence, if we are interested in specifying the mechanisms through which formal sanctions influence perceptions and behavior, we would do well to concentrate on relatively restricted life circumstances and at the same time allow for a strong probability of perceptual instability from one set of circumstances to another.

What can we cull from perceptual deterrence studies by way of guidance for future research? First, it appears that the perceived personal severity of sanctions is a better predictor of behavior than the perceived general severity. Second, formal sanctions are in some sense "filtered" by informal processes. Third, given the personal, informal nature of the sanctioning process, it is reasonable to assume that macro patterns of general deterrence are generated from events within rather restricted interpersonal arenas.

As plausible as these guidelines seem to be, they are supported by rather imperfect data. The cross-sectional nature of most self-report surveys, as well as the frequent reversal of question format, preclude confident assertions. In addition, all self-report surveys depend on recall and on hypothetical situations. Respondents are either asked to imagine their future chances of engaging in specified behavior or to recall past behavior. There is evidence suggesting the validity of self-reported past criminal activity in some situations, but "the fact is the self-report method produces less valid results among those very groups that tend to have high rates of official delinquency" (Hindelang, et al., 1981: 213). This differential validity makes any comparison across highly crime-prone individuals and less crime-prone individuals suspect. Unfortunately, these are exactly the categories that we often want to compare in deterrence research. Thus, the accuracy of reported anticipations of future criminal behavior is anybody's guess at this point.

The safest conclusion seems to be that data on the processes through which subjective and objective sanction properties are linked to one another — and to the probability of criminal behavior — are not easily captured by self-report surveys, and certainly not by official statistics. By comparison, longitudinal observational studies, based on extended contact and in-depth interviews, offer more promise in this regard.

Observational studies have been underutilized in the pursuit of the issues raised above, although an exception is provided by Ekland-Olson and his associates (1982) in a six-year observational study of "restrictive" deterrence among dealers of illicit drugs. Observations and interviews provided information on events surrounding the establishment of contacts, the arrangement of drug deals, calculations of potential risks and payoffs, and the adjustment of associations and activities. A model summarizing the connections between sanctions, fear, interpersonal relations, and the scope and intensity of involvement in drug dealing is depicted in Figure 5.1.

Of particular note for present purposes are the relational anchors of sanction-induced fear. Punishment was perceived as a more or less severe life crisis. Like other crises, it was not limited to the person being arrested, prosecuted, and sentenced; rather, it spilled over into the lives of friends, family, and fellow dealers, thereby affecting the strength of relations with these associates. Thus, the perceived severity of punishment was influenced not only by the number of years a person might spend in prison, but also by a wide variety of police and court practices capable of disrupting interpersonal networks with dealers, friends, and family.

The link between interpersonal relationships and the impact of sanctions has been widely noted. We have already reviewed the

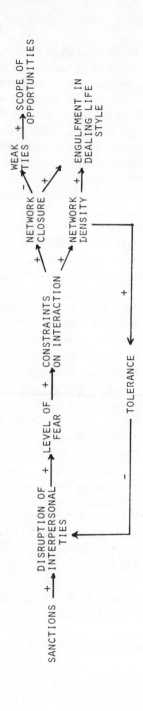

Figure 5.1 Deterrence Mechanism Suggested by Longitudinal Study of Illicit Drug Dealing

studies of Tittle (1980), Grasmick and Green (1981), Grasmick and Bryjak (1980), and Jensen and Erickson (1978). Similarly, the interpersonal implications of sanctions are found throughout Becker's (1963) discussion of "outsiders," Lemert's (1951) conceptualization of "secondary deviance," and Schur's (1971) elaboration of "role engulfment." More specifically, Irwin (1970: 39-40) concluded that among the felons he studied, the period from arrest to disposition was a relatively short-lived life crisis, one central element of which was the disruption of interpersonal networks. Relatedly, Moore (1978: 99) concluded that the severity of imprisonment was in large measure mediated by the presence of supportive interpersonal ties within the prison.

The model in Figure 5.1, with its accompanying propositions (Ekland-Olson et al. 1982), while generated from a case study of drug dealing, may be relevant to a wide range of criminal activity. Although many forms of crime are more solitary than drug dealing (for example, rape), and therefore perhaps less responsive to the deterrence mechanisms implied in Figure 5.1, the model should be quite relevant to the study of deterrence as it affects such behavior as juvenile delinquency (Erickson and Jensen, 1977), prostitution (Bryan, 1965), and fencing stolen goods (Klockars, 1974).

DIRECTIONS FOR FUTURE RESEARCH

Based on our review, two orienting propositions for the measurement of sanction severity are suggested: (1) the severity of punishment depends on the amount of life disruption created; and (2) one critical element of sanction-induced disruption is stress on interpersonal relationships. These simple propositions can be used to account for variations in sentence severity across time, individuals, and circumstances.

Meier and Johnson (1977), among others, suggest that deterrence research be embedded in a broader etiological framework. The relational disruption approach to deterrence is consistent with research growing out of what has been the most influential etiological approach to crime and delinquency during the past decade, namely that by Hirschi (1969). Hirschi's version of control theory centers on the strength of "bonds to society," a particularly important set of which are those defining interpersonal relationships. If the strength and structure of interpersonal relations are the best predictors of crime in etiological studies, there is reason to believe that these same factors should be of central importance in determining the impact of sanctions. Thus, the relational disruption approach to sanction severity puts us in a position to explore the impact of sanctions using the same conceptual framework that has proved so useful in the etiological study of crime and delinquency.

Given the multidimensional nature of interpersonal bonds (Ekland-Olson, 1982), future research on the meaning and impact of sanction severity might move beyond global perceptions of problems (Grasmick and Green, 1981; Grasmick and Bryjak, 1980), the degree of worry (Jensen and Erickson, 1978), and loss of respect (Tittle, 1980) to a comparison of the relative importance of disruption to normative beliefs, patterns of exchange, emotional attachments, and the frequency and pattern of involvement. Such an expansion of interest should enable further specification of the mechanisms through which sanction severity operates.

This approach takes us beyond traditional concern with the psychological fear of sanctions and thus is not a strict test of classical deterrence doctrine (Gibbs, 1975). It is quite consistent, however, with Tittle's (1980: 5) suggestion that the study of deterrence be broadened:

> The deterrence problem really consists of three parts: identifying sanctions or sanction threats in a meaningful way, determining how much and what kind of effect they have on deviance, and specifying the mechanisms by which the effects occur.

Measurement strategies based on a relational disruption conception of sanction severity, and that take into account the multidimensional nature of relationships, offer a promising route toward identifying meaningful dimensions of sanctions, the behavioral effects that sanctions have, and the mechanisms through which those effects take place.

REFERENCES

AKERS, R. L., M. D. KROHN, L. LANZA-KADUCE, and M. RADOSEVICH (1979) "Social learning and deviant behavior: a specific test of a general theory." American Sociological Review 44: 636-655.

ANDERSON, L. S., T. CHIRICOS, and G. P. WALDO (1977) "Formal and informal sanctions: a comparison of deterrent effects." Social Problems 25: 103-114.

ANTUNES, G. and A. L. HUNT (1973) "The impact of certainty and severity of punishment on levels of crime in the United States: an extended analysis." Journal of Criminal Law and Criminology 64: 486-493.

BAILEY, W. C. (1980) Deterrence and the celerity of the death penalty: a neglected question in deterrence research." Social Forces 58 (June): 1308-1333.

——— and R. P. LOTT (1976) "Crime, punishment and personality: an examination of the deterrence question." Journal of Criminal Law and Criminology 67: 99-109.

BAILEY, W. C. and R. W. SMITH (1972) "Punishment: its severity and certainty." Journal of Criminal Law, Criminology and Police Science 63: 530-539.

BAILEY, W. C., L. N. GRAY, and D. J. MARTIN (1971) "On punishment and crime (Chiricos and Waldo, 1970): some methodological commentary." Social Problems 19: 284-289.

BALDUS, D. C. and J. W. L. COLE (1975) "A comparison of the work of Thorsten Sellin and Issac Ehrlich on the deterrent effect of capital punishment." Yale Law Journal 85: 170-186.

BEAN, F. D. and R. G. CUSHING (1971) "Criminal homicide, punishment and deterrence: methodological and substantive reconsiderations." Social Science Quarterly 52: 277-286.

BECKER, G. S. (1968) "Crime and punishment: an economic approach." Journal of Political Economy 76 (March/April): 169-217.

BECKER, H. (1963) Outsiders. New York: Macmillan.

BEYLEVELD, D. (1980) A Bibliography on General Deterrence. Westmead, England: Saxon House.

BIDERMAN, A. (1966) "Social indicators and goals," pp. 68-153 in R. A. Bauer (ed.) Social Indicators. Cambridge, MA: MIT Press.

BLACK, T. and T. ORSAGH (1978) "New evidence on the efficacy of sanctions as a deterrent to homicide." Social Science Quarterly 58: 616-631.

BOWERS, W. J. and G. L. PIERCE (1975) "The illusion of deterrence in Isaac Ehrlich's research on capital punishment." Yale Law Journal 85: 187-208.

BOWERS, W. J. and R. G. SALEM (1972) "Severity of formal sanctions as a repressive response to deviant behavior." Law and Society Review 6: 427-441.

BOX, G. E. P. and G. M. JENKINS (1970) Time Series Analysis: Forecasting and Control. San Francisco: Holden-Day.

BRIAR, S. and I. PILIAVIN (1965) "Delinquency, situational inducements, and commitment to conformity." Social Problems 13: 35-45.

BROWN, D.W. (1978) "Arrest rates and crime rates: when does a tipping effect occur?" Social Forces 57 (December): 671-682.

BRYAN, J. H. (1965) "Apprenticeship in prostitution." Social Problems 12: 287-297.

BUCHNER, D. (1979) "Scale of sentence severity." Journal of Criminal Law and Criminology 70: 182-187.

CARR, B., H. GOLDBERG, and C. FARBAR (1974) "The breathaliser legislation: an inferential evaluation." Ministry of Transport, Ottawa.

CARR-HILL, R. A. and N. H. STERN (1973) "An econometric model of the supply and control of recorded offenses in England and Wales." Journal of Public Economics 2 (Novemver): 289-318.

CHIRICOS, T. G. and G. P. WALDO (1970) "Punishment and crime: an examination of some empirical evidence." Social Problems 18: 200-217.

COLLINS, R. (1981) "On microfoundations of macrosociology." American Journal of Sociology 86: 984-1013.

COOK, P. (1980) "Research in criminal deterrence: laying the groundwork for the second decade," pp. 211-268 in N. Morris and M. Tonry (eds.) Crime and Justice: An Annual Review of Research, Vol. 2. Chicago: University of Chicago Press.

EHRLICH, I. (1977) "Capital punishment and deterrence: some further thoughts and additional evidence." Journal of Political Economy 85 (August): 741-788.

———— (1975a) "The deterrent effect of capital punishment: a question of life and death." American Economic Review 65 (June): 397-417.

———— (1975b) "Deterrence: evidence and inference." The Yale Law Journal 85: 209-227.

———— (1973) "Participation in illegitimate activities: a theoretical and empirical investigation." Journal of Political Economy 81 (May/June): 521-565.

EKLAND-OLSON, S. (1982) "Deviance, social control and social networks," pp. 271-299 in S. Spitzer and R. Simon (eds.) Law and Social Control, Vol. IV. Greenwich, CT: JAI Press.

———— (1981) "The impact of legal sanctions." Presented at the annual meetings of the American Society of Criminology, San Francisco.

———— J. LIEB, and L. ZURCHER (1982) "The paradoxical impact of sanctions: some microstructural findings and propositions." Unpublished.

ERICKSON, M. and J. P. GIBBS (1979) "On the perceived severity of legal penalties." Journal of Criminal Law and Criminology 70: 102-116.

———— (1975) "Specific vs. general properties of legal punishment and deterrence." Social Science Quarterly 56: 390-397.

———— and G. F. JENSEN (1977) "The deterrence doctrine and the perceived certainty of legal punishments." American Sociological Review 42: 305-317.

ERICKSON, M. L. and G. F. JENSEN (1977) "Delinquency is still group behavior: toward revitalizing the group premise in the sociology of deviance." Journal of Criminal Law and Criminology 68: 262-273.

ERICKSON, P. G. (1976) "Deterrence and deviance: the example of cannabis prohibition," Journal of Criminal Law and Criminology 67: 222-232.

FORST, B. (1977) "The deterrent effect of capital punishment: across-state analysis of the 1960's." Minnesota Law Review 61: 743-767.

—— (1976) "Participation in illegitimate activities: further empirical findings."
Policy Analysis 2: 477-492.

FOX, J. A. (1979) "Crime trends and police expenditures: an investigation of the lag
structure." Evaluation Quarterly 3: 41-58.

GEERKEN, M. and W. GOVE (1975) "Deterrence: some theoretical considerations." Law and Society Review 9 (Spring): 497-513.

GIBBS, J. P. (1975) Crime, Punishment and Deterrence. New York: Elsevier Scien-
tific.

—— (1968) "Crime, punishment and deterrence." Southwestern Social Science
Quarterly 48: 515-530.

GRANGER, C. W. J. (1968) "Investigating causal relations by econometric models
and cross-spectral methods." Econometrica 37: 424-438.

—— and P. NEWBOLD (1977) Forecasting Economic Time Series. New York:
Academic.

GRASMICK, H. G. and G. J. BRYJAK (1980) "The deterrent effect of perceived
severity of punishment." Social Forces 59: 471-491.

GRASMICK, H. G. and D. E. GREEN (1981) "Deterrence and the morally committed." Sociological Quarterly 22: 1-14.

—— (1980) "Legal punishment, social disapproval and internalization as inhibitors
of illegal behavior." Journal of Criminal Law and Criminology 71: 325-335.

GRAY, L. N. and J. D. MARTIN (1969) "Punishment and deterrence: another
analysis of Gibbs' data." Social Science Quarterly 50: 389-395.

GREENBERG, D. F. and R. KESSLER (1982) "Model specification in dynamic
analyses of crime deterrence," pp. 15-32 in J. Hagan (ed.) Deterrence Reconsidered. Beverly Hills, CA: Sage.

—— and C. H. LOGAN (1979) "A panel model of crime rates and arrest rates."
American Sociological Review 44: 843-850.

GREENWOOD, M. J. and W. J. WADYCKI (1973) "Crime rates and public expenditures for police protection: their interaction." Review of Social Economy 31:
138-151.

HAMBLIN, R. L. (1974) "Social attitudes: magnitude measurement and theory,"
pp. 61-120 in H. M. Blalock (ed.) Measurement in the Social Sciences. Chicago:
Aldine.

HANSEN, D. A. and R. HILL (1964) "Families under stress," pp. 782-819 in H. T.
Christensen (ed.) Handbook of Marriage and the Family. Chicago: Rand Mc-
Nally.

HANSEN, D. A. and V. JOHNSON (1979) "Rethinking family stress theory: definitional aspects," pp. 582-603 in W. R. Burr et al (eds.) Contemporary Theories
About the Family, Vol. 1. New York: Free Press.

HENSHEL, R. L. and R. A. SILVERMAN [eds.] (1975) Perception in Criminology.
New York: Columbia University Press.

HILL, R. (1949) Families Under Stress. New York: Harper & Row.

HINDELANG, M. J., T. HIRSCHI, and J. G. WEIS (1981) Measuring Delinquency. Beverly Hills, CA: Sage.

HIRSCHI, T. (1969) The Causes of Delinquency. Berkeley: University of California
Press.

HURST, P. (1978) "Blood test legislation in New Zealand." Accident Analysis and Prevention 10: 287-296.

IRWIN, J. (1970) The Felon. Englewood Cliffs, NJ: Prentice-Hall.

JENSEN, G. F. and M. ERICKSON (1978) "The social meaning of sanctions," pp. 119-136 in M. Krohn and R. Akers (eds.) Crime, Law and Sanctions: Theoretical Perspectives. Beverly Hills, CA: Sage.

——— and J. P. GIBBS (1978) "Perceived risk of punishment and self-reported delinquency." Social Forces 57: 57-78.

JOHNSTON, J. (1972) Econometric Methods (2nd ed.). New York: McGraw-Hill.

KAU, J. and P. RUBIN (1975) "New estimates of the determinants of urban crimes." Annals of Regional Science 9 (March): 68-76.

KLECK, G. (1979) "Captial punishment, gun ownership and homicide." American Journal of Sociology 84: 882-910.

KLOCKARS, C. B. (1974) The Professional Fence. New York: Macmillan.

KRAUT, R. E (1976) "Deterrent and definitional influences on shoplifting." Social Problems 23: 358-368.

LAND, K. and M. FELSON (1976) "A general framework for building dynamic macro social indicator models: including an analysis of changes in crime rates and police expenditures." American Journal of Sociology 82: 565-604.

LEMERT, E. (1951) Social Pathology. New York: McGraw-Hill.

LOFTIN, C. and D. McDOWALL (1982) "The police, crime and economic theory: an assessment." American Sociological Review 47: 393-401.

LOGAN, C. H. (1975) "Arrest rates and deterrence." Social Science Quarterly 56 (December): 376-389.

——— (1972) "General deterrent effects of imprisonment." Social Forces 51: 64-73.

——— (1971) "On punishment and crime (Chiricos and Waldo, 1970): some methodological commentary." Social Problems 19: 280-284.

McCLELLAND, K. A. and G. ALPERT (1982) "Factor analysis applied to magnitude estimates of punishment seriousness: patterns of individual differences." Unpublished.

McDOWALL, D. and C. LOFTIN (1982) "ARIMA causal models: an introduction and an application to deterrence research," pp. 135-148 in J. Hagan (ed.) Deterrence Reconsidered. Beverly Hills, CA: Sage.

McDOWALL, D., R. McCLEARY, E. MEIDINGER, and R. HAY (1980) Interrupted Time Series Analysis. Beverly Hills, CA: Sage.

McPHETERS, L. R. and W. B. STRONGE (1974) "Law enforcement expenditures and urban crime." National Tax Journal 27: 633-644.

MEIER, R. F. and W. T. JOHNSON (1977) "Deterrence as social control: the legal and extra legal production of conformity." American Sociological Review 42: 292-304.

MOORE, J. W. (1978) Homeboys: Gangs, Drugs and Prison in the Barrios of Los Angeles. Philadelphia: Temple University Press.

NETTLER, G. (1982) Responding to Crime. Cincinnati, OH: Anderson.

NEWMAN, G. (1978) The Punishment Response. New York: J. B. Lippincott.

NOORDUZIJ, P. (1977) "The introduction of a statutory BAC Limit of 50 mg/100 ml and its effects on drinking habits and traffic accidents," in Proceedings of the

Seventh International Conference on Alcohol, Drugs and Traffic Safety. Canberra: Australian Government Publishing Service.

PALMER, J. (1977) "Economic analysis of the deterrent effect of punishment: a review." Journal of Research in Crime and Delinquency 14 (January): 4-21.

PASSELL, P. (1975) "The deterrent effect of the death penalty: a statistical test." Stanford Law Review 28 (November): 61-80.

—— and J. B. TAYLOR (1977). "Deterrent effect of capital punishment: another view." American Economic Reivew 67: 445-451.

PHILLIPS, L. and H. VOTEY (1975) "Crime control in California." Journal of Legal Studies 4: 327-349.

ROSS, H. (1982) "Interrupted time series studies of deterrence of drinking and driving," pp. 71-98 in J. Hagan (ed.) Deterrence Reconsidered. Beverly Hills, CA: Sage.

—— (1977) "Deterrence regained: the Cheshire constabulary's breathaliser blitz." Journal of Legal Studies 6: 241-249.

—— (1975) "The Scandinavian myth: the effectiveness of drinking-and-driving legislation in Sweden and Norway." Journal of Legal Studies 4: 285-310.

—— (1973) "Law, science and accidents: the British Road Safety Act of 1967." Journal of Legal Studies 2: 1-78.

—— R. McCLEARY, and T. EPPERLEIN (1982) "Deterrence of drinking and driving in France: an evaluation of the law of July 12, 1978." Law and Society Review 16: 345-374.

ROSSI, P. H., E. WAITE, C. E. BOSE, and R. E. BERK (1974) "The seriousness of crimes: normative structure and individual differences." American Sociological Review 39: 224-237.

SALEM, R. and W. J. BOWERS (1970) "Severity of formal sanctions as a deterrent to deviant behavior." Law and Society Review 5: 21-40.

SALTZMAN, L., R. PATERNOSTER, G. P. WALDO and T. CHIRICOS (1982) "Deterrent and experiential effects: the problem of causal order in perceptual deterrence research." Journal of Research in Crime and Delinquency 19 (July): 172-189.

SCHUR, E. (1971) Labeling Deviant Behavior. New York: Harper & Row.

SELLIN, T. (1959) The Death Penalty. Philadelphia: American Law Institute.

—— and M. E. WOLFGANG (1964) The Measurement of Delinquency. New York: John Wiley.

SILBERMAN, M. (1976) "Toward a theory of criminal deterrence." American Sociological Review 41: 442-461.

SJOQUIST, E. (1973) "Property crime and economic behavior: some empirical results." American Economic Review 63: 439-446.

STEVENS, S. S. (1966) "A metric for the social consensus." Science 141: 530-541.

—— (1962) "The surprising simplicity of sensory metrics." American Psychologist 17: 29-39.

—— (1957) "On the psychophysical law." Psychological Review 64: 153-181.

SWIMMER, E. (1974a) "Measurement of the effectiveness of urban law enforcement — simultaneous approach." Southern Economic Journal 40: 618-630.

—————— (1974b) "The relationship of police and crime: some methodological and empirical results." Criminology 12: 293-314.

TEEVAN, J. J., Jr. (1976) "Subjective perceptions of deterrence (continued)." Journal of Research in Crime and Delinquency 13: 155-164.

THURSTONE, L. L. (1927) "A law of comparative judgment." Psychological Review 34: 273-286.

TITTLE, C. (1980) Sanctions and Social Deviance. New York: Praeger.

—————— (1977) "Sanction fear and the maintenance of social order." Social Forces 55 (March): 579-596.

—————— (1969) "Crime rates and legal sanctions." Social Problems 16: 409-423.

—————— and C. H. LOGAN (1973) "Sanctions and deviance: evidence and remaining questions." Law and Society Review 7: 371-396.

TITTLE, C. and A. ROWE (1974) "Certainty of arrest and crime rates: a further test of the deterrence hypothesis." Social Forces 52: 455-462.

TORGESON, W. S. (1954) "A law of categorical judgment." American Psychologist 9: 483.

WALDO, G. P. and T. G. CHIRICOS (1972) "Perceived penal sanction and self-reported criminality: a neglected approach to deterrence research." Social Problems 19: 522-540.

Chapter 6

COMMUNITY CONTEXT AND THE DETERRENT EFFECT OF SANCTIONS

R O B E R T   J.   B U R S I K, J r.

Smith and his associates (1980: 212-213) estimate that the cost of serious juvenile crime in the United States for 1976 was approximately $9.8 billion — 28 percent of our total crime costs. As the agencies most clearly mandated to control such crime, the juvenile courts have come under increasingly severe attack. As early as 1967, it had been concluded that the juvenile courts had not only failed in "reducing or even stemming the tide of juvenile criminality," but also in "bringing justice and compassion to the child offender" (President's Commission, 1967: 7).

While juvenile court sanctions reflect some balance between the traditional philosophic commitment to "individualized treatment"

AUTHOR'S NOTE: *This research has been funded in part through National Institute of Justice grant 82-IJ-CX-001419. I would like to extend my appreciation to Fran Behan, Allen Harden, Don Merten, Michelle Pazul, Emil Peluso, Gary Schwartz, and Jim Webb. They offered insightful comments and suggestions concerning this project while they were my treasured colleagues at the Institute for Juvenile Research prior to the elimination of the research program by forces beyond our control. In recognition of the institute's long tradition of research, this chapter is respectfully dedicated to the memory of Henry McKay, Joseph Puntil, and Clifford Shaw.*

and pressures for "law and order" (Fox, 1974), there is no question that public evaluation of the court is based primarily on perceptions of its ability to deter youths from further illegal activity. Court personnel are very aware of such expectations. In a recent study involving 2000 juvenile court judges, administrators, and probation officers, personnel were asked to describe the performance expectations that they felt were imposed on them by the communities in their jurisdictions (Sarri and Hasenfeld, 1976). The responses of the probation officers, who "bear the major burden of responding to community demands on the court," are most enlightening. Over one-half felt that the community expected them to "protect the community at any cost," "remove offenders with serious behavior problems from the community at any cost," and "make examples of those committing the most serious offenses." On the other hand, less than one-quarter of the probation officers perceived expectations to "consider the needs of the offender" or to "keep offenders in the community as much as possible" (Sarri and Hasenfeld, 1976: 75-76).

Some court systems have self-consciously begun to incorporate community pressures for the strict treatment of serious offenders into their operational procedures. In Cook County, Illinois, for example, the percentage of cases dismissed without prejudice dropped from 21.7 percent to 7.1 percent between 1980 and 1981, while the number of cases with delinquency findings almost doubled. More notably, the commitment of youths to the Department of Corrections increased from 441 to 941, although the total number of adjudications increased by only 258 cases.

Yet as the President's Commission pointed out, the actual ability of the juvenile court to satisfy expectations of "harsher treatment" appears to be rather weak. Critics emphasize two factors directly related to this apparent ineffectiveness: (1) the probability of a youth actually receiving a court sanction is very small, and (2) the severity of the sanctions available is not sufficient to deter offenders from continued delinquency. Even if a juvenile is arrested by the police and referred to court, the odds of him or her being punished are small, and the punishment itself (if received) is fairly inconsequential. Thus, the risks attached to delinquent behavior are relatively low.

Such criticisms cannot be dismissed lightly. In a cohort study of approximately 10,000 male youths in Philadelphia, Wolfgang and his colleagues (1972) found that the deliquents who were recidivists (53.6

percent) accounted for 84 percent of all the offenses committed by the cohort. Moreover, the 18 percent of the sample categorized as chronic offenders (defined as committing five or more offenses) were responsible for 52 percent of all offenses. Likewise, almost 50 percent of the youths referred to the Cook County juvenile court during 1978 had previously been referred on delinquency charges (Institute for Juvenile Research, 1979). However, as Fisher and Erickson (1973: 179) argue, such evidence should be regarded cautiously before reaching conclusions concerning the effectiveness of the juvenile court. The outcome of a court intervention may be highly confounded with various factors, and is often found to be independent of a disposition per se. It is this confounding that will be investigated here.

The President's Commission (1967: 8) suggested that the ineffectiveness of the juvenile court stemmed from a "grossly optimistic view of what is known about the phenomenon of juvenile criminality." This naïveté has also been problematic in studies evaluating the deterrent effectiveness of juvenile court sanctions, with much evaluative work being characterized by an emphasis on individual juvenile offenders and the sanctions that they receive, without a simultaneous consideration of the social context that may influence recidivism. Although actual sanctions are determined within the confines of the court, the ensuing response of the individual occurs outside of this environment— within the context of daily experience. Therefore, the nature of an offender's residential community may have an important mediating effect on the deterrent power of a sanction.

CONTEXTUAL ASPECTS OF
JUVENILE COURT SANCTIONS

Since the landmark work of Shaw (1929) and Shaw and McKay (1931, 1942), sociologists have recognized the important role of community processes in the etiology of delinquent behavior. Many researchers (Lander, 1954; Bordua, 1958-1959; Chilton, 1964) have provided strong evidence that delinquency is not randomly distributed in urban areas. More recently, other analysts (Kapsis, 1978; Bursik and Webb, 1982) have presented evidence that rapidly changing neighborhoods are characterized by relatively high rates of delinquency, regardless of their racial composition.

An awareness of such community processes has been reflected in various social programs directed toward delinquency prevention. For example, the Chicago Area Project (founded by Shaw and his associates in the late 1930s) takes a distinctly community-based approach to delinquency by attempting to mobilize the sentiments of attachment, belonging, and respect on the part of juveniles for community leaders who in turn demonstrate that they are concerned about the welfare of youth in their neighborhoods. A basic assumption of this program is that the effective control of delinquency is only possible through personal relationships within the community (Finestone, 1976: ch. 6). Somewhat similar programs have been instituted in many other parts of the United States, such as Denver (Blew et al., 1977), Boston (Miller, 1962), and Seattle (Berleman and Steinburn, 1967).

Despite the central role of community processes in the formulation of such prevention programs, most investigators of individual-level juvenile deterrence (with the notable exception of Erickson et al., 1977, and Jensen et al., 1978) fail to consider how sanction effectiveness can be mediated by such social contexts. This is an unfortunate omission, for findings indicate (for example, Erickson et al., 1977) that there may be significant differentiation in the "social condemnation" of crimes across communities. As Erickson and his associates (1977: 316) point out: "All purported evidence of general deterrence is suspect without a direct consideration of such variation."

Nevertheless, this failure to consider the effects of community context in most evaluations of the effectiveness of juvenile court sanctions is somewhat understandable. Many of these studies evolved directly from economic models of rational behavior in which it is assumed that an individual decides whether to engage in crime "depending upon the benefits and costs associated with crime and lawful choices" (Palmer, 1977: 5). Although economists have been criticized for not only clearly conceptualizing the nature of these costs in relation to criminal behavior (see Gibbs, 1975: 204), this orientation can be criticized on even more basic grounds. For example, Simon (1955) has argued that we lack any evidence that humans can perform such calculative tasks in situations of any complexity. This stance has been supported by work showing that even in relatively simple situations, people have a hard time simultaneously considering every dimension pertinent to a decision (Shepard, 1964).

Rather, subjects tend to make decisions on the basis of only one or two factors, ignoring the contribution of remaining criteria. Thus, as Simon (1955) argues, people seem to perform substantial simplifications of complex situations and to act on these simplifications.

Obviously, the commission of a delinquent offense is an extremely complex activity. A youth may not only have to consider the probability of apprehension and the type of sanction that he or she may receive, but also the perceived approval or condemnation of peers and family. One certainly cannot expect a potential juvenile offender to calculate accurately the costs and benefits of all relevant deterrent and social factors; indeed, the evidence indicates that it is hardly possible. Hence, some type of simplification is necessary.

While the perceived costs of potential sanctions may be an important consideration prior to recidivism, a youth may give other aspects of the situation greater priority. There are many possible dimensions along which such decisions may be simplified, but the community represents a most powerful referent for juveniles (Suttles, 1972), because it is there that friends are to be found and cultivated. As Berry and Kasarda (1977: 78) conclude, the community becomes a "component of individual identity, a stable judgmental reference against which people are assessed." Therefore, it can also serve as a generalized referent to be used in calculating the costs and benefits of engaging in illegal activities.

Wolfgang and his colleagues (1972) provide evidence highlighting the effect that the community may have in mediating the effectiveness of sanctions imposed on juveniles. For each member of their cohort, they recorded the median income of the tract in which the boy resided; the odds of being a recidivist were much higher in lower-status communities (7.9 to 1) than in higher-status communities (2.8 to 1). Such patterns were noted for both white and nonwhite youths.

For present purposes, we will focus on two general community characteristics: (1) the overall delinquency rate of the neighborhood, as measured by the rate per 1000 juveniles of contact with the police and referral to juvenile court on delinquency matters, and (2) the likelihood that a sanction will be imposed for an officially recorded delinquent act (the probability that police contact will result in an arrest, and that a referral to juvenile court will result in the filing of a delinquency petition).

Although there are a number of potentially relevant community characteristics, this analysis will concentrate on these four variables, for two reasons. First, lacking community-specific measures of how juveniles perceive the seriousness of various kinds of delinquency, rates of such activities can be used as rough surrogates. Second, as an evaluation of sanction effectiveness, the nature of delinquency in a community should have a more straightforward effect on the probability of recidivism than broader (but relevant) contextual factors such as income or residential mobility.

THE DATA

Individual-Level Data

The sanctions handed down to youths first referred to the Cook County, Illinois, juvenile court during 1978 (and the results of their subsequent court appearances) supplied the basic data for this research. These data consitute a continuous record of the officially recorded activities of these youths for a 2-3-year period. The restriction to first offenders is important, since the postsanction histories of these youths are not confounded with previous court handling. The data were drawn from the Youth Data Repository, which has been continuously compiled by the Institute for Juvenile Research in Chicago since 1978. This enormous file is a complete record of all problematic juvenile contact with police, juvenile court, and mental health agencies in the city of Chicago (see Institute for Juvenile Research, 1979, 1980).

Ideally, both police records and court-contact files would have been integrated into this research. Unfortunately, it is impossible to reconstruct the delinquency histories of specific individuals from police data. Although strict confidentiality safeguards are also incorporated into court data, individuals histories can be reconstructed by means of a consistent court identification number. Therefore, this analysis centers on factors that are associated with a reappearance in juvenile court.

Due to the nature of the general project from which this chapter derives, this sample includes only first offenders referred to court on petitions pertaining to burglary, robbery, and aggravated assault. Given the focus on court sanctions and the control of serious delinquency, these three offenses are very pertinent: Burglary is the most common index property crime for which juveniles are arrested, while robbery and assault are the most common violent index crimes. Thus, these are not in any respect marginal offenses.

Of the 15,852 referrals to the Cook County juvenile court during 1978, 938 youths qualified for inclusion in the analysis; 4.4 percent of them appeared on charges on aggravated assault, 67.8 percent appeared on charges of burglary, and 27.8 percent appeared on charges of robbery. There is an important difference in the recidivism for these youths and for first offenders in general. The probability of a reappearance in court for this population was only .388, while other findings presented earlier tended to be over .5. Therefore, regardless of the sanction applied by the court, first-time serious offenders (as defined here) tended not to be referred again. Overall, the sample averaged just over two offenses.

Table 6.1 presents the distribution of the sanctions handed down to these youths for their first offenses. Readers may notice that just over 9 percent of the sanctions are classified as missing. This pattern arises from an unfortunate aspect of the repository — that the only sanctions recorded in the files are those delivered at the screening interview, when the court makes an initial assessment of the youth and decides whether further court action is necessary (Thomas and Fitch, 1981: 39-40). To obtain sanction data on cases filed for further processing by the court, we were forced to go directly to the record library of the court and examine each folder. Those cases classified as missing represent youths who had reached the age of majority by the time of our search (and whose records were subsequently destroyed), or else the cases were currently active, making the folders unavailable to us. These youths were excluded from the analysis.

For our purposes, sanctions were recoded into six dummy variables: SCRSUP (a 90-day supervision period with a probation officer, the youth's parents, or a social agency, handed down during the screening interview); HDIS (a filed petition that is dismissed with or without prejudice); HSUP (a filed petition that results in supervision); HPROB (a filed petition that results in probation); HDOC (a filed petition that results in commitment to the Department of Correc-

TABLE 6.1   Distribution of Sanctions for First Offenses

Sanction	Percentage
At Screening	
Adjusted	21.5
90 Day Supervision—P.O.	8.3
90 Day Supervision—Parent	8.5
90 Day Supervision—Agency	1.0
After Filing of Petition	
Dismissed without prejudice	21.0
Supervision	4.6
Dismissed with prejudice	0.1
Stricken to leave-reinstate	9.8
Move to guardianship calendar	0.1
Commitment to DOC	1.4
Probation	13.4
Unified delinquency intervention	0.1
No action before recidivism	0.6
Missing	9.5
	100.0
N	938

tions); and HNOACT (a filed petition that has been stricken from the docket with leave to reinstate or reappear in court subsequent ot the filing of the initial petition but prior to any court action). The majority of cases that are 0 on all of the dummy variables were adjusted at the screening interview; thus, the effects of the dummy variables represent deviations from the probability of recidivism when no court action is applied.

Four additional pieces of information were drawn from the repository files — ethnicity, gender, living situation, and age at first offense. The first three variables were again dichotomized to reflect being black (64.3 percent of the sample), a girl (6.8 percent of the sample), and living with two parents (40.5 percent of the sample).

The fourth variable was left in continuous form but presents a special problem in the analysis. In Illinois, as in many other states, a youth can no longer be referred to juvenile court on a delinquency petition after turning seventeen. Therefore, the event histories are right-censored by design. Although the sample averages 15.01 years of age at the time of initial referral to court, there is a good deal of variation in this distribution (standard deviation = 1.49 years). Therefore, some youths have a longer period during which they are at risk of becoming a recidivist. In the analyses that follow (except where noted), the effect of age is only entered into the models to control statistically for these varying periods of risk; it should *not* be given a substantive interpretation.

One final adjustment to the data must be made. No referrals to juvenile court that occurred after December 31, 1980, are reflected in the file. Thus, if two youths of the same age committed their first offenses three months apart and had no subsequent petitions referred to court, one youth will have been at risk for three more months than the other. At times in the analysis it will be necessary to adjust the model for this factor. The time between a youth's first referral to court and December 31, 1980 (designated as PERIOD), will be entered into the model to control for this effect.

Community-Level Data

The two indicators of community context were constructed through a maximum-likelihood factor analysis (with varimax rotation) of the four variables listed in Table 6.2. These variables were obtained by aggregating the individual repository records to the community level, of which there are 75 in Cook County, Illinois, officially recognized by the U.S. Census Bureau.

Although these two community characteristics are expected to have independent effects on the probability of recidivism, there is also the possibility that they may be related to the phenomenon through an interaction with court sanctions. For example, probationary sanctions may be more effective in the control of recidivism when they are handed down to youths living in relatively delinquency-free neighborhoods. In order to investigate this possibility, interaction terms involving both community indicators and the six sanction dummy variables were included.

FINDINGS

There are several ways of conceptualizing sanction effectiveness. The strongest formulation is to define effectiveness as the ability to

TABLE 6.2   Statistical Structure of Community Variables

	Factor Pattern		
	Rate	Deter	Communality
Rate of police contacts	.946	−.019	.895
Probability of police contact resulting in an arrest	.616	.549	.681
Rate of court referrals	.986	.081	.979
Probability of court referral resulting in a filed petition	−.027	.944	.892
	Factor Scores		
	Rate	Deter	
Rate of police contacts	.447	−.155	
Probability of police contact resulting in an arrest	.209	.392	
Rate of court referrals	.451	−.073	
Probability of court referral resulting in a filed petition	−.151	.834	

prevent any further illegal activity. Although this is an obvious consideration, the approach is somewhat simplistic in that it neglects the possibility that sanctions can be partially effective.

Partial effectiveness can be reflected in two related postsanction behavior patterns. The first is a lessening of the incidence of delinquent behavior. As Akers (1977: 46) notes, there only has to be a decrease in the rate of behavior for punishment to be considered at least somewhat effective. Serious offenders may not totally desist from delinquent activity, but some youths may commit fewer offenses than they would have if no sanction had been imposed. The second pattern implied by partial effectiveness involves the elapsed time between the imposition of a sanction and the first recurrence of delinquency. Since deterrent effects may decay with time, some deterrence may be reflected in the ability of a sanction to increase significantly the time that elapses until the youth again appears in court. All three of these standards of effectiveness will be investigated in this analysis.

Since total effectiveness is reflected in the dichotomous distinction between the recidivist and the nonrecidivist, discriminant analysis is a natural model for this type of evaluation. In this case, a forward selection, stepwise approach was used to identify those variables that differentiated between the two statuses ($p \leqslant .05$). As Table 6.3 indicates, six variables were associated with the total-effectiveness criterion. As expected, one's age at the time of first referral to court is the strongest predictor of recidivism, with older youths more likely to be nonrecidivists. As noted before, this is primarily a statistical artifact. Surprisingly, the two court sanctions with significant effects have signs that are opposite from what should be expected: Youths who received dismissals or probationary dispositions were more likely to be recidivists than those receiving any other sanction, including a dismissal at the screening interview (the bulk of the residual category).

The interpretation of this finding is not as straightforward as it might seem, since youths whose cases are dismissed at screening are generally seen by the court as less serious offenders than those on whom petitions are filed. Therefore, the negative sign may indicate that these sanctions increase the probability of recidivism, or that the petitions were filed because the court correctly sensed that there was a higher likelihood of recidivism.

Although the individual sanctions handed down to offenders do not strongly affect the probability of recidivism (with the exception of the pattern just noted), the community-specific probability of apprehension and sanctioning (DETER) significantly decreases the odds of become a recidivist. In addition, the effectiveness of commitment to the Department of Corrections is significantly heightened if a youth resides in a high-delinquency neighborhood. In terms of total effectiveness, then, court sanctions appear to have their greatest effect in terms of potential, as opposed to actual, imposition. Also, individual sanctions (or at least commitments) may only be related to recidivism in certain community contexts.

The analysis of the effect of the court's first response to youth on the *degree* of recidivism is limited to those youths who reappeared in court after the initial sanctioning. This dimension of performance was analyzed through a stepwise regression of the natural logarithm of the number of subsequent appearances using the same set of variables as

TABLE 6.3   Variables Significantly Associated With the
             Probability of Recidivism

	Standardized Canonical Discriminant Coefficients
Age at first referral	.826
HDIS	−.288
HPROB	−.426
RSEX	.238
DETER	.310
RATE × HDOC	.340
Group Centroids	
Nonrecidivist (N = 536)	.222
Recidivists (N = 315)	−.578
Eigenvalue = .084	
Canonical correlation = .279	

before (see Table 6.4). The results are again rather discouraging from
a special deterrence perspective. Only one sanction (commitment to
the Department of Corrections) was independently associated with
the suppression of recidivism, and this may not even be due to the
effectiveness of the sanction per se, but may simply reflect the fact
that being incarcerated limits the number of opportunities to engage in
such behavior.

For two of the other three significant effects in the equation, the
community context tends to accelerate the degree of recidivism,
though in a manner that is counterintuitive. Whereas the community-
level probability of apprehension and sanctioning tended to suppress
the probability of recidivism in general (Table 6.3), recidivistic youths
living in areas where this probability was highest tended to be more
active. Although the reason for this pattern cannot be discerned from
these data, two possibilities may be suggested. First, continued contact with the court may jade the youth to the seriousness of these
sanctions. In fact, it may lead a youth to the conclusion that such
sanctions are essentially no punishment at all. The finding in Table
6.4, that youths who receive no court action in areas of high deterrent
probabilities tend to commit more offenses than the rest of the sample,
lends support to this conjecture. Or for the most active offenders, the

TABLE 6.4   Regression Analysis of the LN (number of
postsanction offenses)—Recidivists Only

Variable	B	S.E.	Beta	F
Age at first referral	−.133	.019	−.358	47.236
DETER × HNOACT	.412	.144	.152	8.189
DETER	.069	.026	.144	7.042
DETER × HDOC	−.348	.124	−.182	7.894
HDOC	−.524	.250	−.133	4.405
Constant	3.099			
R^2	.177			
Standard Error	.452			
Overall F Statistic	13.262			

willingness to risk relatively high probabilities of apprehension and sanctioning may increase his or her status among peers involved in delinquency. Such patterns have been noted among gang members in Chicago (Short and Strodtbeck, 1965).

It should be pointed out that the interaction between the delinquency rate of an area (RATE) and the effect of probation was very nearly significant. This near-effect reflects a tendency for such sanctions to be more effective in areas of high delinquency. At the same time, it is apparent that a youth's rate of activity is only weakly associated with individual court sanctions. When such sanctions do have an effect, it is primarily in interaction with community characteristics.

The final dimension of effectiveness — the time between the sanction and the first reappearance in juvenile court — was analyzed through a partial-likelihood proportional hazards model (Cox, 1972, 1975; see also Tuma, 1982). This approach to event histories estimates survivor functions for a single event (such as the time to a death or birth) and is well-suited for analysis of the time to the first instance of recidivism. The estimated regression parameters reflect the effect of each variable on the "instantaneous" rate of recidivism, with positive effects being associated with a shorter period between the sanction and the subsequent offense. The model was again estimated in a stepwise fashion (see Table 6.5).

TABLE 6.5   Effects on Recidivism—Recidivists Only

Variable	B	S.E.	χ^2	P
Age at first referral	.295	.058	25.70	.0000
DETER × HDIS	.587	.211	7.75	.0054
DETER × HNOACT	.828	.351	5.55	.0184
Overall χ^2	46.78			
D.F.	3			
P	0.0			
D*	.145			

*A measure of fit that is comparable to an R^2 statistic.

For this analysis, the age at first offense can be given a substantive interpretation. Since we have limited the analysis to recidivists and have focused on the time to the first reappearance in court, there is by definition no censoring problem. As shown in Table 6.5, older youths tend to become recidivists more quickly than younger ones. Again, individual court sanctions appear to be unable to modify the rate of recidivism, since none of the sanctions has a direct effect on the rate of recidivism. In fact, if a youth's first petition is dismissed at the court hearing or stricken with leave to reinstate, there tends to be an increase in this rate in some communities. We must conclude, then, that court sanctions themselves are fairly ineffective in deterring serious first offenders from speedily resuming their illegal activity. Although individual responses may have an effect in a particular community context, it may be in a direction contrary to the court's intention.

DISCUSSION

Although the preceding analysis indicates that individual juvenile court sanctions are fairly ineffective in deterring serious juvenile offenders, this conclusion must be tempered by three important considerations. First, this analysis could not generally differentiate, on the basis of initial court sanctions, between those who desist and those who recidivate. The primary deterrent for subsequent illegal behavior seems to be the community-specific probability that a police or court contact might result in a sanction being imposed. Nevertheless, the majority of youths (61 percent) do not become recidivists. The court experience may thus be considered a deterrent for most first offenders, although its success is actually derived from processes not reflected in specific sanctioning policies.

Second, it is important to emphasize that our sample consists a fairly select group of individuals who initiated their offense histories with behaviors serious enough to be considered FBI Index offenses. Therefore, the findings in this chapter may not reflect the ability of the court to deter delinquents referred to court on charges of theft or simple assault.

Finally, we have only focused on sanctions imposed for the first appearance in court, assuming that it is this event that has the greatest effect on subsequent behavior. However, with each additional appearance in court, a new sanction is imposed (or old sanctions are modified). Therefore, we have not examined the possibility that special deterrence is achieved through accumulated court sanctions. This is a key issue that will be examined in subsequent work.

Clearly, initial sanctions can only weakly predict who will become a hard-core, serious offender and who will desist after a single appearance in court. In fact, community characteristics, especially the probability of a police or court sanction, play a much stronger role in the decision-making process of youths. This effect is important, for it often works in a direction contrary to that predicted by traditional deterrence theory. While there is some tendency for youths from high-probability areas to refrain from activities that could lead to recidivism (Table 6.3), within the recidivist subsample there is an interaction of this probability with the type of sanction that is handed down. When a sanction was severe, such as commitment to the Department of Corrections, youths in high-probability areas reappeared in court significantly *fewer* times (as shown in Table 6.4; however, recall the caveats of this effect that were noted). However, when a sanction was relatively minor (as in the case of HNOACT in Tables 6.4 and 6.5 and HDIS in Table 6.4, the interaction with the community context resulted in *increased* delinquent activity. Thus, the probability of illegal behavior may be increased in what would otherwise be highly deterrent environments.

We must conclude that community contexts and court sanctions often have a joint effect on recidivism that can reverse the intended effect of a sanction. In closing, we shall reiterate that only one potential aspect of the decision to engage in delinquency has been considered here. At best, the proportion of the variation that has been accounted for is modest; the community is only one aspect of the phenomenon of recidivism. Nevertheless, this analysis indicates that those studying the impact of sanctions must begin to consider how that impact can vary across different environments and the possible interactions between general and specific deterrence in those environments.

REFERENCES

AKERS, R. (1977) Deviant Behavior: A Social Learning Approach (2nd ed.). Belmont, CA: Wadsworth.

BERLEMAN, W. C. and T. W. STEINBURN (1967) "The execution and evaluation of a delinquency prevention program." Social Problems 14: 413-423.

BERRY, B.J.L. and J. KASARDA (1977) Contemporary Urban Ecology. New York: Macmillan.

BLEW, C. H., D. McGILLIS and G. BRYANT (1977) Project New Pride. Washington, DC: Government Printing Office.

BORDUA, D.J. (1958-1959) "Juvenile delinquency and 'anomie': an attempt at replication." Social Problems 6: 230-238.

BURSIK, R.J. and J. WEBB (1982) "Community change and patterns of delinquency." American Journal of Sociology 88: 24-42.

CHILTON, R.J. (1964) "Continuity in delinquency area research: a comparison of studies for Baltimore, Detroit and Indianapolis." American Sociological Review 29: 71-83.

COX, D. R. (1975) "Partial likelihood." Biometrika 62: 269-276.

——— (1972) "Regression models and life tables." Journal of the Royal Statistical Society 34: 177-220.

ERICKSON, M. L., J. P. GIBBS, and G. F. JENSEN (1977) "The deterrence doctrine and the perceived certainty of legal punishment." American Sociological Review 42: 305-317.

FINESTONE, H. (1976) Victims of Change. Westport, CT: Greenwood Press.

FISHER, G. A. and M. L. ERICKSON (1973) "On assessing the effects of official reactions to juvenile delinquency." Journal of Research in Crime and Delinquency 10: 177-194.

FOX, S. J. (1974) "The reform of juvenile justice: the child's right to punishment." Juvenile Justice 7: 2-9.

GIBBS, J. P. (1975) Crime, Punishment and Deterrence. New York: Elsevier.

Institute for Juvenile Research (1980) Youth Problems in the City: 1979 Annual Report. Chicago: Illinois Department of Mental Health.

——— (1979) Youth Problems in the City: 1978 Annual Report. Chicago: Illinois Department of Mental Health.

JENSEN, G. F., M. L. ERICKSON, and J. P. GIBBS (1978) "Perceived risk of punishment and self-reported delinquency." Social Forces 57: 57-78.

KAPSIS, R. E. (1978) "Residential succession and delinquency." Criminology 15: 459-486.

LANDER, B. (1954) Toward an Understanding of Juvenile Delinquency. New York: Columbia University Press.

MILLER, W. B. (1962) "The impact of a 'total community' delinquency control project." Social Problems 10: 168-191.

PALMER, J. (1977) "Economic analyses of the deterrent effect of punishment: a review." Journal of Research in Crime and Delinquency 14: 4-21.

President's Commission on Law Enforcement and the Administration of Justice (1967) Task Force Report: Crime and Its Impact — An Assessment. Washington, DC: Government Printing Office.

SARRI, R. and Y. HASENFELD (1976) Brought to Justice? Juveniles, the Courts and the Law. Ann Arbor: University of Michigan.

SHAW, C. R. (1929) Delinquency Areas. Chicago: University of Chicago Press.

——— and H. D. McKAY (1942) Juvenile Delinquency and Urban Areas. Chicago: University of Chicago Press.

——— (1931) Social Factors in Juvenile Delinquency (Vol. 2 of the Report on the Causes of Crime). Washington, DC: Government Printing Office.

SHEPARD, R. N. (1964) "On subjectively optimum selections among multiattribute alternatives," pp. 257-281 in M. W. Shelley and G. L. Bryan (eds.) Human Judgements and Optimality. New York: John Wiley.

SHORT, J. F., Jr. and F. L. STRODTBECK (1965) Group Process and Gang Delinquency. Chicago: University of Chicago Press.

SIMON, H. (1955) "A behavioral model of rational choice." Quarterly Journal of Economics 69: 302-355.

SMITH, C. P., P. S. ALEXANDER, and D. J. THALHEIMER (1980) A National Assessment of Serious Juvenile Crime and the Juvenile Justice System: The Need for a Rational Response. Washington, DC: Government Printing Office.

SUTTLES, G. (1972) The Social Construction of Communities. Chicago: University of Chicago Press.

THOMAS, C. W. and W. A. FITCH (1981) "The exercise of discretion in the juvenile justice system." Juvenile and Family Court Journal 32: 31-50.

TUMA, N. B. (1982) "Non-parametric and partially parametric approaches to event history analysis," pp. 1-60 in S. Leinhardt (ed.) Sociological Methodology 1982. San Francisco: Jossey-Bass.

WOLFGANG, M. E., R. M. FIGLIO, and T. SELLIN (1972) Delinquency in a Birth Cohort. Chicago: University of Chicago Press.

Chapter 7

EQUITY IN COURT DISPOSITIONS

KENNETH A. HARDY

One of the criteria for measuring the performance of a court system is the equality of treatment accorded the offenders whose cases are processed through it. The issue of equal treatment has been a major concern for criminal justice researchers from a variety of disciplines, including law, economics, sociology, and political science. While a variety of theoretical perspectives have been offered as explanatory frameworks for empirical findings (for example, Chambliss and Seidman, 1971; Hindelang, 1978; Quinney, 1977; Schur, 1971; Turk, 1969), the central empirical question has always been whether extralegal factors play a role in the processing of defendants' cases through the steps of the criminal justice system. More specifically, do defendant characteristics such as race, gender, and socioeconomic status have an effect on outcomes such as incarceration, plea bargaining, or indictment? This chapter will examine the question of equal justice by first discussing the meaning of equal treatment under the law, second, reviewing previous research, third, offering a critique of this research, and fourth, presenting a preliminary analysis of data on a sample of North Carolina homicide cases that illustrates some of the issues raised in the critique.

EQUALITY UNDER THE LAW

Before assessing the degree to which a court system provides equal treatment for defendants, a working definition of equal treatment under the law must be developed and the boundaries of the court system defined. Because it is a simpler concept, the boundaries shall be defined first. For the purposes of this discussion, the court system shall be defined as all aspects of the processing of a defendant's case occurring after arrest and prior to incarceration. Thus, the fairness of the arrest decision, as important as it is, will not be discussed. Indeed, other authors in this volume address the same issue (see also Nettler, 1979: 37-40; Gottfredson and Gottfredson, 1980). The main decision points of concern are, therefore, indictment, plea bargaining, trial verdict, and sentencing.[1]

The concept of equal treatment employed in evaluating the court system is rooted in the Western legal-rational notion of justice acting according to rule (Frankel, 1969). As Nettler (1979) has noted, the criminal justice system's central problem is to protect society while at the same time treating those accused of wrongdoing in an even-handed manner. Although absolute standards concerning methods for determining guilt or innocence and appropriate punishment for the guilty may not exist (Perelman, 1967), there is the expectation that legislatively determined procedures and penalties will be applied in an equitable manner to all, and that only legally relevant matters of fact and legally permissible procedures shall govern the eventual outcome of a case.

The notion of "equal treatment" does not connote equality of outcome, irrespective of the circumstances of a case. Instead, it refers to "equal treatment of those similarly situated with respect to the issue before the court" (Cahn, 1949: 14; see also Nettler, 1979). Moreover, the circumstances used to judge the similarity of cases must be those deemed appropriate under the law; they cannot be factors without legal foundation, such as a defendant's race (Cahn, 1949: 15-18). Indeed, the range of charges and penalties for perhaps the most serious of crimes — murder — clearly indicates that not all killings are judged to be equally heinous and deserving of a single penalty, such as death or life imprisonment. Factors such as the number of victims, the intent of the accused, provocation by the victim, and the concurrent commission of another felony are all circumstances taken into account in determining the legal seriousness of a homicide. The popular notion of "letting the punishment fit the crime," and the more recently discussed concept of "just deserts," reflect this equity-based concept of equal treatment. Thus, equal treatment under the law is more a question of equity in the administration of statutes than it is equality of outcomes for different social groups. The importance of this definition of equal treatment will become clearer when the critique of past research is presented.

Adopting equity of legal administration as the definition of equal treatment leaves open the question of the justness or fairness of the laws being administered. As Cahn (1966: 390-391) has noted: "Reason, experience and history bring forward too many instances where a precept of law, far from serving as a fit model for justice, implements religious bigotry, oppresses the poor, or exploits the weak." History is replete with instances of "unfair" laws enacted by the powerful to the detriment of the disadvantaged. Laws prescribing racial segregation can be fairly administered, but they are not necessarily fair. Moreover, laws can be created that, when applied without prejudice, may still have a disproportionate impact on certain segments of a society. Vagrancy laws are just one example.

The point is that assessing the fairness with which laws are applied is not the same as assessing the fairness of the laws themselves. While assessing the equality of treatment in the construction of law is a very important issue, it is a separate question from assessing the equality of treatment in the administration of law. The distinction is made here merely to facilitate clarity of thought and not to artificially divide the two questions. Clearly, completely equal treatment of citizens in any society requires both equitable laws and equitable administration of those laws. The larger issue is neglected here only to sharpen our focus on equity in administration.

Overall equity in the administration of laws by the court system is the product of the degree of equity accorded defendants at each stage of their journey through the system. While the processing of adult defendants through the court system is a complex process (Gottfredson and Gottfredson, 1980: 1-20) and may differ in some details from jurisdiction to jurisdiction, the process may be generally summarized as the outcome of four major decision points: After arrest, the prosecutor's first basic decision is whether to charge the defendant with a specific crime or crimes, or to dismiss the case. This decision point may be called the "indictment stage." Once a prosecutor has charged a defendant, the next decision to be made is whether to formally try the defendant or to bargain with him or her for a guilty plea. In many jurisdictions, the prosecutor may offer to reduce the number of charges against the defendant, decrease the severity of the charges, recommend lenient sentencing to the judge, or any combination of these and other alternatives. It is also possible (but not common) for the prosecutor to elect to dismiss the charges at this point. Most cases are actually resolved at this "plea bargaining" stage.

If the prosecutor decides to bring the defendant to trial, the third major decision point is then reached. A verdict regarding the guilt or innocence of the defendant on the charge of charges is usually rendered by either a jury or a judge. Finally, if the defendant is found guilty, either by verdict or bargained guilty plea, a sentence is usually pronounced by a judge. In some jurisdictions, the judge's sentencing discretion is constrained by statute, and for some crimes, notably first-degree homicide, a jury decides the penalty. After a verdict and sentence are pronounced, the defendant may appeal them through several levels of appellate courts.

PREVIOUS RESEARCH

Past research concerning the equal treatment of defendants under the law is voluminous and, all too often, contradictory. In part, this is because studies have varied greatly with respect to the offenses and jurisdictions sampled, the variables used, and the methodologies employed. These differences have often been compounded by the use of various theoretical frameworks for the interpretation of findings. Thus, comparing research findings in this area is a difficult task. Given the problems of volume and comparability, no attempt will be made here to make an exhaustive review of the literature. Rather, a synopsis of positive and negative findings will be offered for each major extralegal variable at each stage of the judicial process. The interested reader is encouraged to examine and compare the studies cited in order to resolve questions of comparability and quality.

Racial Discrimination

The issue of racial discrimination in case processing has generated more research than any other major extralegal variable. This literature has examined the effect of race on the equality of treatment from three perspectives — the race of the accused, the race of the victim, and the racial composition of the accused-victim dyad. Three corresponding hypotheses have most commonly been investigated, either separately or in various combinations:

(1) minority-group defendants are treated more harshly than white defendants;

(2) defendants with minority-group victims are treated more leniently than those with white victims; and

(3) minority-group defendants who have victimized whites are treated more harshly than defendants in dyads made up of other combinations.

Discrimination Based on Defendant's Race

Eisenstein and Jacob (1977) present evidence supporting the hypothesis of harsher treatment for minority-group defendants during the dismissal/indictment stage. However, other researchers (Bernstein, Kelly, et al., 1977; Bernstein et al. 1977; Feeley, 1979; La Free, 1980b; Radelet, 1981) have found no support for the hypothesis that discrimination occurs at this stage. Race's role at this stage may thus depend on special circumstances. One study (Boris, 1979) reported an interaction between race of defendant and whether homicide victims were known to defendants. In cases where homicide victims were not friends or relatives of a defendant (that is, nonprimary homicides), blacks were indicted for murder more often than whites.

Findings regarding the effects of the accused's race on the seriousness of the charge for which a defendant is convicted — as the result of either a plea bargain or a trial — are not plentiful. The research of Eisenstein and Jacob (1977) and La Free (1980a) supports the contention of racial discrimination in plea bargaining, while others (Kelly, 1976; Bernstein et al., 1977) found that alternate variables conditioned the relationship. For example, Kelly (1976) noted that the nature of the offense, as well as whether defense counsel was retained or appointed, joined with the race of the accused in a complex interaction on plea-bargain sentences. Bernstein and her colleagues (1977) found that at first appearance, race had no effect on cases, but did have an effect in cases settled by bargains after the first appearance. Eisenstein and Jacob (1977) also found that defendant race affected jury verdicts, but that the magnitude of the effect differed from city to city. Other authors dispute this finding (for example, Garfinkel, 1949; Swigert and Farrell, 1977; La Free, 1980a, 1980b). Finally, Farnworth and Horan (1980) report that race interacted with appointed (versus retained) counsel and offense type for verdicts in district court cases, such that blacks with appointed counsel were convicted more often than whites for certain offenses. They found no racial effects in superior court cases.

The most extensive literature on the effect of the defendant's race on case-processing outcomes concerns the sentencing stage of the judicial process for adults. Here again, sentencing may come after either a bargained guilty plea or a trial verdict. A recent overview of this literature is provided by Kleck (1981); only a brief synopsis of findings is given here. Many studies lend support to the hypothesis that minority-group members, particularly blacks, receive harsher sentences than whites for a given crime (Martin, 1934; Mangum, 1940; Lemert and Rosberg, 1948; Bullock, 1961; Jacob, 1962; Cameron, 1964; Howard, 1967; Janos and Mendelsohn, 1967; Gerard and Terry, 1970; Chiricos et al., 1972; Wolfgang and Reidel, 1973; Cargan and Coates, 1974; Kulig, 1975; Pope, 1975a, 1975b; Tiffany et al., 1975; Hall and Simkus, 1975; Kelly, 1976; Zimring et al., 1976; Adams, 1976; Lizotte, 1978; Lotz and Hewitt, 1977; Uhlman, 1977; Pope, 1978; Unnever et al., 1980; Spohn et al., 1982). Other studies offer no support for this hypothesis (Johnson, 1941; Garfinkel, 1949; Bensing and Schroeder, 1960; Green, 1964; Wolf, 1964; Baab and Ferguson, 1968; Atkinson and Newman, 1970; Mileksi, 1971; Levin, 1972; Rau, 1972; Conklin, 1974; Burke and Turk, 1975; Chiricos and Waldo, 1975; Clarke and Koch, 1976; Perry, 1977; Farrell and Swigert, 1978a, 1978b; Sutton, 1978; Hagan and O'Donnel, 1978; Myers, 1979; La Free, 1980b; Hagan et al., 1980; Radelet, 1981). Two studies (Greenwood et al., 1973; Bernstein, Kelly, et al., 1977) found that, contrary to the hypothesis, whites received harsher sentences than blacks, while several studies indicate that the effect of race of the accused is contingent on other variables.

The most common interaction between race and case outcomes is with type of offense (Kleck, 1981; Rhodes, 1976; Kelly, 1976; Alaska

Judicial Council, 1977), with sentences for certain offenses showing discrimination, while sentences for others show none. Still another study (Foley and Rasch, 1979) found that for female felony defendants, whites received harsher sentences than blacks for homicide, while the reverse was true for property crimes.

Variables such as time period (Thomson and Zingraff, 1981), rural versus urban jurisdiction (Hagan, 1975, 1977), and presiding judge (Gibson, 1978; Uhlman and Walker, 1980) have also been found to condition the relationship. A recent study (Farnworth and Horan, 1980) reported that several variables, including retained versus appointed counsel, severity of offense, past criminal record, and occupational status, interacted with race in explaining sentencing outcomes. However, the specific two-way interactions having an effect differed between district court and superior court cases.

Due to the severity and finality of the penalty, a more specialized literature has developed regarding the relationship between race of the accused and the death penalty. Studies examining the sentencing of homicide defendants are included in the prior discussion of race and sentencing. However, another important aspect of the death penalty involves actually carrying out or commuting the sentence. Several authors (Mangum, 1940; Bridge and Mosure, 1961; Student Special, 1969; Johnson, 1970) conclude that race is a factor in carrying out the death penalty, while others (Johnson, 1941; Bedau, 1964, 1965, 1976) suggest that race of the accused is not the sole factor involved. Another study (Wolfgang et al., 1962) found that the nature of the homicide interacted with race, while yet another (Bowers, 1974) concluded that race was a factor only in the South.

Discrimination Based on Race of Victim

While empirical research investigating the role of the defendant's race in case processing has been extensive and widely published, research examining the role of the victim's race or the racial composition of the victim/offender dyad is more scarce. Radelet (1981) found that suspects in homicide cases with black victims were indicted less often for first-degree murder than were those in cases with white victims. Victim race, however, had no effect on sentencing. La Free (1980a) analyzed the processing of rape cases and found that victim race had no effect on whether a case was bargained or tried, but did affect verdicts in cases that went to trial.

Some studies examining the racial composition of the victim/offender dyad (Bowers and Pierce, 1980; La Free, 1980b) have found that black offenders who victimized whites were indicted more often than others for homicide and rape cases. However, while Garfinkel (1949) noted that this combination was more likely to result in a guilty verdict in homicide cases, La Free (1980b) reports no such relationship for rape cases.

With respect to severity of sentence, many authors (Johnson, 1941; Garfinkel, 1949; Green, 1964; Wolfgang and Reidel, 1973; Zimring et al., 1976; Bowers and Pierce, 1980; La Free, 1980b) have found evidence to support the hypothesis that black offenders with white victims are given harsher sentences than other offenders, although Farrell and Swigert (1978a, 1978b) found no such effect in their data. In his extensive review of the literature, Kleck (1981) concludes that the research supporting this hypothesis has been confined primarily to rape cases.

Class Bias

The role of the socioeconomic status of defendants in case processing has received a great deal of theoretical attention, particularly by sociologists developing conflict models of the criminal justice system (for example, Chambliss and Seidman, 1971; Quinney, 1977). However, the empirical research relating to this topic is not nearly so voluminous as that on race.

The basic hypothesis guiding much of this research is that lower-class defendants are treated more harshly than middle- or upper-class defendants. One study of homicide cases (Boris, 1979) reported evidence supporting this hypothesis for decisions to indict versus those to dismiss, but only for felony homicides. Swigert and Farrell (1977) also found support for this hypothesis with regard to verdicts in homicide cases. Yet another (Farnworth and Horan, 1978) reported that occupational status had a direct effect on the probability of a guilty verdict in district court cases, but not in superior court cases.

Turning to sentencing decision, many studies (Chiricos et al., 1972; Clarke and Koch, 1976; Lizotte, 1978; Kruttschnitt, 1980; Spohn et al., 1982) found evidence supporting harsher treatment of lower-status offenders. However, several studies yielded contrary findings (Landes, 1974; Willick et al., 1975; Chiricos and Waldo, 1975; Myers, 1979). Swigert and Farrell (1977) noted that lower-status offenders with higher-status victims were given more severe sentences than those with low-status victims. Occupational status and race were found to interact for incarceration decisions, but had no effect on length of sentence (Farnworth and Horan, (1978).

Gender Bias

The central assumption about the role of a defendant's gender in the processing of cases has been that females are treated more leniently than males (see Hagan and O'Donnel, 1978, for a review). The role of the victim's gender or of the gender composition of the victim-offender dyad is less well defined. It may also be contingent on the relationship between the victim and offender; however, relatively few empirical studies have sought to examine the role of gender in case processing and, not surprisingly, their results have been somewhat mixed. An investigation of dismissals (Feeley, 1979) found no relationship between the defendant's gender and case dismissals; however, another study of dismissals (Williams, 1978) did find that defendants whose victims were female had their cases dismissed more often than those with male victims. Relatedly, Bernstein et al., (1977) reported no effect of defendant gender on plea bargaining outcomes at first appearance, but did report that males pled guilty more often than females after the first appearance. Two other studies (Swigert and Farrell, 1977; Cousineau and Veevers, 1972) report that women were found guilty less often than men in trial verdicts.

With regard to sentencing, Cousineau and Veevers (1972) and Pope (1975a, 1975b, 1978) found that women received shorter sentences than men, while Feeley (1979) found that females were treated more harshly than males in these decisions. On the other hand, several authors (Green, as reanalyzed by Hagan, 1974;

Chiricos et al., 1972; Hagan and O'Donnel, 1978; Sutton, 1978; Hagan et al., 1980) found no such effect for gender. Moreover, no effect of either defendant or victim gender on judges' decisions to incarcerate was found by Meyers (1979). Finally, Farnworth and Horan (1978) also reported no effect for defendant gender on sentencing. However, they did find a relationship between gender and verdicts favoring women in district court cases.

A CRITIQUE

It is always easier to point out flaws in the research of others than to improve one's own research. Nevertheless, synopses and critiques of past research do help to improve the quality of future undertakings. The preparation of this chapter has drawn on several such works (Gottfredson and Gottfredson, 1980; Hagan, 1974; Kleck, 1981; Nettler, 1979), to which the reader is referred. This section will try to summarize critiques of research on the equality of treatment, in addition to making some original contributions to those critiques.

One problem with many of the studies noted above is their selection of a limited range of offenses to test for the effects of extralegal variables in the court system as a whole. Some studies are confined to a particular type of crime, such as murder, shoplifting, or rape. However, these offenses still represent only a portion of the total spectrum of crimes, ranging from traffic offenses, to robbery, to murder, to embezzlement. In particular, so-called "white collar" crimes, such as embezzlement, fraud, and income tax evasion are seldom considered. The review of the literature conducted for this chapter encountered only one such study (Hagan et al., 1980). On the other hand, other studies examine only broad classes of offenses, such as all felonies or all misdemeanors, paying little attention to the possibility that unequal treatment might occur in only a few such offenses.

The difficulties involved in collecting data for this type of research are considerable. It is, therefore, perhaps a bit unfair to criticize past researchers for dealing with limited ranges of offenses. At the same times, conclusions drawn about the lack of effect of extralegal variables for a particular offense or range of offenses do not necessarily mean that those variables have no effect for crimes not included in that range. In fact, it does not seem unreasonable to assume that extralegal variables may have effects for certain offenses and no effects for others. For example, would the race of a defendant be expected to have the same effect for a rape case as for a tax evasion case?

The situation becomes more problematic if one expects the extralegal variables employed in the study to be correlated with the offenses examined. Hindelang (1978) has pointed out that race and socioeconomic status may be highly related to offense type. If this is the case in a particular study, the range of variation in the correlated extralegal variables is restricted. Thus, any effects of these variables may well be disguised. For example, if income tax evasion is committed primarily by upper-middle-class whites, finding a race effect is highly unlikely, unless the sample of offenders is very large or the degree of discrimination quite high. While the conclusion of "no race effect" is warranted in such a circumstance, it is restricted to cases of income tax evasion and cannot be generalized to other offenses or to other distributions of offenders.

Criticism concerning the range of offenses examined is actually an important subset of a more general problem: Many studies fail to control relationships between extralegal variables and outcome measures for relevant legal variables such as type of offense, prior criminal record, and the strength of evidence against the defendant. While the first two variables have been controlled for in recent studies (for example, Unnever et al., 1980; Spohn et al., 1982; Radelet, 1981), the results are still mixed. Although few studies attempt to control for the strength of evidence because of the difficulty of obtaining reliable data and of developing suitable scaling procedures, it is clearly a critical variable. If, as the literature of the past decade strongly suggests, legal variables have a much stronger relationship to outcome measures than do extralegal variables (Hagan, 1974; Kleck, 1981; Nettler, 1979), the conclusions of any study not controlling for some or all of these factors must be viewed with a great deal of skepticism.

In addition to a lack of control for legal variables, many studies do not control for what may be termed "legal process" variables, such as appointed versus retained counsel; jury trial versus plea bargaining; and jury composition versus presentencing report recommendations to sentencing judges. All of these factors have been found to be important in determining case outcomes (Hagan, 1975, 1977; Chiricos et al., 1972; Swigert and Farrell, 1977). In addition, it can be argued that some of these variables are highly related to extralegal variables. For example, socioeconomic status is certainly related to whether or not a defendant can secure retained counsel (Clarke and Koch, 1976).

It is important to distinguish between the direct and indirect effects of extralegal variables. Direct effects support conflict or labeling-theory interpretations of the judicial process, while indirect effects support structural interpretations. For example, a direct effect of race on sentence would indicate, ceteris paribus, overt discrimination. However, an indirect effect of race, perhaps mediated by retained versus appointed counsel, would not support such a contention. Rather, it would indicate a form of "economic discrimination" (Kleck, 1981), wherein the discrimination is structurally rooted in the economic status of defendants rather than overtly practiced by prosecutors, judges, or juries. Likewise, an indirect effect of race mediated by prior criminal record would not support a conclusion of overt racial discrimination. It would, however, indicate a form of "institutional racism" whereby nonwhites would be overpenalized for committing more crimes than whites. As a result, the criminal statutes would prescribe more severe treatment for offenders with prior records.

Yet another class of variables often omitted in studies of equal treatment may be termed "contextual" variables. Among them are region, time period, jurisdiction, stage of process, and relationship between victim and offender (Thomson and Zingraff, 1981). The literature review just presented clearly indicates that these variables often condition relationships. Indeed, it does not seem unreasonable to assume that outcomes might differ among judges, time periods, or regions. Moreover, states and provinces often differ in the range of charging and sentencing options available for particular categories of crimes. The most obvious example is the difference among various states in the availability of the death penalty as a punishment for first-degree murder.

Not only do studies of the equality of treatment differ considerably with respect to the variables controlled for when examining the effects of extralegal variables, but also in how these variables are controlled for. Such differences are reflected not only in the statistical technique employed, but also in the conceptualization of the type of effects that extralegal variables can have on outcomes. Most recent studies, particularly those employing path analytic techniques, hypothesize and test for direct, additive effects of extralegal variables while controlling for a variety of contextual, legal, or legal process variables. The coefficients of the extralegal variables are examined for statistical significance, and conclusions are drawn about the effects of race, gender, or economic status. If statistically significant effects are found, a conclusion of inequality of treatment is usually warranted, provided that relevant legal variables have been controlled for; however, if no significant coefficients for extralegal variables appear, a conclusion of equal treatment is usually made. But such a conclusion is not necessarily correct. Interactions among the variables may exist that are not detected by the linear, additive, statistical models employed.

Conceptually, such interaction effects may be interpreted in two ways. The first interpretation is that legal variables determine outcomes differently for different social groups (Farnworth and Horan, 1978). Therefore, such variables as severity of offense, prior record, and type of legal counsel may produce different outcomes for blacks compared with whites, and/or for women compared with men. The second interpretation is that defendant attributes determine outcomes differently for different levels of legal variables (Radelet, 1981; Phillips and Dinitz, 1982). Thus, being black may result in unequal treatment only for certain types of offenses, such as rape, or only for rapes of white women by black men in the South. Favorable treatment for some offenses and unfavorable treatment for others may even cancel each other out, thus masking the unequal treatment.

Regardless of which of these two conceptualizations may apply to a particular study, unequal treatment involving interactions among variables cannot be detected by simple, additive, statistical models which test only for the significance of parameters representing social subgroup membership. Such tests assume either that the same processes hold for both majority and subgroup offenders, or that subgroup membership has the same average effect on outcome, irrespective of the levels of legal and contextual variables.

A final problem with much of the past research in assessing the equality of treatment is that most studies examine only a single stage of the process. Moreover, the stage examined is usually either the verdict or the sentencing stage, which is almost the last stage in the process. This has been noted by several authors (for example, Hagan, 1974; Boris, 1979; La Free, 1980b; Kleck, 1981; Thomson and Zingraff, 1981). The central problem with single-stage studies that focus on the latter stages of the judicial process is that they cannot take into account the filtering of cases in prior stages.

Since most cases are settled by plea bargains, studies examining trial verdicts and sentences are dealing with a very select sample of cases relative to the population of cases at arrest. Moreover, such studies do not monitor the decisions of prosecutors in discretionary matters prior to trial, such as indictment charges and plea bargains. Therefore, conclusions about the overall equity of the process cannot be drawn from such studies. A preferable, though more time-consuming and costly, research design would be to follow a cohort of arrested cases through the system, noting the important variables that affect *each* major decision point. Unfortunately, the cost entailed in a longitudinal approach may place a limit on the range of offenses that can be investigated in a single study.

AN EXAMPLE

In order to illustrate the need for careful examination of the flow of cases through the court system, a brief, preliminary analysis of data gathered on indictments and plea bargains in homicide cases in North Carolina will be presented. Data were gathered on all deaths in North Carolina between June 1, 1977, and May 31, 1978, that were initially ruled homicides by the Office of the State Medical Examiner, or by a county medical examiner.[2] Deaths by vehicle homicides were not considered, because they are handled as traffic-related offenses rather than as criminal homicides.

Interviews were conducted with police officers, prosecutors, and defense attorneys. In addition, the court records for each case were examined. While a great deal of information was compiled for each case, only a small portion — relating to indictment charges, plea bargains, race of the defendant, judicial division of the state in which the homicide took place, the defendant's prior criminal record, and the strength of the prosecutor's case against the accused — will be dealt with here. The question of interest is whether nonwhite defendants are treated differently than white defendants at the early stages of case processing. More specifically, are nonwhites indicted for first degree murder in greater proportions than whites? Finally, are their cases more frequently bargained rather than tried?

Table 7.1 gives the rates of indictment for first-degree and second-degree murder or less for white and nonwhite defendants. The table shows that the first-degree indictment rates do not differ substantially, and that both nonminority and minority defendants are indicted for first-degree murder in about three out of every four cases. In addition, the data indicate that, if anything, whites tend to be indicted for first-degree murder slightly more often than nonwhites. Thus, a conclusion of discrimination against minority defendants would not be sustained on the basis of these data.

A more complicated picture emerges when two other factors — quality of evidence and judicial division — are considered.[3] Tables 7.2 and 7.3 present an analysis of the effects of evidence quality, judicial division, and race of the accused on the seriousness of the indictment charge, using weighted least squares estimates of a linear model, with all main and interaction effects for these variables included in the model.[4] The important sources of explained variation for this model are summarized by the chi-square statistics in Table 7.2. The table shows:

(1) Evidence quality is the best single predictor of the severity of an indictment ($p < .0001$).

(2) There is a systematic difference among prosecutors in different judicial divisions in their propensity to indict for first-degree murder ($p < .02$).

(3) Despite the fact that there is no main effect of race, a complex interaction exists between all three variables such that for certain levels of the quality of evidence, white and nonwhite defendants are indicted for first-degree murder at different rates, and that these differences vary among judicial divisions. However, the direction of the difference in rates for first-degree murder does not show that nonwhites are consistently overpenalized ($p < .001$).

The presence of the strong three-way interaction among the variables indicates that a simple additive model containing just the main effects

TABLE 7.1   Degree of Homicide Indictment Charge by Race
             of Defendant

| | Race of Defendant | | |
Indictment Charge	White	Nonwhite	Total
Second or less	22.0% (50)	27.1% (80)	24.9% (130)
First	78.0% (178)	72.9% (215)	75.1% (493)
Total	43.6% (228)	56.4% (295)	100% (523)

NOTE: Frequencies in parentheses.

TABLE 7.2   Weighted Least Squares Regression Analysis of Various
             Effects on Probability of First-Degree Indictment

Source	DF	Chi Square	Probability
Intercept	1	209.32	.0001
Evidence quality	3	24.04	.0001
Judicial division	3	9.90	.02
Defendant race	1	1.33	.25
Evidence * Division	9	8.20	.50
Evidence * Race	3	1.96	.60
Division * Race	3	5.81	.15
Evidence * Division * Race	9	28.20	.001

of the three variables would not have fit the data as well. Indeed, the chi square for goodness of fit for such a model is 45.44, with 24 degrees of freedom, indicating a lack of fit with a probability of error less than .005.

An examination of the proportions indicted for first-degree murder reveals that there is no pattern of first-degree indictments that indicates consistent discrimination against nonwhite defendants (see Table 7.3). For example, just for strong first-degree cases, nonwhites were indicted for first-degree murder at a much higher rate than whites in Judicial Division I (94 percent versus 54 percent), at about the same rate in Divisions II (88 percent versus 82 percent), and at lower rates in Divisions III and IV (71 percent versus 94 percent, and 84 percent versus 94 percent, respectively). However, the pattern for weak murder-one cases is not the same. In Division I, whites were indicted at a much higher rate than nonwhites (95 percent versus 44 percent), reversing the trend for strong murder-one cases. In addition, whites were indicted less often in Division II (54 percent versus 92 percent), while the indictment rates for Divisions III and IV were close to equal (82 percent versus 73 percent, and 96 percent versus 95 percent). Thus, from this evidence one might conclude that non-whites are treated unfairly only in certain judicial divisions, and only for certain types of cases. Of course, other factors, such as race of the victim, might account for this varied pattern. However, since over 90 percent of the homicides in this study were intraracial, and only 6 percent of the cases involved murders of whites by nonwhites, such an explanation does not seem likely.

A separate analysis of the same independent variables' effects on whether a case was plea bargained or tried revealed a different pattern of their relative importance. Due to space limitations, the results will be summarized here. A weighted least squares regression analysis revealed that prosecutors' propensities to bargain cases differed among judicial divisions. Furthermore, while neither evidence quality nor race had strong independent effects on the probability of a case being bargained, a significant interaction between the two indicated that bargaining depended on both. An examination of the proportions revealed that prosecutors in Divisions I and III were more likely to bargain cases. In addition, more nonwhite, strong first-degree and strong second-degree cases were settled by plea bargains than were corresponding cases against whites (75.9 percent versus 64.8 percent, and 78.2 percent versus 64.4 percent, respectively). The reverse was true for weak first-degree cases, and the bargaining rates were about equal for weak second-degree cases.

What does this preliminary analysis show? Substantively, it would seem that, compared to each other, neither white nor nonwhite defendants received equal treatment under the law for the cases examined here. However, the degree and type of inequality were contextually dependent. Different factors affected the processing of cases differently at each of the two decision points examined. At indictment, the probability of being charged with first-degree murder was not

TABLE 7.3   Probability of First-Degree Indictment by Evidence Quality, Judicial Division, and Race of Defendant

Evidence Quality	Judicial Division	Race of Defendant	Indictment Probability	N
Strong Murder-One Cases	I	W	.54	14
		NW	.94	25
	II	W	.82	14
		NW	.88	28
	III	W	.94	23
		NW	.71	19
	IV	W	.94	24
		NW	.84	16
Weak Murder-One Cases	I	W	.95	10
		NW	.44	8
	II	W	.54	12
		NW	.92	33
	III	W	.82	14
		NW	.73	24
	IV	W	.96	12
		NW	.95	11
Strong 2nd-Degree Murder Cases	I	W	.66	16
		NW	.58	13
	II	W	.46	12
		NW	.45	19
	III	W	.79	12
		NW	.43	15
	IV	W	.55	10
		NW	.71	12
Weak 2nd-Degree Murder Cases	I	W	.68	11
		NW	.64	21
	II	W	.72	9
		NW	.40	24
	III	W	.79	12
		NW	.72	16
	IV	W	.69	24
		NW	.78	16

consistently determined by a defendant's race. Rather, it depended also on the strength of the evidence and the area of the state in which the homicide occurred. This may indicate that prosecutors' attitudes toward nonwhites may vary by geographic location, and that the expression of negative attitudes may be conditioned by a prosecutor's assessment of the strength of the evidence in a case. However, at the bargaining stage the effect of a defendant's race on whether a case is bargained or tried depends on evidence quality, not location. Nonwhites with strong cases against them pled guilty more often than whites. Whether this was the result of prosecutor leniency toward nonwhites or of nonwhites' fears of harsher treatment at trial is an open question.

Since the analysis presented here is somewhat limited, the main lesson to be learned from these data relates to the methodological criticisms of prior studies in the previous section. Rather than examine a range of offenses, this study concentrated on one serious offense — homicide. Although the results cannot be generalized to other types of offenses, this approach does lend itself to examining case processing longitudinally. Moreover, if evidence quality had not been controlled, or if only linear, additive, statistical models had been employed, or if only one later stage of the process had been examined, important information regarding the processing of these cases through the judicial system prior to trial would not have been uncovered. Granted, many questions remain unexplored at this point. However, the analysis presented should help to illustrate the need for taking these points into consideration when empirically assessing the equality of treatment of various social groups under the law.

NOTES

1. Since juvenile law and court procedures differ substantially from the laws and procedures applied to adult offenders, the equality of treatment of juvenile offenders will not be considered here.

2. Support for this project was provided by NSF grant #SOC-7812178 to Barry Nakell, principal investigator. Any results presented herein are provisional and used only as methodological examples. A complete report on the substantive results of the project is forthcoming.

3. While no table is presented here in order to conserve space, there was no difference between white and nonwhite defendants with respect to prior convictions.

About 24 percent of each group had been convicted of a prior violent felony. Thus, any differences in rates of indictment for first-degree homicide between the two groups are probably not due to differences in prior records.

4. For this regression technique, the proportion indicted for first-degree murder for each cell is treated in a manner similar to a cell mean in a conventional analysis of variance. Also, the chi-square statistic associated with each effect is analogous to the conventional sum of squares in an analysis of variance (Grizzle et al., 1969; Swafford, 1980).

REFERENCES

ADAMS, S. N. (1976) "The black shift phenomenon in criminal justice." Justice System Journal 2: 185-194.

Alaska Judicial Council (1977) Alaska Felony Sentencing Patterns: A Multivariate Statistical Analysis. Anchorage: Alaska Judicial Council.

ARKIN, S. D. (1979) "Discrimination and arbitrariness in capital punishment: an analysis of post-Furman murder cases in Dade County, Florida, 1973-1976." Stanford Law Review 33: 75-101.

ATKINSON, D. N. and D. A. NEWMAN (1970) "Judicial attitudes and defendant attributes: some consequences for municipal court decision making." Journal of Public Law 19: 68-87.

BAAB, G. A. and W. R. FERGUSON (1968) "Texas sentencing practices: a statistical study." Texas Law Review 45: 471-503.

BEDAU, H. A. (1976) "Felony murder, rape and the mandatory death penalty." Suffolk University Law Review 10: 494.

———— (1965) "Captial punishment in Oregon 1903-1964." Oregon Law Review 45: 1-39.

———— (1964) "Death sentences in New Jersey." Rutgers Law Review 19: 1-55.

BENSING, R. C. and O. J. SCHROEDER (1960) Homicide in an Urban Community. Springfield, IL: Charles C. Thomas.

BERNSTEIN, I. N., A. J. CARDASCIA, and C. E. ROSS (1979) "Defendant's sex and criminal court decisions," in R. Alvarez (ed.) Discrimination in Organizations. San Francisco: Jossey-Bass.

BERNSTEIN, I. N., W. R. KELLY, and P. A. DOYLE (1977) "Societal reaction to deviants: the case of criminal defendants." American Sociological Review 42: 743-755.

BERNSTEIN, I. N. et al. (1977) "Charge reduction: an intermediate stage in the process of labelling criminal defendants." Social Forces 56: 362-384.

BORIS, S. B. (1979) "Stereotypes and disposition of criminal homicide." Criminology 17: 139-158.

BOWERS, W. J. (1974) Executions in America. Lexington, MA: D.C. Heath

———— and G. L. PIERCE (1980) "Arbitrariness and discrimination under post-Furman capital statute." Crime and Delinquency 26: 563-635.

BRIDGE, F. M. and J. MOSURE (1961) Capital Punishment. Columbus: Ohio Legislative Service Commission, Staff Research Report No. 26.

BROSI, K. (1979) A Cross-City Comparison of Felony Case Processing. Washington, DC: Institute for Law and Social Research.

BULLOCK, H. A. (1961) "Significance of the racial factor in the length of prison sentences." Journal of Criminal Law, Criminology and Police Science 52: 411-417.

BURKE, P. and A. TURK (1975) "Factors affecting postarrest disposition: a model for analysis." Social Problems 22: 313-332.

CAHN, E. N. (1966) "The shift to a consumer perspective," in L. L. Cahn (ed.) Confronting Injustice: The Edmond Cahn Reader. Boston: Little, Brown.

——— (1949) The Sense of Injustice. New York: New York University Press.

CAMERON, M. O. (1964) The Booster and the Snitch. New York: Free Press.

CARGAN, L. and M. A. COATES (1974) "Indeterminate sentence and judicial bias." Crime and Delinquency 20: 144-156.

CHAMBLISS, W. J. and R. B. SEIDMAN (1971) Law, Order and Power. Reading, MA: Addison-Wesley.

CHIRICOS, T. and G. P. WALDO (1975) "Socioeconomic status and criminal sentencing: an empirical assessment of a conflict proposition." American Sociological Review 40: 753-772.

CHIRICOS, T., P. D. JACKSON and G. P. WALDO (1972) "Inequality in the disposition of the criminal label." Social Problems 19: 553-572.

CLARKE, S. H. and G. G. KOCH (1976) "The influence of income and other factors on whether criminal defendants go to prison." Law and Society Review 11: 57-92.

CONKLIN, J. E. (1974) Criminal Violene. Lexington, MA: D. C. Heath.

COUSINEU, D. F. and J. E. VEEVERS (1972) "Incarceration as a response to crime: the utilization of Canadian prisons." Journal of Criminology and Corrections 14: 19-31.

EISENSTEIN, J. and H. JACOB (1977) Felony Justice: An Organizational Study of Criminal Courts. Boston: Little, Brown.

FARNWORTH, M. and P. HORAN (1978) "Separate justice: an analysis of race differences in court processes." Social Science Research 9: 381-399.

FARRELL, R. A. and V. L. SWIGERT (1978a) "Legal disposition of inter-group and intra-group homicides." Sociological Quarterly 19: 566-576.

——— (1978b) "Prior offense as a self-fulfilling prophecy." Law and Society Review 12: 437-453.

FEELEY, M. M. (1979) The Process Is the Punishment. New York: Russell Sage Foundation.

FOLEY L. A. and C. E. RASCH (1979) "The effect of race on sentence: actual time served and final disposition," in J. CONLEY (ed.) Theory and Research in Criminal Justice: Current Perspectives. Cincinnatti: Anderson.

FORST, B. and K. BROSI (1977) "A theoretical and empirical analysis of the prosecutor." Journal of Legal Studies 6: 177.

FORST, B., J. LUCIANOVIC, and S. COX (1977) What Happens after Arrest? Washington, DC: Government Printing Office.

FRANKEL, C. (1969) "Justice and rationality," in S. Morgenbesser et al. (eds.) Philosophy, Science and Method: Essays in Honor of Ernest Nagel. New York: St. Martin's Press.

GARFINKEL, H. (1949) "Research note on inter- and intra-racial homicides." Social Forces 27: 369-381.

GERARD, J. and T. R. TERRY (1970) "Discrimination against negroes in the administration of criminal law in Missouri." Washington University Law Quarterly 1970: 415-437.

GIBSON, J. L. (1978) "Race as a determinate of criminal sentences: a methodological critique and case study." Law and Society Review 12: 455-478.

GOTTFREDSON, M. R. and D. M. GOTTFREDSON (1980) Decision Making in Criminal Justice: Toward the Rational Exercise of Discretion. Cambridge, MA: Ballinger.

GOVE, W. L. [ed] (1980) The Labelling of Deviance: Evaluating a Perspective (2nd ed.). Beverly Hills, CA: Sage.

GREEN, E. (1964) "Inter' and intra-racial crime relative to sentencing." Journal of Criminal Law, Criminology and Police Science 55: 348-358.

GREENWOOD, P. W. et al. (1973) Prosecution of Adult Felony Defendants in L. A. County: A Policy Perspective. Washington, DC: Government Printing Office.

GRIZZLE, J. E., F. STARMER and G. G. KOCH (1969) "Analysis of categorical data by linear models." Biometrics 25: 489-504.

HAGAN, J. (1977) "Criminal justice in rural and urban communities: a study of the bureaucratization of justice." Social Forces 55: 597-612.

——— (1975) "The social and legal construction of criminal justice: a study of the pre-sentencing process." Social Problems 22: 620-637.

——— (1974) "Exta-legal attributes and criminal sentencing: an assessment of a sociological viewpoint." Law and Society Review 8: 357-383.

——— and N. O' DONNEL (1978) "Sexual stereotyping and judicial sentencing: a legal test of the sociological wisdom." Canadian Journal of Sociology 3: 309-319.

HAGAN, J., I. H. NAGEL, and C. ALBONETTI (1980) "The differential sentencing of white-collar offenders in ten federal court districts." American Sociological Review 45: 802-820.

HALL, E. L. and A. A. SIMKUS (1975) "Inequality in the type of sentence received by Native Americans and Indians." Criminology 13: 199-222.

HINDELANG, M. (1978) "Race and involvement in crimes." American Sociological Review 43: 93-109.

HOWARD, J. C., Jr. (1967) "Rape death penalty study." New York Times, September 18, p. 33.

JACOB, H. (1962) "Politics and criminal prosecution in New Orleans." Tulane Studies in Political Science 8: 77-98.

JANOS, D. and R. I. MENDELSOHN, (1967) "The judicial role and sentencing behavior." Midwest Journal of Political Science 11: 471-488.

JOHNSON, G. (1941) "The Negro and crime." Annals of the American Academy of Political and Social Science 217: 93-104.

JOHNSON, O. C. (1970) "Is the punishment of rape equally administered to Negroes in the State of Louisiana?" in W. Patterson (ed.) We Charge Genocide. New York: International.

KELLY, H. E. (1976) "A comparison of defense strategy and race as influences in differential sentencing." Criminology 14: 241-249.

KINGSWORTH, R. and L. RIZZO (1979) "Decision making in criminal courts." Criminology 17: 3-14.

KLECK, G. (1981) "Racial discrimination in criminal sentencing: a critical evaluation of the evidence with additional evidence on the death penalty." American Sociological Reivew 46: 783-805.

KRUTTSCHNITT, C. (1980) "Social status and sentences of female offenders." Law and Society Review 15: 247-265.

KULIG, F. (1975) "Plea bargaining, probation and other aspects of conviction and sentencing." Creighton Law Review 8: 938-954.

LA FREE, G. (1980a) "Variables affecting guilty pleas and convictions in rape cases: toward a social theory of rape processing." Social Forces 58: 837-850.

——— (1980b) "The effect of sexual stratification by race on official reactions to rape." American Sociological Review 45: 842-854.

LANDES, W. (1974) "Legality and reality: some evidence on criminal procedure." Journal of Legal Studies 3: 287-338.

LEMERT, E. M. and J. ROSBERG (1948) The Administration of Justice to Minority Groups in L.A. County. Berkeley: University of California Press.

LEVIN, M. A. (1972) "Urban politics and judicial behavior." Journal of Legal Studies 1: 220-221.

LIZOTTE, A. J. (1978) "Extra-legal factors in Chicago's criminal courts: testing the conflict model of criminal justice." Social Problems 25: 564-580.

LOTZ, R. and J. D. HEWITT (1977) "The influence of legally irrelevant factors on felony sentencing." Sociological Inquiry 47: 39-48.

LUNDMAN, R. J. (1974) "Routine police arrest practices: a commonweal perspective." Social Problems 22: 127-141.

LUNDSGAARDE, H. P. (1977) Murder in Space City: An Analysis of Houston Homicide Patterns. New York: Oxford University Press.

MANGUM, C. S., Jr. (1940) The Legal Status of the Negro. Chapel Hill: University of North Carolina Press.

MARTIN, R. (1934) The Defendant and Criminal Justice. Austin, TX: Bureau of Research in Social Science.

MAYNARD, D. W. (1982) "Defendant's attributes in plea bargaining: notes on the modeling of sentencing decisions." Social Problems 29: 347-360.

MILESKI, M. (1971) "Courtroom encounters: an observation of a lower criminal court." Law and Society Review 5: 473-538.

MILLER, F. (1970) The Decision to Charge a Suspect with a Crime. Boston: Little, Brown.

MYERS, M. A. (1979) "Offended parties and official reactions: victims and the sentencing of criminal defendants." Sociological Quarterly 20: 529-540.

NAGEL, S. (1969) The Legal Process from a Behavioral Perspective. Homewood, IL: Dorsey Press.

NETTLER, G. (1979) "Criminal justice," in A. Inkeles et al. (eds.) Annual Review of Sociology, Vol. 5.

PARTINGTON, D. (1965) "The incidence of the death penalty for rape in Virginia." Washington and Lee Law Review 22: 43-75.

PERELMAN, C. (1967) Justice. New York: Random House.

PERRY, W. (1977) "Justice system and sentencing: the importance of race in the military." Criminology 15: 225-234.

PHILLIPS, C. D. and S. DINITZ (1982) "Labelling and juvenile court dispositions: official responses to a cohort of violent juveniles." Sociological Quarterly 23: 267-268.

POPE, C. (1978) "Sentence dispositions accorded assault and burglary offenders: an explanatory study in twelve California counties." Journal of Criminal Justice 6: 151.

—— (1975a) Sentencing of California Felony Offenders. Washington, DC: Government Printing Office.

—— (1975b) The Judicial Processing of Assault and Burglary Offenders in Selected California counties. Washington, DC: Government Printing Office.

QUINNEY, R. (1977) Class, State and Crime. New York: David McKay.

RADELET, M. L. (1981) "Racial characteristics and the imposition of the death penalty." American Sociological Review 46: 918-927.

RAU, R. M. (1972) Sentencing in the Federal Courts. Washington, DC: Government Printing Office.

RHODES, W. M. (1976) "The economics of criminal courts: a theoretical and empirical investigation." Journal of Legal Studies 5: 311-340.

ROSEN, L. (1973) "Policemen," In P. Rose et al. (eds.) Through Different Eyes. New York: Oxford University Press.

SCHUR, E. (1971) Labelling Deviant Behavior. New York: Harper & Row.

SKOLNIK, J. H. (1966) Justice Without Trial: Law Enforcement in Democratic Society. New York: John Wiley.

Southern Regional Council (1969) Race Makes the Difference. Atlanta: Southern Regional Council.

SPOHN, C., J. GRUHL, and S. WELCH (1982) "The effect of race on sentencing: a re-examination of an unsettled question." Law and Society Review 16: 71-88.

STANKO, E. (1982) "The impact of victim assessment on prosecutor's screening decision: the case of the New York County District Attorney's office." Law and Society Review 16: 225-239.

Student Special Edition (1969) "A study of the California penalty jury in first-degree murder cases." Stanford Law review 21: 1297.

SUTTON, P. (1978) Variations in Federal Criminal Sentences: A Statistical Assessment at the National Level. Washington, DC: Government Printing Office.

SWAFFORD, M. (1980) "Three parametric techniques for contingency table analysis: a nontechnical commentary." American Sociological Review 45: 664-690.

SWIGERT, V. L. and R. A. FARRELL (1977) "Normal homicides and the law." American Sociological Review 42: 16-32.

THOMSON, R. J. and M. T. ZINGRAFF (1981) "Detecting sentencing disparity: some problems and evidence." American Journal of Sociology 86: 869-880.

TIFFANY, L., Y. AVICHAI, and G. PETERS (1975) "A statistical analysis of sentencing in the federal courts: defendants convicted after trial, 1967-1968." Journal of Legal Studies 4: 369-390.

TURK, A. (1969) Criminality and Legal Order. Chicago: Rand McNally.

UHLMAN, T. (1977) "The impact of defendant race in trial-court sentencing decisions," in J. A. Gardner (ed.) Public Law and Public Policy. New York: Praeger.

——— and D. WALKER (1980) "He takes some of my time, I take some of his: an analysis of judicial sentencing patterns in jury cases." Law and Society Review 14: 323-341.

UNNEVER, J. D., C. E. FRAZIER, and J. C. HENRETTA (1980) "Race differences in criminal sentencing." Sociological Quarterly 21: 197-205.

Vera Institute of Justice (1977) Felony Arrests: Their Prosecution and Disposition in New York City's Courts. New York: Author.

WILLIAMS, K. (1978) The Role of the Victim in the Prosecution of Violent Offenses. Washington, DC: Government Printing Office.

WILLICK, D. H., G. GEHLKER, and A. M. WATTS (1975) "Social class as a factor affecting judicial disposition." Criminology 13: 57-77.

WOLF, G. M. (1964) "Abstract analysis of jury sentencing in capital cases." Rutgers Law Review 19: 56-64.

WOLFGANG, M. E. and M. REIDEL (1973) "Race, judicial discretion and the death penalty." Annals of the American Academy of Political and Social Science 407: 119-133.

WOLFGANG, M. E., A. KELLY, and H. C. NOLDE (1962) "Comparison of the executed and commuted among admissions to death row." Journal of Criminal Law, Criminology and Police Science 53: 301-311.

WYNNE, D. F. and T. F. HARTNAGEL (1975) "Race and plea negotiation: an analysis of some Canadian data." Canadian Journal of Sociology 1: 147-155.

ZIMRING, F. E., J. EIGEN, and S. O'MALLEY (1976) "Punishing homicide in Philadelphia: perspectives on the death penalty." University of Chicago Law Review 43: 227-252.

III

THE PERFORMANCE
OF PRISONS

Chapter 8

PRISON EFFECTIVENESS MEASUREMENT

MARY ELLEN MARSDEN
THOMAS ORSAGH

Recent studies of the effectiveness of prisons have tended to base their assessment of prison performance on the attainment of one goal — rehabilitation — and have largely relied on a single performance measure — recidivism — to gauge success in attaining that goal. However, recent shifts in the basic assumptions underlying and guiding correctional practice suggest the need for a reconsideration of this concentration on rehabilitation in studies of prison effectiveness. At the same time, advances in evaluation methodology require changes in traditional methods of evaluating prison performance. While goal attainment and outcome measures continue to be the most meaningful ways of evaluating prison performance, consideration should also be given to process and efficiency issues. Moreover, two trends — greater emphasis on accountability in publicly financed programs, and increasing attention to the provision of cost-effective services — have intensified the demand for revisions in the evaluation of prison effectiveness.

This chapter first describes the current state of performance measurement for prisons. The focus is on the basic theoretical model that has, until recently, guided correctional practice. Correctional goals

AUTHORS' NOTE: *We are indebted to David A. Smith of the Department of Sociology at the University of North Carolina at Chapel Hill for assistance in reviewing relevant literature.*

and performance measures relevant to that model are then discussed. Next, the research design guiding most current evaluation studies is examined and evaluated. Methodological problems inherent to current studies of correctional performance are also considered. Finally, a suggested direction for improved evaluation is developed, one that takes account of both advances in evaluation design, and of the heightened status of correctional goals other than rehabilitation. Performance measures appropriate to that plan are then discussed.

THE CURRENT STATE OF PERFORMANCE MEASUREMENT

The conventional approach to performance measurement for prisons involves the ascription of explicit goals to prison activity, as well as the evaluation of prison performance with reference to the attainment of those goals (see Rutman, 1977: 28-29; Connolly and Deutsch, 1980: 36-37; Schulberg and Baker, 1977: 56-59; Janeksela, 1977: 4; Adams, 1975: 45). This goal-attainment model of evaluation assumes that correctional goals can be identified and program impacts measured relative to those goals. The focus here is on the outcome of the prison experience, rather than on the process by which that outcome is produced.

The goals most frequently evaluated are general ones of correctional practice, although certain administrative goals may also be of interest.[1] General goals rest on criminological theory concerning the causes of crime and the appropriate and effective societal response to it. Typically, these goals involve outcomes occurring outside the prison environment and require the participation of other criminal justice agencies for achievement. General goals also describe the ideological component of prison functioning, thereby providing overall direction for the allocation of resources within the prison.

Administrative goals focus attention on the processes occurring within prisons. Typically, though not exclusively, these goals emphasize efficiency — the accomplishment of tasks, such as the general goals noted above, with minimal resource use. The attainment of administrative goals has little or no direct effect on crime rates and is usually of interest only to prison administrators and others concerned with effective prison management. Examples of performance measurement directly related to administrative goals, such as efficiency, are found in a later chapter.

The general goals commonly ascribed to prisons are rehabilitation, deterrence, incapacitation, and retribution (see Sutherland and Cressey, 1978: 533-537; Grizzle, 1980: 11; Marshall, 1981: 15). Rehabilitation involves the provision of treatment in prison that will reduce the likelihood of offenders engaging in criminal activity once they are released. Deterrence can be achieved in two ways: Either the prison experience can dissuade individual prisoners from recidivating because of the threat of another term of incarceration (specific deterrence), or potential offenders, contemplating the risk of imprisonment, can decide not to commit a crime (general deterrence). Incapacitation is said to reduce crime in that incarcerated offenders are prevented from committing other crimes against society for the period of their incarceration. The goal of retribution assumes that the purpose of prison is to inflict punishment on an offender, thereby righting some wrong done society. A related goal, restitution, has recently regained prominence. It provides a mechanism by which offenders can repay victims or society for the harm caused by their acts.

These general goals have guided correctional practice over the past decades. Each has been an expressed goal of corrections, although the relative importance of each has generally not been addressed, and the emphasis attached to each has undoubtedly varied over time.[2] What is clear, however, is that until the last decade, first and foremost has been the goal of rehabilitation.

The Primacy of the Rehabilitative Goal

While the goals of deterrence, incapacitation, and retribution have substantial public support, the long-standing, dominant view found in the criminological literature, and that voiced frequently by criminal justice decision makers, has been that these goals are secondary to rehabilitation (Allen, 1959). Some have even rejected these goals outright as morally reprehensible and/or unworthy of a civilized society. The American Correctional Association, for example, has asserted that the only legitimate purpose of prison is to rehabilitate (Carter et al., 1972: 22; See also the reviews of the development of the rehabilitative ideal in Marshall, 1981: 20-23).

Support for the rehabilitative ideal has been based on the nearly universal acceptance of the assumption that society can effect favorable behavioral changes in offender populations by deliberate, individualized intervention — that is, treatment. This stance emerges from the positivistic social thought of the last century and the liberal orientations of this century. The centrality of rehabilitation to prison performance may also be due to two additional factors. First, the professional literature on prison management and performance has been dominated by criminologists rather than prison administrators. The former are more concerned with general goals, such as rehabilitation, that directly affect crime rates, while the latter are more frequently concerned with administrative goals and management issues in the provision of custody and care for inmates.

Second, rehabilitation is the one general goal whose attainment was once widely believed to be within the discretionary power of the prison. Prisons may have little active control over the attainment of general goals other than rehabilitation, but these alternative goals can usually be achieved through the normal, routine performance of the prison function. For instance, prisons contribute to incapacitation through the provision of facilities that reduce escape risks to an acceptable minimum, while deterrent and retributive goals may be achieved through the simple fact of incarceration. Thus, it is argued, if social engineering in a prison is to affect the crime rate, it must come through its rehabilitative effect.

The concept of rehabilitation is not, however, unidimensional. Adopting the distinction posed by Sutherland and Cressey (1978: 360; see also Halleck and Witte, 1977: 374), two forms of the rehabilitative ideal may be distinguished, each with different implications for the design of rehabilitative treatment and the performance measurement of prisons: (1) the *medical* model, which stresses the notion that "individual criminal should be cured of what ails them" (see Morris, 1974: 13-16; Shover, 1979; 61-62); and (2) the *social structural* model, which stresses changing crime rates by changing the social order — that is, by effecting favorable changes in the offender's environment. The former conception emphasizes changing those aspects of an offender's own personality, preferences, or proclivities that foster involvement in criminal activity. Rehabilitation programs based on this concept include psychoanalysis, individual and group counseling, and drug and alcohol therapy. The latter model emphasizes changing variables, independent of an offender's value system or personality, that decrease criminal activity by increasing opportunities for legitimate activity and making legitimate activity more attractive. Such rehabilitation programs include vocational training and education, and job placement.

These interventions are designed to heighten an individual's socioeconomic status by improving his or her productivity or marketability, and by generating greater community acceptance of ex-offenders. Both conceptions of the rehabilitative model have guided correctional practice, but they have not typically been distinguished in correctional evaluations. The melding of the two conceptions is exemplified in the use of recidivism to measure the effectiveness of treatment, since this measure cannot distinguish between the two causal models.

Performance Measures Relating to Rehabilitation

Recidivism. The index used almost universally to measure the effectiveness of rehabilitation programs is the recidivism rate. Of the 231 studies of correctional effectiveness conducted between 1945 and 1967 and reviewed by Lipton et al. (1975), 48 percent of the outcome measures used to gauge program effectiveness were measures of recidivism. Similarly, in 95 studies conducted between 1973 and 1978 and reviewed by Gendreau and Ross (1979), the majority used recidivism as the primary measure of program effectiveness. Citing a "slavish adherence" to the recidivism measure, Gendreau and Ross (1979: 487) maintain that the measurement of treatment outcome in terms of the single recidivism measure has obscured other positive accomplishments of prisons. Bennett (1979: 92) also discusses the frequent use of postrelease arrests as measures of effectiveness, arguing that arrests are a more adequate indicator of police activity than of rehabilitation or individual behavior.

Other Performance Measures Related to Rehabilitation. While recidivism has been the primary measure of rehabilitative effectiveness, other measures can be found. Lipton et al. (1975), for instance, reviewed six additional, frequently employed measures of the rehabilitative effect of prison programs: institutional adjustment, vocational adjustment, educational achievement, drug and alcohol readdiction, personality and attitudinal change, and community adjustment. However, these six measures *combined* accounted for only 52 percent of the outcome measures used in such studies, compared with 48 percent for recidivism measures alone. Other than recidivism, the most frequently used measures (23 percent) were of personality and attitude change (see Lipton et al., 1975: 8). The other measures individually accounted for no more than 8 percent of the total. Gendreau and Ross (1979) cite other outcome measures, such as educational achievement and interpersonal adjustment, but they also found recidivism to be the preeminent measure of prison outcome.

Other Goals and Associated Performance Measures

While rehabilitation has been the primary goal of corrections, and recidivism the primary performance measure, the importance of deterrence, incapacitation, and retribution has also been recognized. As a result, some attention has been directed toward performance measures that assess the effectiveness of prisons in attaining these goals. Consider specific and general deterrence: Both assume that an increase in the likelihood of being sanctioned or in the severity of the sanction will induce some persons to refrain from a contemplated offense.[3] Performance measures relating to general deterrence tend to rely on an offense rate index — most commonly, the per capita number of Part I Uniform Crime Report offenses. Other studies use indices of particular offenses such as homicide, robbery, or larceny (see Palmer, 1977; Nagin, 1978). The number of studies concerned with evaluating general deterrent effects is vast; Beyleveld's (1980) annotated bibliography contains 568 references. An extensive literature has also emerged recently that examines the incapacitative effects of imprisonment, with particular attention to separating the effects of incapacitation and general deterrence (Blumstein et al., 1978; Brier and Fienberg, 1980).

In contrast, specific deterrence has not been subject to general evaluation. Zimring and Hawkins (1973) provide the most recent comprehensive survey, and Grasmic and Green (1980) performed a survey of methodological issues related to the measurement of specific deterrence. While general deterrence research relies on aggregate-level offense rates, studies of specific deterrence tend to use either individual-level measures of recidivism or measures of offender and nonoffender attitudes toward crime.

In the hierarchy of general goals, retribution has received the least attention. Consonant with its low priority is an almost total absence of discussion concerning how it might be measured. Measures exist, but they are discovered more through inference than direct suggestion. Quite generally, goal attainment is assumed by the fact of imprisonment.[4] However, if retributive justice requires that the punishment fit the crime — that the offender receives his or her "just deserts" — a more subtle measure of goal attainment is needed. Such a measure would allow us to evaluate the correspondence between the severity of an offense and the severity of its punishment. No attempts to operationalize this index of goal attainment are currently known to exist. Rather, most programmatic plans based on the retributive goal simply call for a return to determinate sentencing, in which the length of sentence is determined at the time of sentencing, independent of any judgment concerning rehabilitation (Clear, 1978: 36; see also Pugsley, 1979).

In an important sense, then, the vast sentencing-variation literature only addresses the performance issue indirectly. If sentencing decisions are influenced by the race, gender, or socioeconomic status of an offender, this implies that the principle of retributive justice is violated. Thus, empirical measures of the sentencing bias attributable to these characteristics might be used as indicators of goal attainment.

CURRENT BELIEFS REGARDING THE EFFECTIVENESS OF PRISONS

Rehabilitation

A multitude of studies have addressed the effectiveness of prisons by examining their role in effecting rehabilitation. For instance,

Bailey's (1966) review of 100 studies conducted between 1940 and 1960 found many programs claiming rehabilitative effectiveness. However, he maintained that the evidentiary basis of most of these claims was seriously defective and could not support the asserted success. A later review by Lipton et al. (1975) of 231 studies also concluded that there is little basis for assertions of rehabilitative effectiveness. The findings of these and other surveys of existing literature are reviewed by Adams (1975), Shover (1979), and Bennett (1979). The result of these and other assessments of prison performance with respect to rehabilitation has been the belief that "nothing works," or at least not very well.[5] These pessimistic findings have stimulated a search for more effective prison interventions, a demand for more rigorous evaluation of programmatic efforts, and perhaps most importantly, a decrease in support for the implementation of rehabilitative programs.

The Shift Away From Rehabilitation

The decline of the rehabilitative ideal is due to a complex set of forces. It is closely linked to the recommendations of Morris (1974) concerning the need to rehabilitate the medical model itself, and to the publication of the comprehensive reviews of correctional effectiveness studies noted above. These works and others, combined with a broad shift to more conservative social thought and public policy, have resulted in a rethinking of the validity of the rehabilitative ideal and of the relative importance of this goal within the prison goal hierarchy. Consequently, the emphasis has shifted from rehabilitation to crime control and retribution. This erosion of support for the rehabilitative model among criminal justice practitioners and within the research community has been accompanied by increased support for the just deserts model, with its general goals of retribution, incapacitation, and deterrence (see Allen, 1978, 1981; Bayer, 1981; Fogel, 1975, 1979; MacNamara, 1977; von Hirsch, 1976).

These models — the medical/social structural models of rehabilitation and the just deserts model — differ radically in the goals they espouse for corrections and in their methods of evaluating the effectiveness of correctional performance. The primary goal of corrections under the medical model is rehabilitation, and only secondarily deterrence, incapacitation, and retribution; hence, the emphasis is on changing the offender. In the just deserts model, on the other hand, the emphasis is on the offense, with deterrence, incapacitation, and retribution given more centrality.

The shift from the rehabilitative to the just deserts model implies a reorientation away from treatment — where the intent is not to diminish the well-being of the offender (or potential offender) — and toward punishment, where the intent, by definition, is to diminish well-being. This shift also represents movement away from goals that are offender-oriented in favor of goals that are offense-oriented. Figure 8.1 portrays these trends. The figure depicts movement away from the goal of rehabilitation toward goals of incapacitation, specific and general deterrence, and retribution.

Analysis of expenditures for inmate care and confinement in the federal prison system provides a further indication of the changing priority assigned to rehabilitation relative to other prison goals. In Figure 8.2, the federal prison system's aggregate expenditures designated for education, narcotics addiction treatment, and vocational expenses associated with prison industries are displayed as a percentage of total prison expenditures, excluding capital expenditures. These data exclude many rehabilitation programs operating at the time within the federal system, as well as general operating costs.[6] Assuming that they are representative of all programs, and that overhead costs are a constant proportion of reported expenditures, these data show that as a proportion of total prison expenditures, federal expenditures for rehabilitation rose to a peak in 1975, when the foregoing three programs accounted for 7.4 percent of the budget, and declined thereafter.

These data are consistent with the argument presented above, that in recent years there has been a decline in support for rehabilitation as a goal for prisons. Interestingly, the peak expenditure year coincides with the publication of the Lipton et al. (1975) monograph, which is said to have been a significant contributor to the decline in interest in rehabilitation.

Deterrence and Incapacitation

As opinion began to shift away from the belief that rehabilitation was (or could be) effective, it began to shift toward the belief that crime control (that is, the combined effect of deterrence and inca-

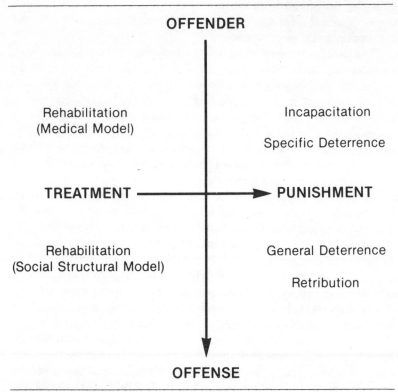

Figure 8.1 Shifting Emphasis on Prison Goals

pacitation) might be more effective. The older view — predominantly sociological — was that legal sanctions have little or no effect on criminal behavior. Instead, man was assumed to be a product of his environment, constantly subject to pressures that could induce, encourage, or impel criminal activity with a force far greater than that possessed by legal sanctions. This view, largely based on conjecture and simple correlations, has been replaced in recent years by a large body of research literature utilizing sophisticated statistical analyses to estimate crime-control effects. This newer research almost always reveals the existence of crime-control effects when offense rates are associated with the risk of imprisonment (see recent reviews by Palmer, 1977; Fattah, 1977; Blumstein et al. 1978; Beyleveld, 1980; Orsagh, 1982).[7]

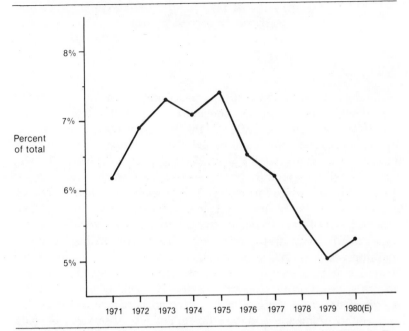

Figure 8.2 Percentage of Federal Prison System Budget for Inmate Rehabilitation, 1971-1980

SOURCE: U.S. Office of Management and Budget, *The Budget of the United States Government, Fiscal Years 1972-1981.*

The most serious criticism of deterrence research is that research purporting to measure deterrent effects usually fails to distinguish deterrence from incapacitation. While incarceration may have a deterrent effect, there is no question about its incapacitative effect.[8] Nonetheless, while the distinction is of theoretical interest, in practical terms the issue is inconsequential, for estimates made of the incapacitation effect tend to show that its contribution to crime control is small relative to that of deterrent effects (Cohen, 1978; Greenberg, 1975; Ehrlich, 1973; Clarke, 1974; but also see Chinnar and Shinnar, 1975).[9]

In summary, the literature strongly supports the position that legal sanctions, including imprisonment, deter criminal activity.[10] Yet two important questions remain: (1) How strong a deterrent effect does the risk or length of imprisonment have on crime? (2) How great is the prison's contribution to the production of that effect?

PROBLEMS IN THE EVALUATION OF
PRISON EFFECTIVENESS

Scope

Studies of correctional effectiveness number in the thousands. Despite this volume, major conceptual and methodological difficulties severely limit the value of this research. On the whole, the studies utilize goal-attainment models for evaluation. They typically examine success in attaining a single general goal — usually rehabilitation — and they tend to rely on a single performance measure — usually recidivism. Unfortunately, this research paradigm offers an exceedingly restricted view of prison effectiveness. By slighting other general goals of imprisonment, overall prison effectiveness may be understated. Concentrating on recidivism blinds one to the possibility that imprisonment may produce positive outcomes — for example, better job performance or a more stable family life — whether or not it effects a cessation of criminal activity. Particularly ignored is the accomplishment of those administrative goals related to the health and welfare of inmates and the efficient delivery of services — goals that provide the necessary underlying conditions for the attainment of the overarching, general goals of imprisonment.

The attainment of prison goals is not the only way to conceptualize prison performance. Evaluations can be made without reference to explicit goals, and without focusing on outcome measures. Alternative methods of evaluation include systems analysis or operations research (Schulberg and Baker, 1977), process evaluation (Deutscher, 1976; Krisberg, 1980), and cost-benefit analyses (Richmond, 1972). These approaches direct attention away from outcomes toward processes, and away from effectiveness toward efficiency issues. Before examining how performance measurement might be improved, several specific methodological problems inherent to current, goal-oriented evaluations are examined.

Multiple Goals

If it is recognized that four general goals guide correctional practice, it must then be conceded that the process of goal achievement may involve serious inconsistencies. For example, the rehabilitative ideal calls for the release of an offender once he is "cured." According to the rehabilitative principle, a person who has deliberately committed the most heinous of crimes could serve a very short sentence if he or she were judged to be rehabilitated. Meanwhile, an incorrigible shoplifter could be incarcerated for life if he or she were not so judged. Thus, rehabilitation could be in obvious conflict with the goal of retribution, and may be in conflict with the goals of general deterrence and incapacitation as well.

Because of such goal inconsistencies and contradictions, improved performance with respect to one goal may hinder progress toward another. Consequently, the achievement of one goal does not imply better overall system performance. That judgment depends on the net marginal effect of simultaneous movements toward one goal and away from others. Even if goals are complementary, as retribution and deterrence may be, reliance on one performance measure will tend to understate overall system performance as long as that measure ignores the joint outcome. Thus, performance measures that relate to individual goals are but a first step in system evaluation. A composite performance measure is also needed that recognizes goal inconsistencies and complementarities, that presumes the existence of an optimum goal mix, and that indexes the achievement of that optimum.

Empirical Measures of Performance

Typically, performance measures emphasize a single dimension of a behavioral outcome. For example, most recidivism studies use an extremely simple, dichotomous measure — the subject either recidivates or not. More sophisticated studies usually compare the proportion of failures in an experimental and a control group, typically using rearrests occurring within some specified time period. Thus, recidivism measures often ignore a number of important factors in an offender's postincarceration history, including the number of offenses committed, the seriousness of these offenses, and the follow-up time period. These factors depict the offender's length of exposure to risk and the seriousness of his or her involvement in post prison crime. They also provide a fuller description of the outcome and permit a richer analysis of the effects of imprisonment on recidivism than do simple dichotomous measures of success and failure. Unlike Ehrlich (1977), most general deterrence studies measure the effects of sanctions on offense rates without regard for the possible effects of sanctions on offense seriousness.

When prisons are evaluated in terms of their effectiveness in achieving particular goals, it is essential that performance measures be precisely and demonstrably linked to the goals they are presumed to serve. For example, the risk and length or incarceration can be directly linked via rational-choice theory to offense rates (Heineke, 1978). Sometimes, however, recidivism has been used as a performance measure of both the rehabilitative and specific deterrent effects of imprisonment. Such analyses go forward without recognizing that both types of effects are confounded by this measure. The failure to separate rehabilitation's effect on recidivism from that of specific deterrence makes the rational allocation of resources exceedingly difficult, and substantially diminishes the policy relevance of recidivism as a performance measure.

Lack of Concern for Efficiency

The goal-attainment model of evaluation places primary emphasis on measures of effectiveness, such as recidivism, while neglecting efficiency issues such as cost/benefit and cost effectiveness. Because goal attainment usually calls for a supply of scarce resources — labor, machinery, buildings, and capital — success cannot be accurately gauged without asking: What benefit at what cost? Because resources are scarce, expenditures to attain one goal (for example, rehabilitation) may come at the expense of some other goal, especially if the goals are inconsistent. Thus, when costs are taken into account, rehabilitation programs may not be as beneficial as those aspects of prison that promote general deterrence or other prison goals (see Shover, 1979: 274-297).

Neglect of Strength and Integrity Issues

The widespread use of the goal-attainment method of evaluation focuses attention on the outcomes of correctional practice to the virtual exclusion of process; that is, of how those outcomes were achieved. This focus has resulted in global assessments of prison performance based on one or more outcome measures that do not (indeed, cannot) indicate in sufficient detail how a given outcome was actually produced. The consequence is that research findings associated with a particular goal are of limited use to correctional planners or administrators, since they fail to establish the essential linkage between an outcome and the actual processes and activities involved.

One important process issue that has been largely ignored concerns the strength and integrity of rehabilitative treatment (see Quay, 1977; Sechrest and Redner, 1979). Strength of treatment refers to program design, as well as the intended intensity and quality of treatment. The integrity of treatment is determined by how well the program is implemented. Relevant measures of program strength include the number of training sessions, hours per session, the staff/student ratio, and the length of the treatment process. Measurements of the quality of treatment might include the qualifications and dedication of the staff, or the quality (and quantity) of equipment used to carry out the program.

Questions relating to program integrity concern the actual implementation of the program: Were staff and clients actually in attendance? Were other activities substituted for those called for by program planners? Were requisite resources available during program operation? Another set of questions concerns the quality of implementation. Did the staff believe in, and were they dedicated to, the program? How motivated were the inmates? What degree of monitoring and supervision was employed? Were inmates and staff appropriately matched with respect to personality characteristics?

Because of the neglect of strength and integrity issues in evaluations of rehabilitation programs, it is rarely possible to identify the cause of program failure, to determine why a particular intervention — vocational training, education, and the like — has not worked. Was the failure due to conceptual or theoretical flaws that would lead to failure regardless of how the program was implemented? Was failure the result of factors such as inadequate staff training or a misconception of the program's mission? Perhaps failure was due to factors that had nothing to do with the rehabilitative program itself.

Program Design and Evaluation

Typically, evaluation is conducted within an atheoretical frame-work. The inappropriate use of recidivism measures and the failure to attend to strength and integrity issues may be ascribed, in part, to this neglect of theoretical issues. Theory asserts that a particular treat-ment will have a particular effect, and detailed articulation of the theory usually reveals or implies that the specified treatment will have its effect through a particular causal mechanism. Yet treatments are generally applied and evaluated without considering the causal mechanisms linking specific treatments to predicted outcomes. For example, the Panel on Research and Rehabilitative Techniques of the National Academy of Sciences (Sechrest et al., 1979: 35) maintains that most interventions are derived from "conventional wisdom," not from any careful analysis of crime causation or the rehabilitative process. Similarly, Bailey (1966) noted that few studies made explicit the behavioral theory underlying the treatment approach used. Specification and testing of the causal theory underlying rehabilita-tion programs can only strengthen program design and evaluation by identifying that set of conditions necessary to achieve a desired outcome with a particular treatment.[11]

The result of failure to design, implement, and evaluate rehabilita-tion programs on the basis of explicit theory is perhaps best illustrated by the fact that most rehabilitation programs have been implemented and most evaluation designs planned without regard for the possibility that such programs may not be equally effective for all offenders. That is, matching treatments with offender types may appear to increase the success rates of programs merely because the treatment addresses specific problems or deficiencies on the part of certain offenders (see Warren, 1977; Palmer and Lewis, 1980; Gibbons, 1975; Hawkins et al., 1980). The idea of individualized treatment is, of course, central to both the medical and social-structural model var-iants of the rehabilitative ideal. One may even fault program designers for not having provided individualized rehabilitative treatment. But one must also fault the evaluators of rehabilitation programs. Re-searchers have failed to interpret the results of rehabilitative programs in a theoretical context; hence, they have reaced conclusions unwarranted by the data. Possibly, they have concluded much too readily that "nothing works."

IMPROVING THE EVALUATION OF PRISONS

The preceding discussion of current beliefs regarding the effectiveness of prisons and problems with the empirical measurement of prison performance has documented the need for broader conceptions of correctional goals and outcomes. Evaluation should be considered in the context of multiple goals, cost effectiveness, and process. Concerns for the attainment of general goals should be joined by concerns for administrative goals such as efficiency and cost. Likewise, concerns for outcomes of the prison experience should be integrated with concerns for the processes by which those outcomes are produced.

The common practice of assessing success in rehabilitation by means of the single performance measure of recidivism ignores the level of attainment, if not the existence, of other correctional goals. Such analysis provides an incomplete and imperfect assessment of overall prison performance. Moreover, it fails to recognize shifts in correctional practice and goal orientation. The result is that non-recidivistic outcomes and general goals other than rehabilitation remain essentially unevaluated. Thus, assessments of prison effectiveness that rely on single measures or single goals are suspect.

Evaluations that ignore efficiency issues are also deficient, in that the attainment of general goals requires resources, and prisons operate with fixed budgets. Clearly the degree of goal attainment is directly related to efficiency. Moreover, because resources are scarce, focusing more effort on the attainment of one goal often entails a diminished effort with respect to other goals. Thus, concerns for efficiency and cost effectiveness should underlie the choice of procedures for achieving a specific goal and the establishment of priorities with respect to the attainment of competing goals.

Including process issues in evaluations requires us to consider the strength and integrity of a program's implementation, the matching of offenders with specific treatments, and the interrelations between program characteristics and observed outcomes. Such investigations enable us to assess how and why a program produced certain observed outcomes, thus providing useful information for policy choice. Accordingly, evaluations must consider a multiplicity of general goals within a framework of concerns for efficiency and cost effectiveness. As a first step in the evaluation of the effectiveness of prisons, the multiple general and administrative goals must be specified. The level of attainment of each of the general goals would then be separately assessed, using relevant outcome and efficiency measures. These investigations would also require us to separate the effects of the prison experience from the effects of other criminal justice agencies on the attainment of each goals. No study to date has incorporated this degree of detail.

Separate evaluation of the attainment of each general goal vis-à-vis the administrative goals would facilitate the assessment of prison performance during a time in which prison goals are changing. Some, however, might still desire an overall measure of a prison's performance. This difficult, if not impossible, task first requires the specification of the differential value of each general goal. A theory providing for the estimation of these values, or weights, has been developed,[12] and its application to managerial decision making may be found, for example, in Zeleny (1982). The question of which decision-making body shall assign the various weights, however, is open to discussion. If and when these weights are established by a relevant decision-making body, it will be possible to develop a comprehensive measure of overall effectiveness that will enable the comparison of prison effectiveness within a single system or across different systems.

Within this expanded framework for evaluation, performance measures must also be improved. The first priority is the development of uniform outcome measures. The measurement of recidivism, for example, requires a standard follow-up period, permitting the extent and seriousness of recidivism to be compared across prisons, treatments, and studies. Improved performance measurement also demands more attention to the multiple sources of variation in performance measures. For example, the well-established phenomenon of declining age-specific offense rates implies that the simple passage of time involved in incarceration tends to generate lower postprison offense rates for an inmate cohort. Thus, a recidivism index may reflect a maturation process, as well as rehabilitation and specific deterrence effects. Sound evaluation requires that the rehabilitative and deterrent effects of imprisonment be identified and distinguished, and that the confounding effect of maturation be taken into account. Multivariate statistical procedures provide one means for doing so.

Performance measures must be multidimensional so as to describe more fully the outcome under observation. Dichotomous measures based on arrests or remission of a drug habit are simply inadequate. Empirical studies (Waldo and Chiricos, 1977; Maltz and McCleary, 1977; Hoffman and Stone-Meierhoeffer, 1980) in which recidivism is viewed multidimensionally provide examples of the work that is moving in this direction.

These improvements in evaluation methodology also require the integration of theory, research, and practice, in addition to program planning and evaluation. For instance, investigations of the specific ways in which program outcomes are produced should result in more effective planning. Criminological and criminal justice theory and research can suggest effective routes by which prisons can produce desirable postprison outcomes through controlled evaluation of these propositions in order to determine which programs and program components are most effective. Further, theory and research provide for the determination of mechanisms by which programs produce results, and of the specific populations for which certain programs might be more effective.

The foregoing describes an optimal plan for the evaluation of prison performance. In the end, it may be unattainable. What is clear, however, is that the current scope of evaluations must be broadened to include measures of process and efficiency, and correctional goals other than rehabilitation.

NOTES

1. This distinction parallels that of Duffee (1975: 4-7) for the production, maintenance, and adjustment functions of prisons defined by organizational theory. Production functions (corresponding to our general goals) describe the goal-oriented activities of prison such as rehabilitation, while maintenance functions (our administrative goals) describe internal activites directed toward the functioning of the system. Adjustment functions, not considered here, define the external relations of the prison, such as political and social pressures on prison functioning.

2. Note also that the relative importance of each of the goals may vary across prisons. Duffee (1975: 172-174), for instance, found that prisons differed in their social climates and in the relative importance attached to the goals of rehabilitation, reform, and restraint. See also the Street et al. (1966) discussion of three models describing dominant correctional goals of prisons, which vary along a continuum from treatment to custody.

3. Deterrence theory assumes a spectrum of responses to a sanction, from those who would not commit an offense even if the probability of a sanction being imposed slightest sanction were absolutely zero, to those who would commit such act even though punishment was certain to follow. Deterrence obtains its leverage from the marginal group — those within these extremes — and particularly from those at the threshold, as it is this latter group for whom small, marginal changes are significant.

4. Retribution may be based on the moral imperative that requires punishment for a criminal act, or on the utilitarian principle that exacts punishment so that the victims of the criminal act will feel better. Both bases imply that the offender's well-being ought to be diminished, and it is assumed that imprisonment accomplishes this end. Thus, von Hirsch (1976) proposes, though Gardner (1976) disputes the suggestion, that prisons be organized on principles of just deserts and recrimination.

5. The findings of empirical social science research are generally and ineluctably tainted by methodological shortcomings, and evaluations of rehabilitative effectiveness are no exception. Thus, the conclusion that nothing works is quite conceivably false.

6. Vocational programs, counseling services, alcohol treatment programs, furloughs, and work release are among the programs omitted. Light, heat, physical facilities, and general administration are among the overhead expenses that ought to be allocated to programs.

7. This literature also supports the argument that arrest itself has a crime-control effect, and possibly that the length of a prison sentence may have an effect. Evidence with reference to the efficacy of the death penalty is wholly ambiguous.

A recent vigorous denial of the efficacy of sanctions is found in Brier and Feinberg (1980), but their survey and analysis is restricted to a very small, select set of studies and focuses mostly on the effect of the death penalty.

8. This point is made, implicitly and explicitly, throughout Blumstein et al. (1978) and is probably their most telling criticism of deterrence research.

9. This distinction is also inconsequential if crime control (rather than deterrence or incapacitation) is the goal.

10. The empirical regression analysis literature since 1970 uniformly supports this contention with respect to the sanctions of arrest, incarceration, and length of imprisonment. For example, of the 22 models that have tested the hypothesis that an increase in the probability of incarceration for homicide results in fewer homicides, all reported negative coefficients (Orsagh, 1982). These models were estimated by different authors and include both cross-sectional and longitudinal data sets. Controversy still exists, of course. Those who assert that sanctions deter or have crime-control effects (largely economists) use rather sophisticated empirical modeling, while those who assert there is no effect (largely sociologists) tend to argue that empirical analyses have serious conceptual flaws (Palmer, 1977).

11. The medical model presupposes a different set of causal factors and a different set of outcome measures from those associated with the social-structural model of rehabilitation.

12. The theory is found in the specialized literature of welfare economics.

REFERENCES

ADAMS, S. (1975) Evaluative Research in Corrections: A Practical Guide. Washington, DC: U.S. Department of Justice.

ALLEN, F. A. (1981) The Decline of the Rehabilitative Ideal: Penal Policy and Social Purpose. New Haven, CT: Yale University Press.

—— (1978) "The decline of the rehabilitative ideal in American criminal justice." Cleveland State Law Review 27: 147-156.

—— (1959) "Criminal justice, legal values and the rehabilitative ideal." Journal of Criminal Law, Criminology, and Police Science 50 (September-October): 226-232.

ANDENAES, J. (1975) "General prevention revisited: research and policy implications." Journal of Criminal Law and Criminology 66: 338-365.

BAILEY, W. (1966) "Correctional outcome: an evaluation of 100 reports." Journal of Criminal Law, Criminology, and Police Science 57: 153-160.

BAYER, R. (1981) "Crime, punishment, and the decline of liberal optimism." Crime and Delinquency 27: 169-190.

BENNETT, L. A. (1979) "Probation, parole and correctional programs — review of evaluation," in How Well Does It Work? Review of Criminal Justice Evaluation, 1978. Washington, DC: U.S. Department of Justice.

BEYLEVELD, D. (1980) A Bibliography on General Deterrence. Hampshire, England: Saxon House.

BLUMSTEIN, A., J. COHEN, and D. NAGIN (1978) Deterrence and Incapacitation — Estimating the Effects of Criminal Sanctions. Washington, DC: National Academy of Sciences.

BRIER, S. S. and S. E. FEINBERG (1980) "Recent econometric modeling of crime and punishment: support for the deterrence hypothesis?" Evaluation Review 4: 147-191.

CARTER, R. M., D. GLASER, and L. T. WILKINS [eds.] (1972) "Development of modern correctional concepts and standards," in Correctional Institutions. Philadelphia: J. B. Lippincott. (Reprinted from American Correctional Association, Manual of Correctional Standards.)

CLARKE, S. H. (1974) "Getting 'em out of circulation: does incarceration of juvenile offenders reduce crime?" Journal of Criminal Law and Criminology 65 (December): 528-535.

CLEAR, T. R. (1978) "Correctional policy, neo-retributionism, and the determinate sentence." The Justice System Journal 4: 26-48.

COHEN, J. (1978) "The incapacitative effect of imprisonment: a critical review of the literature," in A. Blumstein et al. (eds.) Deterrence and Incapacitation — Estimating the Effects of Criminal Sanctions. Washington, DC: National Academy of Sciences.

CONNOLLY, T. and S. J. DEUTSCH (1980) "Performance measurement: some conceptual issues." Evaluation and Program Planning 3: 35-43.

DEUTSCHER, I. (1976) "Toward avoiding the goal trap in evaluation research," in C. C. Abt (ed.) The Evaluation of Social Programs. Beverly Hills, CA: Sage.

DUFFEE, D. (1975) Correctional Policy and Prison Organization. Beverly Hills, CA: Sage.

EHRLICH, I. (1977) "Capital punishment and deterrence: some further thoughts and additional evidence." Journal of Political Economy 85: 741-788.

——— (1973) "Participation in illegitimate activities: an economic analysis," in G. S. Becker and W. M. Landes (eds.) Essays in the Economics of Crime and Punishment. New York: National Bureau of Economic Research.

EMPEY, L. T. (1969) "Contemporary programs for convicted juvenile offenders: problems of theory, practice, and research," in Crimes of Violence. Washington, DC: National Commission on the Causes and Prevention of Violence.

FATTAH, E. A. (1977) "Deterrence: a review of the literature." Canadian Journal of Criminology and Corrections 19(2): 1-119.

FOGEL, D. (1979) "Justice, not therapy: a new mission for corrections." Judicature 62: 373-380.

——— (1975) We Are the Living Proof: The Justice Model for Corrections. Cincinnati: W. H. Anderson.

GARDNER, M. R. (1976) "The renaissance of retribution — an examination of doing justice." Wisconsin Law Reivew 76: 781-815.

GENDREAU, P. and B. ROSS (1979) "Effective correctional treatment: bibliotherapy for cynics." Crime and Delinquency 463-489.

GIBBONS, D. C. (1975) Changing the Lawbreaker: The Treatment of Delinquents and Criminals. New York: Prentice-Hall.

GRASMICK, H. G. and D. E. GREEN (1980) "Legal punishment, social disapproval and internalization as inhibitors of illegal behavior." Journal of Criminal Law and Criminology 71: 325-335.

GREENBERG, D. F. (1975) "The incapacitative effect of imprisonment: some estimates." Law and Society Review 9 (Summer): 541-580.

GRIZZLE, G. A. (1980) Measuring Corrections Performance. Raleigh, NC: Osprey.

HALLECK, S. L. and A. D. WITTE (1977) "Is rehabilitation dead?" Crime and Delinquency 23: 372-382.

HAWKINS, J. D., P. A. PASTOR, Jr., M. BELL, and S. MORRISON (1980) Report of the National Juvenile Justice Assessment Centers: A Typology of Cause-Focused Strategies of Delinquency Prevention. Washington, DC: Government Printing Office.

HEINEKI, J. M. (1978) "Economic models of criminal behavior: an overview," in J. M. Heineke (ed.) Economic Models of Criminal Behavior. Amsterdam: North-Holland.

HOFFMAN, P. B. and B. STONE-MEIERHOEFFER (1980) "Reporting recidivism rates: the criterion and follow-up issues." Journal of Criminal Justice 8: 53-59.

HOLLISTER, R. G., P. KEMPER, and J. WOOLDRIDGE (1979) "Linking process and impact analysis: the case of supported work," in T. D. Cook and C. H. Reichardt (eds.) Qualitative and Quantitative Methods in Evaluation Research. Beverly Hills, CA: Sage.

JANEKSELA, G. M. (1977) "An evaluation model for criminal justice." Criminal justice review 2: 1-11.

KELLOGG, F. R. (1977) "From retribution to 'desert': the evolution of criminal punishment." Criminology 15: 179-192.

KRISBERG, B. (1980) "Utility of process evaluation: crime and delinquency programs," in M. W. Klein and K. S. Teilman (eds.) Handbook of Criminal Justice Evaluation. Beverly Hills, CA: Sage.

LIPTON, D., R. MARTINSON, and J. WILKS (1975) The Effectiveness of Correctional Treatment: A Survey of Treatment Evaluation Studies. New York: Praeger.

MacNAMARA, D. E. J. (1977) "The medical model in corrections: requiescat in pace." Criminology 14: 439-448.

MALTZ, M. D. and R. McCLEARY (1977) "The mathematics of behavior change: recidivism and construct validity." Evaluation Quarterly 1: 421-438.

MARSHALL, I. H. (1981) "Correctional treatment processes: rehabilitation reconsidered," in R. R. Roberg and V. J. Webb (eds.) Critical Issues in Corrections: Problems, Trends, and Prospects. St. Paul, MN: West.

MORRIS, N. (1974) The Future of Imprisonment. Chicago: University of Chicago Press.

NAGIN, D. (1978) " General deterrence: a review of the empirical evidence," in A. Blumstein et al. (eds.) Deterrence and Incapacitation — Estimating the Effects of Criminal Sanctions. Washington, DC: National Academy of Sciences.

ORSAGH, T. (1982) "A meta-statistical analysis of deterrence research." Presented at the annual meetings of the American Society of Criminology, Toronto.

PALMER, J. (1977) "Economic analyses of the deterrent effect of punishment: a review." Journal of Research in Crime and Delinquency 14: 4-21.

PALMER, T. B. (1975) "Martinson revisited." Journal of Research in Crime and Delinquency 12: 133-152.

—— and R. V. LEWIS (1980) "A differential approach to juvenile diversion." Journal of Research in Crime and Delinquency 17: 209-227.

PUGSLEY, R. A. (1979) "Retributionism: a just basis for criminal sentences." Hofstra Law Review 7: 379-405.

QUAY, H. C. (1977) "The three faces of evaluation: what can be expected to work," Criminal Justice and Behavior 4: 341, 354.

RICHMOND, M. S. (1972) "Measuring the cost of correctional services." Crime and Delinquency (July): 243-252.

RUTMAN, L. (1977) Evaluation Research Methods. Beverly Hills, CA: Sage.

SCHULBERG, H. C. and F. BAKER (1977) "Program evaluation models and the implementation of research findings." American Journal of Public Health 58: 1248-1255.

SECHREST, L. and R. REDNER (1979) "Strength and integrity of treatments in evaluation studies," in How Well Does It Work? Review of Criminal Justice Evaluation, 1978. Washington, DC: U.S. Department of Justice.

SECHREST, L., S. O. WHITE, and E. D. BROWN [eds.] (1979) The Rehabilitation of Criminal Offenders: Problems and Prospects. Washington, DC: National Academy of Sciences.

SHINNAR, R. and S. SHINNAR (1975) "The effects of the criminal justice system on the control of crime: a quantitative approach." Law and Society Review 9 (Summer): 581-611.

SHOVER, N. (1979) A Sociology of American Corrections. Homewood, IL: Dorsey.

STREET, D., R. VINTER, and C. PERROW (1966) Organization for Treatment. New York: Free Press.

SUTHERLAND, E.H. and D.R. CRESSEY (1978) Principles of Criminology (10th ed.). Philadelphia: J.B. Lippincott.

von HIRSCH, A. (1976) Doing Justice: The Choice of Punishments. New York: Hill & Wang.

WALDO, G.P. and T.G. CHIRICOS (1977) "Work release and recidivism: an empirical evaluation of a social policy." Evaluation Quarterly 1: 87-107.

WARREN, M.Q. (1977) "Correctional treatment and coercion: the differential effectiveness perspective." Criminal Justice and Behavior 4: 355-516.

—— (1969) "The case for differential treatment of delinquents." Annals of the American Academy of Political and Social Science 38: 47-59.

ZELENY, M. (1982) Multiple Criteria Decision Making. New York: McGraw-Hill.

ZIMRING, F.E. and G.J. HAWKINS (1973) Deterrence: The Legal Threat in Crime Control. Chicago: University of Chicago Press.

Chapter 9

THE SPECIAL DETERRENT EFFECT OF INCARCERATION

CHARLES DAVID PHILLIPS
BRUCE W. McCLEARY
SIMON DINITZ

The agencies that administer the criminal law are our society's instruments for distributing a social cost. As Benthan (1948: 71) recognized in the late eighteenth century: "The business of government is to promote the happiness of the society, by punishing and rewarding. The part of its business which consists in punishing, is more particularly the subject of the penal law." It is this part of the state's business that we have given to police, courts, and penal institutions, and it is an unhappy business. After all, "all punishment is mischief: all punishment in itself is evil" (Bentham, 1948: 171). We allow these institutions to do their "evil" because it is hoped that their deeds will be repaid with increases in the general level of happiness. These increments are

AUTHORS' NOTE: *An earlier version of this chapter was presented at the annual meetings of the American Society of Criminology, Toronto, 1982. This research uses data originally collected as part of the Dangerous Offenders Project (Simon Dinitz and John Conrad, co-principal investigators), a study supported by a grant from the Lilly Endowment to the Academy for Contemporary Problems in Columbus, Ohio. The University Research Council of the University of North Carolina at Chapel Hill provided support for this analysis.*

believed to derive from punishment's salutory effects on citizens' behavior. One dimension of these effects relies on the idea of deterrence. As Bentham (1948: 171, note 1) expressed it:

> The immediate end of punishment is to control action. This action is either that of the offender, or of others: that of the offender it controls by its influence . . . on his will, in which case it is said to operate in the way of reformation . . . that of others . . . by its influence on their wills . . . in the way of example.

What Bentham outlined in 1780 are, of course, two fundamental goals for criminal justice agencies — special and general deterrence. Two centuries later, however, we are still unsure whether the punishment meted out by these agencies does indeed have such salutory effects. The literature addressing the issue of general deterrence (the effects of punishment levels on the overall crime rate) is now quite substantial but remains contradictory (see Nagin, 1978; Cook, 1980; Ekland-Olson et al., this volume, for reviews). In contrast, the study of special deterrence (the effects of punishment on those specific individuals receiving punishment) is not so well developed.

Some analysts find special deterrence "difficult to distinguish from other forms of rehabilitation" (Nagin, 1978: 95). Thus, they see all studies of rehabilitation, which are quite numerous (see Lipton et al., 1975), as studies reflecting on special deterrence. In an abstract sense, Nagin is correct; rehabilitation studies do focus on individual behavior in response to punishment or treatment, and we use the same focus for studies of special deterrence. However, most studies of rehabilitation programs give us little real insight into whether special deterrence succeeds. Such studies are usually constructed to discover whether the members of Group X (who received some special form of treatment) display postpunishment behavior that differs from the postpunishment behavior of Group Y (who did not receive this special treatment). Most of these studies also use an exceedingly narrow concept of "effect" — whether an individual at any point after punishment participates in criminal activity (see Marsden and Orsagh, this volume, for a discussion of the study of rehabilitation).

What we need in order to investigate special deterrence is an approach that differs from the one classically used in even the best analyses of rehabilitation. We need studies that, as Murray and Cox (1979a) argue, "compare behavior prior to the correctional program with behavior following the correctional program." Such projects must not ask whether criminality is "in any sense cured, but whether things got better. The reference point is not zero, but the preintervention state" (Murray and Cox, 1979a: 32). When one searches for such studies — those dealing directly with the degree to which sanctions change the behavior of those on whom they are imposed — the universe of relevant research shrinks drastically.

As one recognizes that most studies of rehabilitative programs have little to say about special deterrence, one's faith in the conclusion that "recent evidence tends to suggest that special deterrence . . . is not operating" (Nagin, 1978: 95) shrinks precipitously. This conclusion is based on studies indicating "the invariance of recidivism to any type of special rehabilitative program" (Nagin, 1978: 95-96). Also, after perusing the small body of literature that analyzes differences in prepunishment and postpunishment behavior, one cannot accept such sweeping conclusions as: "There is no evidence to support this [special deterrence] notion" (Cook, 1980: 218). In fact, in the area of juvenile justice, a stream of research arguing that special deterrence *does* work is growing in both size and respectability (see Thornberry, 1971; Empey and Lubeck, 1971; Empey and Erickson, 1972; Murray and Cox, 1979a).

It is this research, which analyzes the effects of institutionalization on delinquency, that will provide the focus for this discussion of the performance of criminal justice agencies. We will review and analyze certain contributions to this body of work, add the results of our own study to it, point out a number of serious methodological problems in studies of this ilk, and consider the appropriate course for future inquiries that hope to measure performance by studying the effects of institutionalization.

EFFECTS OF INSTITUTIONALIZATION
ON DELINQUENCY

Despite the growing body of research on special deterrence and delinquency, much of the theoretical work on delinquency eschews the idea of special deterrence. An entire school of scholars — adherents of the labeling perspective — sees official responses to delinquency as causes of, rather than cures for, youths' tendencies to violate the criminal law (see Tannenbaum, 1938; Lemert, 1951; Erikson, 1962; Becker, 1963; Cicourel, 1968; Schur, 1969, 1971). Such scholars argue that the labeling of a youth, which occurs when juveniles are processed by officials, generates "secondary deviance." As Tannenbaum (1938: 20) put it: "The harder they work to reform the evil, the greater the evil grows under their hands." Much of the research spawned by this perspective analyzes the effects of juvenile court contact on a youth's self-image and on family members, friends, or school officials (see Mahoney, 1974). Some researchers have focused their attention on the negative responses of juvenile justice agencies to "previously stigmatized" youth (McEachern and Bauzer, 1967; Phillips and Dinitz, 1982; Terry, 1967; Werthman and Piliavin, 1967).

Other researchers have searched for the effects of labeling by analyzing the impact of sanctions on subsequent delinquency. Some of these studies support the labeling perspective (Gold and Williams, 1969; Williams and Gold, 1970). The implications of others are not as clear (McEachern, 1968). Even the classic Philadelphia birth cohort study gives labelers' contentions some support. As the authors indicate: "The more severe the dispositions, the higher the probability of [a youth] committing a subsequent offense" (Wolfgang et al., 1972: 226).

As is almost always the case, other evidence points in the opposite direction — to the efficacy of sanctions (especially institutionalization) in reducing later delinquency. Thornberry's (1971) work on the Philadelphia cohort indicated that, while certain court dispositions may have amplified delinquency, institutionalized youth were arrested less frequently after their release. Also, a field experiment done by Empey and Lubeck (1971) provides some support for the efficacy of incarceration. Though the experiment was designed to test the effects of a rehabilitative program, its pretest/posttest design allowed a closer look at the effects of institutionalization than is usually available. In the Silverlake experiment, both the group involved in the community-based residential program and the group sent to a more traditional environment experienced more than a 70 percent reduction in their respective delinquency rates (Empey and Lubeck, 1971: 259-260).

Probably the most noteworthy recent effort to investigate special deterrence is Murray and Cox's (1979a) report of their evaluation of the UDIS (Unified Delinquency Intervention Services) in Chicago. The authors report significant reductions that they attribute to special deterrence (1979a: 38):

> In the year before they were [institutionalized] . . . , the 317 . . . subjects were arrested an average of 6.3 times each. After they were released, the same 317 boys were arrested an average of 2.9 times during an average follow-up period of 16.8 months on the street. . . . This, in elementary form, is the phenomenon we have called the supression effect.

In fact, roughly 90 percent of the juveniles in the Chicago study seemed to respond to their institutionalization by reducing their participation in delinquency (Murray and Cox, 1979a: 39). To explain these findings, Murray and Cox suggest that "something very like deterrence was at work" (1979a: 178).

INTERNAL VALIDITY ISSUES

Such startling claims, which run contrary to much conventional academic wisdom, deserve serious attention. In the course of discussing some of the potential problems in the Chicago study, we will highlight methodological problems that arise in all efforts to demonstrate the efficacy of incarceration and lay the necessary groundwork for later discussion of our own research. The various threats to the validity of results derived from quasi-experimental studies fall into four general categories as sources of internal, external, construct, or statistical conclusion invalidity (see Cook and Campbell, 1979: 37-94; Campbell, 1973; Campbell and Stanley, 1963). Only a few of these potential sources of invalidity will apply to any single piece of research, and each research question will have its own unique constellation of problems. Our major focus here will be on those threats to internal validity that are most troublesome in studies of special deterrence. Each threat to internal validity represents an alternative explanation for a finding that an intervention had a significant impact on the problem that it was designed to remedy.

In analyses that purport to demonstrate the effect of institutionalization on juveniles, two of the most serious validity issues derive from a single alternative hypothesis: They may have reduced their involvement in delinquency after they were institutionalized, but not because of the institutionalization. The first variant of this argument is based on the idea of maturation. If one sees delinquency as something that the young "grow out of," one must wonder whether the intervention simply caught the subjects as they naturally matured out of their involvement in criminal activity. Murray and Cox (1979a: 67-78) identify two types of maturation that may threaten suppression findings — age and career stage. Analyses of interventions that fail to control for a juvenile's age at institutionalization and where he or she is in a delinquency career (that is, the number of previous arrests) must be considered suspect. Thus, the authors of the Chicago study enter age and previous arrests into their analysis in order to show that, in fact, institutionalization has a significant effect, independent of a youth's age and the length of his or her career prior to the intervention (Murray and Cox, 1979a: 77).

A more troublesome variant of the "they would have stopped anyway" argument derives from the problem of regression. As McCleary et al. (1979) indicate, research on special deterrence creates the possibility for two types of regression artifacts. The first type of artifact occurs when "subjects are selected [for study] due to abnormal pretest scores." Such groups "on a posttest . . . will regress to their population means, thus guaranteeing a pretest/posttest difference" (McCleary et al., 1979: 632). The second type of regression artifact occurs when an intervention takes place in reaction to an abnormal level of activity on the part of the subjects. McCleary and his associates (1979: 633) argue that both types may be occurring in the Chicago study because (1) the juveniles were chosen for involvement in the study because of their relatively high arrest rates, and (2) the exact timing of their institutionalization may have been in reaction to an unusually high level of activity on a youth's part. These possibilities lead the authors to conclude that "a regression artifact is a reasonable and viable alternative for the effect" reported in the Chicago study (McCleary et al., 1979: 648).

In response to this criticism, Murray and Cox (1979b) argue force-fully against the efficacy of regression artifacts as an explanation for their findings. Much of the debate between these researchers re-volves around how well one can model delinquency careers as stochastic processes, what assumptions can be used in such models and, finally, whether the models devised by the critics fit the process that generated the Chicago data. Given the present state of knowl-edge, such issues are not fully resolvable.

McCleary and his associates make two interesting points about special deterrence and the "suppression effect." First, the amount of suppression should be dependent in part on the amount of time a juvenile spends in custody. If institutionalization operates as a true deterrent, it is because juveniles respond to the increased "costs" associated with custody. This implies that those who have paid the highest costs (been in custody longest) should evidence the greatest changes in behavior. Second, the degree of suppression should not be positively correlated with the level of a youth's preintervention activ-ity. That is, youths with high levels of preinstitutionalization delin-quency should not be more receptive to the costs imposed by institutionalization than youths with lower levels of preintervention activity (McCleary et al., 1979) If anything, the correlation between suppression and earlier activity should be negative. One can easily argue, within the utilitarian tradition of the deterrence argument, that the greatest suppression should occur among those with the least commitment to delinquency, and among those who have benefited least from it (that is, those with low rates of activity). If one finds either of the relationships outlined above, then one can be more confident that special deterrence, rather than a regression effect, is operating.

The external validity (generalizability) of research findings with regard to special deterrence is also troublesome. For example, in the Chicago study, subjects averaged ten arrests and three detentions prior to inclusion in the study (see Glaser, 1979) — hardly a random sample of all juvenile offenders. This is a fault shared by all research in this area. Only after the accumulation of a large body of research dealing with the effects of incarceration can one hope to resolve the issues raised above. The research reported here is an attempt to contribute to this body of research and, more importantly, to discuss the problems noted above in the context of a different research setting.

ANALYSIS USING THE COLUMBUS COHORT

The data for the present study were collected for the Dangerous Offenders Project in Franklin County, Ohio (see Hamparian et al., 1978). The cohort of juveniles included in the study was defined by the following conditions:

(1) all were born during the period from 1956 through 1960;
(2) all resided, during their delinquent careers, in Franklin County, Ohio (that is, Columbus, its suburbs, and the surrounding area); and
(3) each had an arrest for at least one violent offense while a juvenile.

Data on the 1138 youths in the cohort were assembled from both police records (provided by the Columbus Police Department Juvenile Bureau) and commitment records (provided by the Ohio Youth Commission). The data collection ended in 1976, so the delinquent careers of those born in 1959 and 1960 had not been completed. Complete juvenile career data (that is, arrests and official action up to age 18) are therefore available only for the 811 youths born from 1956 through 1958.

For our purposes, two more defining conditions were added to the original three. We selected only those juveniles

(1) whose juvenile history was complete at the time of the data collection; and
(2) who had had at least one commitment to an Ohio Youth Commission facility.

The second condition was added for obvious reasons. We confined the analysis to those for whom a complete juvenile history was available because of our desire to base our "before and after" institutionalization comparisons on entire careers. This reduced the size of the sample to 251 youths.

The data base was further reduced for other reasons. Nineteen youths had no postinstitutionalization arrests, but they were not released from custody until their eighteenth birthday, or until that birthday was only a month away. Thus, their reduction in activity may have been the result of incapacitation rather than deterrence, so they were dropped from the sample. The data for one youth were so incomplete that he was dropped from our analysis. Also, 21 youths had some record of postinstitutionalization arrests, but no postrelease time. Either the data were missing, or we showed no release for them. These arrests may have involved escapes and rearrests, or they may have been arrests that occurred during short furloughs. In any case, inability to calculate a postinstitutionalization arrest rate for these youths forced us to drop them from the analysis.

The remaining sample, on which we base the first stage of our analysis, contained 210 juveniles. Descriptive statistics on the institutionalized cohort, presented in Table 9.1, shed some light on the types of youths in our study and offer some interesting comparisons to the larger data base from which these youths were drawn. It was expected that the institutionalized cohort would contain worse delinquents than the original cohort (see Hamparian et al., 1978). Institutionalization is the severest sanction available to the juvenile courts and is not usually the preferred method of dealing with less serious delinquents. The most obvious statistic for comparing the two groups is the average number of arrests. The institutionalized cohort compiled almost twice as many arrests per individual (6.9) as did the members of the original cohort (4.2), although the mean number of violent arrests for the institutionalized cohort (1.7) was only slightly larger than that for the entire cohort (1.2). Two other interesting comparisons involve age at onset and age at cessation. In general, the institutionalized cohort started younger (age 12.3 vs. 13.3 years) and quit later (age 16.4 vs. 15.7 years) than did those in the original cohort.

The average youth in our smaller group was first institutionalized roughly two and one-half years after his or her first arrest. Each youth spent an average of eight months in an institution, followed by a year and one-half on the street between the first institutionalization and last arrest. The average member of our group received a wide variety of dispositions, including two bouts of institutionalization. Nevertheless, our cohort was very similar to the larger cohort in terms of

TABLE 9.1   The Institutionalized Cohort (N = 210)

Careers	Mean	Standard Deviation
Total arrests	7.1	4.6
Violent arrests	1.7	1.0
Serious violent arrests	0.6	0.7
Age at first arrest[a]	12.1	2.47
Age at last arrest[a]	16.4	0.90
Age at first institutionalization[a]	14.5	1.65
Time between first arrest and first institutionalization[b]	28.7	24.4
Street time after first institutionalization to last arrest[b]	18.1	12.8
Time institutionalized[b]	7.7	7.7

Legal Responses[c]	Mean	
Releases	0.9	—
Informal supervisions	1.8	—
Formal supervisions	0.9	—
Detentions	0.9	—
Institutionalizations	2.1	—

Personal Attributes	Percentage	
Gender		
Male	83.3	—
Female	16.7	—
Race		
White	44.3	—
Minority	55.7	—

a. Juveniles' age in years.
b. Time in months.
c. Average number of times a youth in the group received this disposition.

personal attributes. While 85 percent of the original group were male, 83 percent of those institutionalized were also male. Of those institutionalized, 55 percent were minorities, as were 56 percent of the original cohort.

Estimating the Impact of Institutionalization

Hamparian and her associates (1978: 22) define a juvenile's delinquent career as "the period extending between the onset and cessation of delinquent acts." Since our interests were in analyzing the effects of institutionalization on delinquent careers, we divided these youths' delinquent careers into two parts: the preinstitutionalization career, measured by the number of months between his or her first arrest and first institutionalization; and the postinstitutionalization career, measured by the number of months a youth was on the street between the first institutionalization and last arrest (taking subsequent institutionalizations into account). For those with no arrests after their release, "street time" was defined as the time from release until their eighteenth birthday.

These two time periods, in conjunction with a youth's arrest record during each period, constituted our measures of activity and formed the basis on which the impact of institutionalization was to be evaluated. We chose to use arrests per month, rather than simply the number of arrests, for obvious reasons. For example, suppose a juvenile were arrested four times, then institutionalized. Upon release, he is arrested twice more. Knowing nothing more, one might think that he "got better." But if one found that his preinstitutionalization arrests were accumulated over a period of two years, while his postinstitutionalization arrests occurred within two months of his release, one would recognize that the opposite conclusion is more justified. The exact operationalizations of our measures of pre- and postintervention activity appear below:

$$\text{Prerate} = \frac{\text{number of arrests prior to institutionalization}}{\text{number of months between first arrest and institutionalization}}$$

$$\text{Postrate} = \frac{\text{number of arrests following first institutionalization}}{\text{months of "street time" following release from the first institutionalization}}$$

If a youth's postrate is lower than his or her prerate, one can begin to consider the possibility that the youth's delinquency was suppressed. However, if the postrate exceeds the prerate, the possibility that institutionalization may have amplified the youth's delinquency becomes a consideration.

We used arrests as surrogates measures of delinquency, although we know that all delinquency does not result in an arrest. Given our purposes, however, this is problematic only if the correlation between "real" delinquency and arrests is affected by institutionalization. If institutions are indeed "schools of crime," then the young who go there may learn how better to avoid arrest upon their release, thus changing the correlation between arrest and delinquency. This argument also implies some degree of offense specialization: One learns to be a better purse snatcher, car thief, burglar, or whatever. However, the best available evidence indicates that there is serious question as to whether such specialization actually occurs (Wolfgang et al., 1972; Rojek and Erickson, 1982).

One might also make the opposite argument — that institutionalization increases the correlation between delinquency and arrest. As Werthman and Piliavin (1967) point out, police research methods frequently involve focusing investigatory efforts on a group of suspects identified on the basis of their past behavior. At the same time, it is previous contact with the police that is thought to heighten the probability of arrest in an encounter. While a previous institutionalization may affect the responses of juvenile court officials (Phillips and Dinitz, 1982), however, there is no real evidence that it affects arrest decisions in encounters with juveniles.

The Impact of Institutionalization

Using the operationalizations outlined above, the results obtained in the analysis of the Columbus birth cohort differ dramatically from those obtained in the Chicago study. While the Chicago study indicated a reduction in the arrest rate for approximately 90 percent of the 317 juveniles studied (Murray and Cox, 1979a: 39), only 65 percent of the 210 Columbus juveniles showed potential evidence of reduced activity. Of this population, 35 percent "desisted" — that is, they had no recorded arrests following release. The remaining 30 percent were arrested after their release, but they had postrelease arrest rates lower than their preinstitutionalization arrest rates; their activity was suppressed. However, 35 percent of the youths had postrelease arrest rates that were higher than their preinstitutionalization rates; their activity was amplified.

These results cast the effects of incarceration in a much darker light than did the UDIS findings. While only some 10 percent of the Chicago youth showed evidence of amplification, over one-third of the Columbus youth seemed to respond to institutionalization by increasing their criminal activity. Furthermore, the Columbus results are very likely an underestimation of the deleterious effects of imprisonment. Our data include all juvenile arrests for those youth who stayed in Columbus during their entire juvenile careers. We have no idea, however, how many of the population may have moved out of the Columbus area at some point after their release.

Any "mortality" in our population should result in an overestimation of the number of youth who desisted or whose activity was suppressed. For example, if we make the reasonable assumption that an equal percentage of those who would fall into each outcome category did leave town, the true desistees would be correctly identified in our data. However, depending on how soon after their release they left the Columbus area, true suppressees might be identified as either suppressees or desistees. Those youths whose activity levels increased, depending on when they left, could be classified as members of any of our three categories. Thus, those whose delinquency was amplified could be incorrectly identified as successes, although no departing desistees or suppressees could be incorrectly identified as failures. The 65 percent of the population on whom prison seems to have had a salutary effect must include a number of failures who committed their crimes elsewhere. Thus, the deleterious effects of institutionalization in this population, which are already substantial, are underestimated to some unknown degree.

Table 9.2 presents descriptive statistics for the three groups of youths as they are identified by our data. As one would expect, those whose delinquent activity increased had more total arrests, on the average, than did either suppressees or desistees. They were also institutionalized more frequently than other youths. However, the most interesting differences among these three groups relate to when they were first involved with the juvenile justice system and when they were first institutionalized. Those whose activities were amplified began their delinquent careers over a year earlier than the suppressees and over two years earlier than the desistees. However, their ages at first institutionalization do not follow this pattern. The

TABLE 9.2   Career Characteristics of the Institutionalized
            Cohort (means)

	Desisted N = 74	Suppressed N = 63	Amplified N = 73
Total arrests	3.9	8.1	9.4
Violent arrests	1.3	1.8	2.1
Serious violent arrests	.5	.6	.6
Age at first arrest[a]	13.1	12.2	11.0
Age at first institutionalization[a]	15.4	13.5	14.4
Age at last arrest	—	16.5	16.6
Preinstitutionalization arrests	3.9	4.2	5.3
Time between first arrest and first institutionalization[b]	27.6	14.3	42.1
Preinstitutionalization arrest rate	.42	.58	.18
Postinstitutionalization arrests	0	3.9	4.1
Street time after first institutionalization to last arrest[b]	20.1	23.0	11.7
Postinstitutionalization arrest rate	0	.19	.62
Time of institutionalization[b]	5.7	8.4	9.0
Total institutionalizations	1.0	2.4	3.0

a. Juveniles' age in years.
b. Time in months.

average age at institutionalization for suppressees is two years earlier than that for desistees and one year earlier than the average age for youths whose activities increased. Thus, the amplified had a preinstitutionalization arrest rate that was much lower than the rate for either suppressees or desistees. Such a result is not what one would expect. Why would those with the seemingly highest commitment to delinquency (highest rate of involvement) be "reformed" while those with seemingly the least commitment to delinquency would get worse? Such a counterintuitive finding suggests the operation of regression artifacts or some other source of internal invalidity. The use of multivariate analysis strategy may allow us to get a better idea of how much of the change that we see in these youths' behavior might be attributable to alternative hypotheses.

Discriminant Analysis of Amplification, Suppression, and Desistence

The 210 youths in our analysis fall into one of three categories, each representing a possible response to institutionalization (that is, desistence, suppression, or amplification). Since these categories — our dependent variable — constitute a nominal variable, discriminant analysis was used (Anderson, 1958; Cooley and Lohnes, 1971; Klecka, 1980). The basic question that this technique answers is whether individuals' scores on certain independent variables are helpful in distinguishing among those who fall into different categories of the dependent variable. To put it somewhat differently, do those individuals who are in different categories of the dependent variable differ in their scores on certain independent variables? For our purposes, the technique helps us to address the specific question of whether youths who seem to respond differently to institutionalization also differ in their scores on our independent variables. Our independent variables represent the various sources of internal invalidity that threaten this style of research. Thus, this analysis gives us some idea of how much of a role a number of alternative hypotheses may play in determining whether a youth seems to desist, to exhibit amplification, or to show what seems to be evidence of suppression.

The variables included in our analysis will represent three of the most troublesome alternative explanations for what seem to be the effects of institutionalization — history, maturation, and statistical regression. The analysis, though it does not address the question directly, may also shed some light on how seriously amplification may be underestimated due to mortality in our population. History and maturation can easily be controlled for by the inclusion of three variables; historical effects usually result from an uncontrolled change that occurs during the course of observation. Since this sample includes juveniles institutionalized in different years, it is possible that our results may be affected by temporal changes in delinquency or in official responses to that delinquency. By including the year of institutionalization in our analysis, it can be ascertained whether history plays some role in generating our results. Maturation can be a serious challenge to any analysis such as ours, since any observed change may be due to (1) chronological age or (2) career stage (Murray and Cox, 1979a). The latter suggests that each career has a peak activity point; therefore, the number of preinstitutionalization arrests is included in the analysis. Chronological age is controlled for by including a variable for age at first institutionalization.

Finally, two types of regression artifacts may plague this type of analysis. One type of regression artifact can occur whenever an intervention is cued by an abnormal high in an ongoing stream of behavior. If intervention occurs at one of these peaks, the posttreatment stream will automatically be relatively lower. Juvenile court judges may institutionalize delinquents when they are at a peak in their delinquent activities. When this occurs, the subsequent return to the average level may be erroneously interpreted as a treatment effect (either deterrence or rehabilitation).

The problem can be addressed by including a variable that measures velocity changes in the preinstitutionalization behavior stream. The measure used in this analysis is:

$$\text{velocity change} = (\text{diff}_{a \text{ and } b}) - (\text{diff}_{b \text{ and } c})$$

diff = time (in months) between arrests
a = arrest resulting in first institutionalization
b = arrest immediately prior to a
c = arrest immediately prior to b

While this variable is rather crude, it will control, to a limited degree, abnormal perturbations in the preinstitutionalization stream of arrests. However, it carries the unfortunate condition that some cases have to be dropped. This is because a minimum of three arrests is necessary to make the computation. For this reason, 34 cases were dropped and an exploratory regression performed, using the three categories of youths as the dependent variable. The acceleration variable came late into the regression equation (using a R^2 maximizing procedure that adds variables in order of importance). In addition, the coefficient for this variable in the final regression equation was small and insignificant.

Previous research on this cohort also indicates that no regression artifact of this type seems to be occurring. According to earlier analyses, the decision to institutionalize a youth is dependent on the number of previous arrests and the seriousness of the offense with which he or she is charged (Phillips and Dinitz, 1982). This court seemed to respond more heavily to the number of infractions than to the rate of infraction. Given our findings, the results of this earlier research, and the already small sample size, this variable was dropped from our analysis so that the 34 affected cases could be retained.

The second type of regression artifact that may be present does not involve capturing any individual at some career trough or peak. Instead, it involves applying the intervention (institutionalization) to groups with exceedingly high or low levels of preintervention activity. The members of these groups should "regress" toward the mean level of activity in the postintervention period. We attempt to control for this possibility by including a youth's preintervention arrest rate in the analysis.

One measure of how important history, maturation, and regression may be in our analysis is based on how well the variables representing these factors predict the type of behavioral change that occurs after institutionalization. If the variables included in our model can accurately predict whether a youth desists, seems to reduce his or her delinquency, or seems to increase such activity, there may be some serious question as to whether these changes in behavior are the result of the treatment (that is, institutionalization) or simply the operation of various alternative causal mechanisms. If, on the other hand, our model cannot predict a youth's response, these changes can probably be attributed to the effects of treatment.

Table 9.3 presents a comparison of our 210 youths' measured responses to institutionalization with their predicted responses, based on our model. As the summary statistics for that table indicate, our model correctly classifies 63 percent of the population — over one-half of the desistees and suppressees, and over 80 percent of those whose delinquency was amplified. The Tau$_b$ indicates what proportion of the errors in guessing a youth's category is reduced when guesses are based on the variables in our model rather than on prior probabilities; our model generates a 44 percent reduction in guessing errors.

Interestingly, most of the misclassifications generated by the model placed those whom we had identified as desistees or suppressees in the amplification category. Such a result is exactly what

TABLE 9.3   Comparison of Classifications Based on Functions
With True Group Membership

	Predicted		
Actual	*Desisted*	*Suppressed*	*Amplified*
Desisted	40	5	29
	54%	7%	39%
Suppressed	9	33	21
	14%	52%	33%
Amplified	10	4	59
	14%	5%	81%

Percentage Correctly Classified = 63%
Tau_b = .44

one would expect if the mortality problems discussed earlier (such as youths moving out of the area) are indeed occurring. Thus, this result represents only a minimum estimate of the effects of various sources of internal invalidity on the youths' behavior.

Exactly which invalidity issues play the largest roles in generating the correct classifications in Table 9.3 is an issue addressed in Table 9.4, which displays the two functions on which the classifications in Table 9.3 were based. Function 1 separates suppressees most clearly from desistees, while Function 2 separates (somewhat less clearly) those whose activities were amplified from both other groups. The major differences among the youths falling into each group seem to be in the year in which their first institutionalization occurred and in their preinstitutionalization arrest rates. Since a youth's age at first institutionalization is, in these data, very highly correlated with the year of that institutionalization, it is difficult to ascertain whether one is seeing history or maturation in operation. However, if maturation were operating, one would expect those displaying amplification to have been incarcerated earlier than any other group. Since that is not the case, the argument is probably stronger for an interpretation of these coefficients as representing some type of historical effect. The importance of the preinstitutionalization arrest rate reflects the operation of a regression artifact.

TABLE 9.4   Functions and Standardized Canonical Discriminant
Function Coefficients

	Function 1		Function 2
Eigen Values	.44		.18
Group Centroids			
	.69	Desisted	Desisted .36
	.11	Amplified	Suppressed .24
	−.94	Suppressed	Amplified −.57
Coefficients			
	.239	Age at first institutionalization (history/maturation)	.162
	.926	Year of first institutionalization (history/maturation)	.244
	−.018	Total preinstitutionalization arrests (maturation)	−.162
	−.306	Preinstitutionalization arrest rate (regression)	.983

Such results indicate that the various sources of invalidity may play a significant role in generating the behavioral changes displayed by these youths. However, alternative hypotheses alone cannot predict the correct classification for all of these youths. It seems that some portion of the observed changes, though not all of them, may indeed be the result of institutionalization.

Invalidity and Estimates of the Magnitude of Amplification and Suppression

When one recognizes that institutionalization can generate amplification as well as suppression, estimates of the magnitude of change take on vital importance. Without accurate estimates of both the positive and negative effects of institutionalization, assessments of the costs and benefits of any sanctioning strategy become impossible. Of course, we must again be concerned about the effects of various sources of invalidity on such estimates. In this section, we used two of our three groups of youths (those amplified and those suppressed) to explore the degree to which maturation, history, and regression may distort the results of analyses of this type. Through OLS, we determined the amount of variation in amplification and suppression that can be attributed to the independent variables included in the discriminant analysis discussed above.

As part of this analysis, we also explored the effects of using different measures of the magnitude of change. The first measure of change that we used is based on the percent reduction statistic used by McCleary and his associates (1979):

$$\text{percent reduction} = 1 - \frac{\text{postrate}}{\text{prerate}}$$

This statistic ranges from minus infinity to $+1$. Positive values, therefore, do not have strictly the same meaning as negative values. We used the following computation for a different change statistic so that negative and positive values would be more comparable:

$$1 - \frac{\text{postrate}}{\text{prerate}}, \text{ when prerate} > \text{postrate,}$$

$$\text{change} = 0, \text{ when prerate} = \text{postrate, and}$$

$$-1 + \frac{\text{prerate}}{\text{postrate}}, \text{ when prerate} < \text{postrate}$$

This statistic ranges from -1 to 0 for those whose delinquency was amplified and from 0 to $+1$ for those who were suppressed. This symmetry makes the comparison more meaningful of how much better and how much worse the groups actually were.

The second measure that we used was the measure of suppression found in Murray and Cox (1979a):

$$\text{difference} = \frac{\text{postrate} - \text{prerate}}{\text{prerate}}$$

This measure ranges from -1 to 0 for suppressees and from 0 to infinity for those whose activities were amplified. For our third measure, we simply used a youth's postinstitutionalization arrest rate.

While this is not a true "change" measure, it provides important supplementary information.

While we consider these operationalizations to be reasonable constructs representing important aspects of the underlying phenomenon with which we are concerned, certain warnings are appropriate. Were one to accept a different concept of a youth's "delinquent career," different results might be obtained. For example, if one simply considered a delinquent career to be those eight years that an Ohio youth's behavior is under the jurisdiction of the juvenile court, one would greatly lengthen most careers, thus deflating all our measures.

The results of the analysis appear in Table 9.5. These results are not so much interesting in the conclusions to which they lead as they are important in the problems that they emphasize. The analyses using the "change" and "difference" statistics indicate that the only source of internal invalidity that is of any consequence seems to be regression. The analyses using these two measures imply that something between one-half and 90 percent of the variation in suppression can potentially be attributed to a regression artifact. However, the results for postrate lead to a different conclusion: The correlation between pre- and postrates of delinquency was positive. If a regression artifact were operating, one would expect a negative relationship.

These disparate results are to some degree the result of the different computational strategies underlying these statistics and the effects on the statistics of the differences in our population, which contained both "amplifieds," and suppressees. For example, since the prerate was included in the computation of both the difference and the change statistics, some correlation between these measures and the prerate was built into the analysis. For suppressees, the prerate varied much more than the postrate, while for amplifieds, it was the postrate that varied much more than the prerate. Thus, the correlation of these two measures with the preratte was much higher for suppressees than it was for those whose delinquency was amplified. Using either of these two traditional change measures, it is very difficult to get an accurate assessment of the importance of regression. The third measure, though not troubled by these specific problems, is of limited utility because it is not a true measure of behavioral change.

TABLE 9.5   Stepwise OLS Using Different Indicators of
            Amplification and Suppression

| | I | | II | | III | |
| | Change (+) | | Difference (−) | | Postrate | |
Suppression (N = 63)	b	R^2	b	R^2	b	R^2
Preinstitutionalization arrest rate (regression)	.45*	.49	−.87*	.92	.13*	.19
Year of institutionalization (history/maturation)	−.03	.51	.01	.92	.01	.24
Age at institutionalization (history/maturation)	.02	.51	.01	.92	.01	.24
Number of arrests prior to institutionalization (maturation)	.01	.51	−.002	.92	−.002	.24
	Change (−)		Difference[a] (+)		Postrate	
Amplification (N = 73)	b	R^2	b	R^2	b	R^2
Preinstitutionalization arrest rate (regression)	.42*	.14	−.29	.07	.71*	.06
Age at institutionalization (history/maturation)	−.03	.17	.08	.06	.08	.11
Number of arrests prior to institutionalization (maturation)	.02	.20	−.02	.08	−.02	.12
Year of institutionalization (history/maturation)	.003	.20	.001	.08	.001	.12

*p < .05
a. In this instance, age at first institutionalization was entered first.

IMPLICATIONS AND CONCLUSIONS

The substantive implications of our analysis are fairly clear; our
results indicate that the seeming effects of institutionalization were
not as overwhelmingly positive in our population as they appear to

have been in other populations. Thirty-five percent of our institutionalized population seemed to increase their activity following their release, and due to mortality, this figure represents only a minimal estimate of the negative outcomes following incarceration. We are not lead by this finding to question the validity of previous research so much as its generalizability. There may indeed be populations of juveniles in which the effects of incarceration are almost uniformly positive; the question that we must now face is: What are the characteristics of those populations and incarceration programs? Only through undertaking analyses in a large number of settings, with a variety of populations and corrections programs, will we be able to get a clearer picture of whose delinquency gets amplified and whose gets suppressed, and by what kinds of treatment.

It is imperative that such analyses be guided by theoretical statements identifying the types of characteristics that generate differential responses to incarceration. Only when we attach the empirical findings in this area to some theoretical framework, rather than simply lumping results together based on outcome, will we be able to have any real confidence in the generalizability of our findings. For example, one might compare our results with those of Murray and Cox (1979a) and conclude that institutionalization only works on those youths with the highest rates of activity. One might then be tempted to suggest that this response be used in other environments on this type of offender. However, high rates of activity may be the result of a variety of environment/population interactions. Some of these causal structures may generate very active individuals susceptible to behavioral change, while other structures may generate active youths immune to this form of intervention. Only when we have some clear idea of the causal structure underlying the effects of institutionalization will we be able to determine which environments and populations will display positive results for this form of intervention.

Our findings also emphasize the necessity of developing accurate estimates of the magnitude of suppression and amplification in treatment populations. Given our findings that in some populations, incarceration may involve a significant cost in increased criminal activity, cost-benefit calculations for any sanctioning policy become dependent on accurate measures of behavioral change. Such measures must be purified of any effects attributable to the various sources of invalidity discussed above. Lacking accurate measures, we cannot speak with any degree of precision about the nature of changes in aggregate delinquency that might result from institutionalizing a specific group of juveniles.

Our work also emphasizes certain methodological problems shared by many analyses of the effects of institutionalization. Our results indicate that both the nature and magnitude of the behavioral changes that follow incarceration may be influenced by various sources of internal invalidity — most noticeably, in this case, history and regression artifacts. The problems that were discussed in our analysis of the potential effects of regression on the magnitude of change emphasize the shortcomings of research in this field based solely on measures of behavioral change. Without detailed information on the attitudinal changes, if any, wrought by institutionalization, one's ability to separate the effects of artifacts from true treatment effects is quite limited.

Putting aside "common-term" and distribution problems, suppose that one found a consistent positive correlation between the degree of suppression and either the acceleration or the velocity of youths' preinstitutionalization streams of activity. This would look very much like a regression artifact; however, it would not have to be such an artifact. Only data that could assure us that these behavioral changes mirrored attitudinal changes would really allow us to ascertain whether we were seeing a true treatment effect or an artifact. It is only such attitudinal measures that will allow researchers to specify clearly whether it is deterrence (that is, fear of punishment) or some other form of reformation (for example, rehabilitation) that is generating true treatment effects. Analyses such as ours, based solely on behavioral measures, will always be troubled by their inability to specify the mechanism of change, and that inability will seriously hamper the usefulness of such studies in policy development.

Finally, our analysis deals with only one form of intervention — institutionalization. Thus, we cannot speak to a central issue: Did institutionalization have an effect over and above that which would have been generated by some other intervention? Of our population, 65 percent seemed to reduce their activity. What might have happened had these youths received only supervision? Until we can answer this type of question, we can offer little useful guidance to policymakers. More generally, if one views delinquency as a "natural process" with its own mechanisms generating a base-level of "natural cessation," we need to know how much of a gain over this natural cessation rate are the results obtained through intervention. The idea of chronological maturation is now in some disrepute as the key to natural cessation, since other factors (that is, other sets of life experiences) may be powerful forces toward cessation. If such a process exists, until we discover its mechanisms and who it affects, comparisons among the various forms of intervention may not be terribly useful.

The utility of our findings in this study may be small in scope, but they should sound a clear note of caution to those who advocate what Erickson (1979: 303-305) calls the "heavy hands" approach to juvenile justice. Deterrence may work; some of the young may respond favorably to serious interventions in their lives. Those youths, however, may be only a subset of all the youths processed by juvenile institutions — at present, an unidentifiable subset. The indiscriminate use of institutionalization could generate, as it may have done in our cohort, as many crimes as it prevents. To borrow Tannenbaum's (1938) image, evil may grow greater under those "heavy hands."

REFERENCES

ANDERSON, T. W. (1958) An Introduction to Multivariate Statistical Analysis. New York: John Wiley.

BECKER, H. (1963) Outsiders: Studies in the Sociology of Deviance. New York: Free Press.

BENTHAM, J. (1948) An Introduction to the Principles of Morals and Legislation. New York: Hafner.

CAMPBELL, D. (1973) "Reforms as experiments," pp. 182-225 in J. Caporaso and L. Roos (eds.) Quasi-Experimental Approaches: Testing Theory and Evaluating Policy. Evanston, IL: Northwestern University Press.

——— and J. STANLEY (1963) Experimental and Quasi-Experimental Designs for Research. Chicago: Rand McNally.

CICOUREL, A. (1968) The Social Organization of Juvenile Justice. New York: John Wiley.

COOK, P. (1980) "Research in criminal deterrence: laying the groundwork for a second decade," pp. 211-268 in N. Morris and M. Tonry (eds.) Crime and Justice: An Annual Review of Research. Chicago: University of Chicago Press.

COOK, T. and D. CAMPBELL (1979) Quasi-Experimentation: Design and Analysis Issues for Field Settings. Chicago: Rand-McNally.

COOLEY, W. A. and P. R. Lohnes (1971) Multivariate Data Analysis. New York: John Wiley.

EMPEY, L. and M. ERICKSON (1972) The Provo Experiment: Evaluating Community Control of Delinquency. Lexington, MA: D. C. Heath.

EMPEY, L. and S. LUBECK (1971) The Silverlake Experiment: Testing Delinquency Theory and Community Intervention. Chicago: Aldine.

ERICKSON, M. (1979) "Some empirical questions concerning the current revolution in juvenile justice," pp. 277-311 in L. Empey (ed.) The Future of Childhood and Juvenile Justice. Charlottesville: University of Virginia Press.

ERIKSON, K. (1962) "Notes on the sociology of deviance." Social Problems 9 (Spring): 307-314.

GLASER, D. (1979) "Disillusion with rehabilitation: theoretical and empirical questions," pp. 234-276 in L. Empey (ed.) The Future of Childhood and Juvenile Justice. Charlottesville: University of Virginia Press.

GOLD, M. and J. WILLIAMS (1969) "National study of the aftermath of apprehension." Prospectus 3: 3-12.

HAMPARIAN, D., R. SCHUSTER, S. DINITZ, and J. CONRAD (1978) The Violent Few: A Study of Dangerous Juvenile Offenders. Lexington, MA: D. C. Heath.

KLECKA, W. R. (1980) Discriminant Analysis. Beverly Hills, CA: Sage.

LEMERT, E. (1951) Social Pathology. New York: McGraw-Hill.

LIPTON, D., R. MARTINSON, and J. WILKS (1975) The Effectiveness of Correctional Treatment: A Survey of Treatment Evaluation Studies. New York: Praeger.

MAHONEY, A. (1974) "The effect of labelling upon youths in the juvenile justice system: a review of the evidence." Law and Society 8 (Summer): 583-614.

McCLEARY, R., A. GORDON, D. McDOWALL, and M. MALTZ (1979) "How a regression artifact can make any delinquency intervention program look effective," pp. 626-652 in L. Sechrest and associates (eds.) Evaluation Studies Review Annual, Vol. 4. Beverly Hills, CA: Sage.

McEACHERN, A. (1968) "The juvenile probation system." American Behavioral Scientist 11 (January-February): 3-43.

———— and R. BAUZER (1967) "Factors related to disposition in juvenile police contacts," pp. 148-160 in M. Klein (ed.) Juvenile Gangs in Context: Theory, Research and Action. Englewood Cliffs, NJ: Prentice-Hall.

MURRAY, C. and L. COX (1979a) Beyond Probation: Juvenile Corrections and the Chronic Delinquent. Beverly Hills, CA: Sage.

———— (1979b) "The suppression effect and the institutionalization of children," pp. 653-663 in L. Sechrest and associates (eds.) Evaluation Studies Review Annual, Vol. 4. Beverly Hills, CA: Sage.

NAGIN, D. (1978) "General deterrence: a review of the empirical evidence," pp. 90-139 in A. Blumstein et al. (eds.) Deterrence and Incapacitation: Estimating the Effects of Criminal Sanctions on Crime Rates. Washington, DC: National Academy of Sciences.

PHILLIPS, C. and S. DINITZ (1982) "Labelling and juvenile court dispositions: official responses to a cohort of violent juveniles." Sociological Quarterly 23 (Spring): 267-279.

ROJEK, D. and M. ERICKSON (1982) "Delinquent careers: a test of the career escalation model." Criminology 20 (May): 5-28.

SCHUR, E. (1971) Labeling Deviant Behavior: Its Sociological Implications. New York: Harper & Row.

——— (1969) "Reactions to deviance: a critical assessment." American Journal of Sociology 75 (November): 309-322.

TANNENBAUM, F. (1938) Crime and the Community. Boston: Ginn.

TERRY, R. (1967) "The screening of juvenile offenders." Journal of Criminal Law, Criminology, and Police Science 58 (June): 173-181.

THORNBERRY, T. (1971) "Punishment and crime: the effect of legal dispositions on subsequent criminal behavior." Ph.D. dissertation, University of Pennsylvania.

WERTHMAN, C. and I. PILIAVIN (1967) "Gang members and the police," pp. 56-98 in D. Bordua (ed.) The Police: Six Sociological Essays. New York: John Wiley.

WILLIAMS, J. and M. GOLD (1970) "From delinquent behavior to official delinquency." Social Problems 20 (Fall): 209-229.

WOLFGANG, M., R. FIGLIO, and T. SELLIN (1972) Delinquency in a Birth Cohort. Chicago: University of Chicago Press.

Chapter 10

EFFICIENCY IN CORRECTIONS AGENCIES

G L O R I A   A.   G R I Z Z L E
A N N   D.   W I T T E

This chapter explores the problem of providing performance information for corrections agencies. Suggested in the sections below are an
appropriate theoretical perspective from which to view an agency's
performance, types of performance measures consistent with this
theoretical perspective, and statistical models by which one can
interpret performance. The cost and production function approach is
then developed in more detail as a method of measuring an agency's
efficiency. Data from prisons illustrate the use of this approach.

THEORETICAL PERSPECTIVE

Performance measurement means obtaining information useful to
someone in assessing how well an organization or program is working. What measures are relevant to this task depend on one's theoretical perspective. Organizational theory provides a number of different
models by which to assess an organization's success (Cameron, 1981;

AUTHORS' NOTE: *Supported in part by grant 80-IJ-CX-0033 from the
National Institute of Justice, U.S. Department of Justice. Views and opinions
are those of the authors and do not necessarily reflect the official position or
policies of the U.S. Department of Justice. We would like to thank Peter
Schmidt of Michigan State University for his aid in obtaining estimates of
inefficiency for each prison in our sample.*

Quinn and Rohrbaugh, 1981). The principal models are listed below. In the parentheses following each model are the criteria that best conform to that model's perspective on organizational success.

- human relations model (human need satisfaction, human resource development, morale, cohesion);
- rational goal model (organization's stated goals);
- System resource model (organizational growth, resource acquisition, external support);
- internal process model (stability, smooth functioning, absence of internal strain); and
- strategic constituencies model (satisfaction of important constituent groups).

Quinn and Cameron (reported in Anderson, 1981) review seven models of organizational life cycles and develop a model suggesting that organizations progress through four stages:

(1) entrepreneurial — early innovation and creativity;
(2) collectivity — informal communication and structure, sense of family and cooperation among members, personalized leadership;
(3) formalization and control — organizational stability, efficiency of production, rules and procedures; and
(4) elaboration of structure — decentralization of structure, orientation to external environment, adaptation.

Except for some community-based programs, corrections organizations in the United States generally seem to be in the formalization and control stage.

Quinn and Cameron also suggest that the appropriate model by which to judge an organization's performance depends on the organization's stage in its life cycle. They believe that the rational goal and internal process models provide the most appropriate perspectives for measuring the success of organizations in the formalization and control stage. Of these two, the rational goal model would seem the more useful in serving such purposes as public accountability, program planning, resource allocation, and operations analysis.

Assuming that the rational goal model is the most appropriate model for measuring corrections performance, which performance dimensions conform to this model? Public administrationists, economists, and political scientists have all advocated performance dimensions consistent with this model.

The Technique of Municipal Administration (ICMA, 1958), for example, suggests a variety of dimensions for measuring performance: costs, efforts (man-hour units), performance (work units, production), results, effectiveness, needs, and ability of the tax base to support a certain level of expenditure. Other researchers have adopted an economist's orientation and look at public sector programs as production functions that transform inputs into outputs. Bradford et al. (1969) expanded the classic input-program-output concept by distinguishing between outputs directly produced and the consequences of those outputs. More recently, Bahl and Burkhead (1977) added an additional component to this set of performance dimensions — the environment (or needs of the citizenry).

While economists have focused primarily on the relationship between inputs and outputs, political scientists have argued that the distribution of outputs must also be considered (Bodily, 1978; Coulter, 1980; Jones, 1981; Lineberry and Welch, 1974; Ostrom et al., 1979; Wilenski, 1980-81). Suggested standards for measuring the equitable distribution of service include input equality, output equality, categorical equality, and demand. Recently, Jones (1981) tied equity concerns to the dimensions derived from the production function concept. He sees government programs as service production processes that involve four transformations:

inputs ⟶ activities ⟶ outputs ⟶ outcomes ⟶ impacts

He argues that each step in the process has distributional effects, benefiting some people and costing others.

It is this last conceptualization of performance that seems most useful in identifying the information that should be available when assessing corrections performance. This conceptualization draws attention to the following questions:

- What do corrections agencies produce?
- What are the benefits?
- Who benefits?
- Who pays?
- How cost effective are corrections agencies?
- How efficiently do corrections agencies operate?

We focus the remainder of this chapter on the question of how to measure and interpret a corrections agency's efficiency. In our discussion, we address both technical and allocative efficiency. An agency is considered technically efficient if, given some set of resources, no more output can be produced by changing the way the resources are combined (Levine, 1981). Allocative efficiency exists when one uses the production process that maximizes physical output per dollar value of input (Levine, 1981).

BASES FOR COMPARISONS

Measuring performance implies the ability to compare two types of data. First, one needs data that describe how an agency is operating over some specific time period — a performance measure. An example of such a measure might be Agency A's cost per probationer supervised in 1982 (for example, $1000). Standing alone, this measurement does not permit one to conclude whether $1000 is adequate or inadequate performance. The second type of needed data consist of benchmarks to which one can compare performance measurements in order to judge how well an agency is operating. Continuing with the unit cost example, assume that lower unit costs indicate better performance and that the benchmark is $1300. After comparing Agency A's unit cost of $1000 to the benchmark of $1300, one would conclude that its performance (as measured by unit cost) was good.

What is the source of the benchmark against which one compares a performance measurement? Possible sources include an agency's goals, objectives, or targets; standards established by relevant professional associations; the performance of other agencies; the agency's own historical performance record; and optimal or technically efficient performance levels (Cameron, 1981; Grizzle et al., 1980; Hatry, 1980).

Decision makers above the agency level will probably want to compare performance across agencies. The great diversity of missions, programs, and clientele groups among corrections agencies, however, requires that one exercise special care when comparing agencies. Performance comparisons are most appropriate when these conditions exist:

(1) when performance is measured in terms of unit cost, the agencies to be compared have common products or outputs, similar conditions under which to operate, and similar inputs;

(2) when performance is measured in terms of equity, potential clientele groups of the agencies to be compared have similar characteristics;

(3) when performance is measured in terms of outcomes, the agencies to be compared have similar outcome objectives or missions and work in similar external environments;

(4) agencies use the same definitions, accounting methods, and data collection and reduction procedures;

(5) data collection and reduction techniques are practical and relatively cheap;

(6) agencies have an opportunity to explain unusual situations;

(7) timely data collection and reporting occur;

(8) agencies operate under similar laws and procedural regulations; and

(9) agencies operate under similar incentives for collecting and reporting performance measurements accurately.

MODELS FOR GENERATING A SINGLE MEASURE OF OVERALL AGENCY EFFICIENCY

Much of the effort that has gone into performance measurement research during the past twenty years has been devoted to the problem of how to combine multiple measures into a single performance measure. Three such approaches, discussed below, are multiattribute decision theory, data envelopment analysis, and cost and production functions.

Multiattribute Decision Theory

Many multiattribute techniques have been developed for combining multiple attributes or outcomes into a single measure. All of these techniques rely on weights for each individual attribute. These weights are used as coefficients for the attributes and, through an aggregating function, the weighted attributes are combined into a single measure. Applications of these techniques may differ in terms of

(1) who identifies the important attributes;
(2) who sets the weights;
(3) how the performance of each agency for each attribute is determined;
(4) the aggregating (or utility) function used; and
(5) how overall performance is calculated.

We discuss four of these techniques — decision analysis, simplified multiattribute rating technique, the analytic hierarchy procedure, and social judgment theory — and summarize an application of each.

Decision Analysis (DA). Decision analysis may be the best known of the multiattribute methods discussed here (Keeney and Raiffa, 1976). It is also the most complicated to explain. This technique divides the performance measurement process into several tasks — identifying the dimensions against which an agency's performance shall be assessed, measuring each agency's performance in terms of each dimension, determining weights by estimating the relative importance of each dimension, and combining the performance measurements and weights so as to generate an overall performance measurement for each agency. The decision analysis application discussed here involves designing police sectors for a city (Bodily, 1978).

The purpose of this New Haven-based exercise was to determine which police sector designs would perform best, taking into account two different performance dimensions. The participants included a consultant, an administrator, a citizen representative, and a police representative. The consultant identified two performance dimensions — equality of travel time and equality of workload — and estimated each design alternative's performance on these dimensions, using a hypercube queueing model. The administrator judged the relative importance of these two dimensions. A citizen representative specified a travel time for which he was indifferent between two sector designs. One design offered a travel time of one minute in the first sector and ten minutes in the second sector. The second design offered equal travel times for the two sectors, with the equal time being that specified by the citizen representative. A police representative followed a similar procedure in determining his preferences regarding the distribution of workload across sectors.

Assuming constant inequality aversion and mutual utility independence, the consultant then combined into a single overall utility function the citizen's preference regarding travel time equality and the policeman's preference regarding workload distribution equality with the administrator's relative weights for travel time and workload equality.

Inserting travel times and workload distribution estimates for a given sector design into this function and evaluating the function yields a single overall performance measurement for that sector design. The sector design with the highest overall measurement would be expected to perform best in terms of the two performance dimensions addressed.

Simplified Multiattribute Rating Technique (SMART). Edwards (1979), who developed this technique, has used it to evaluate alternative desegregation plans for Los Angeles schools. As the name implies, SMART is designed to simplify the kinds of judgments required by Keeney and Raiffa's (1976) decision analysis technique. Edwards assumes that the organization, rather than a single individual, is the decision maker. Following this assumption, he partitions the decision problem and looks to individuals with different expertise to render judgments for different parts of the problem (Edwards, 1980).

In the Los Angeles application, school board members identified the performance dimensions in terms of which the alternative desegregation plans would be judged. They also determined the relative importance of these dimensions. Examples of the dimensions selected include the plan's effect on the racial-ethnic composition of schools, educational quality, community acceptance, and stability. Edwards used a direct scaling technique to elicit each board member's judgment of the relative importance of these dimensions and then averaged the individual weights to produce a single set of weights.

School district staff then estimated how well each desegregation plan would perform in terms of each dimension. Estimates were located on a 0 to 100 percent scale. The utility function used was linear and additive — that is, the utility for each plan was calculated by multiplying each outcome times its respective weight and summing the products.

Analytic Hierarchy Process. Saaty developed this technique in 1971 and has since applied it to many policy issues. The application reviewed here considers the effects of seven higher-education policies on four performance dimensions (Saaty, 1980). The alternative policies evaluated were (1) the status quo, (2) vocational-technical orientation, (3) subsidized education for all, (4) education for those with money or exceptional talent, (5) all public (government-owned) institutions, (6) technology-based instruction, and (7) part-time teaching without research. A group of 28 college-level teachers identified four performance dimensions to which they believed higher education policies should contribute: prosperity, civil order, profit for industry, and perpetuation and power for industry. The relative importance of these performance dimensions was established through a two-step procedure. The teachers first reached a consensus on the relative importance between each pair of dimensions. These consensus ratings were then set in a matrix and the eigenvector of the matrix calculated. This eigenvector is an array of numbers that reflect the weight, or relative importance, of each dimension (subsequently referred to as the importance vector).

Next, the teachers determined how well each policy would perform on each of the four dimensions, using a similar two-step procedure. Through pair-wise comparisons, the teachers first reached a consensus on the relative degree to which each policy alternative would affect each dimension. These consensus judgments were then set in a matrix for each performance dimension and an effect vector calculated for each. A dimension's effect vector thus reflects each policy's relative contribution toward that dimension.

The final step in the analytic hierarchy process (AHP) was to construct a matrix consisting of the four effect vectors and to multiply this matrix by the importance vector. The resulting priority vector contains a single number for each alternative that reflects its overall performance across all four dimensions.

Social Judgment Theory. All three of the multiattribute techniques discussed above elicit performance dimensions weights directly, either from direct scaling or paired comparisons. These techniques then multiply performance on each dimension by its respective weight and sum the resulting products to get a single overall performance measurement. Social judgment theory, in contrast, is a holistic approach that first requires people to give a single overall performance rating. The technique then infers the weights for each dimension from the overall performance ratings. The SJT application discussed below deals with the type of handgun ammunition to be used by Denver police (Hammond, 1976).

SJT broke the decision problem into several parts. The debate over which bullet to use centered on the bullets' performance on three dimensions: (a) stopping effectiveness, (b) amount of injury, and (c) threat to bystanders. City officials and other interested people rated 30 profiles of hypothetical bullets that varied in terms of the extent to which each performed across these three dimensions. These ratings were regressed against the hypothetical performance indicators to infer the relative importance, or weights, for each performance dimension.

In a separate process, five ballistics experts judged the performance of 80 real but unnamed bullets on the same three performance dimensions. For each bullet, these performance scores were multiplied by the weights inferred from the earlier regression analysis and summed to provide an overall performance measurement.

Summary

Table 10.1 summarizes the important characteristics of these four multiattribute techniques. Each offers a systematic means of eliciting judgments about the relative importance of different performance measures. The applications discussed vary in terms of who participates in identifying the dimensions against which an agency's performance is to be measured, determining the relative importance of these dimensions, and scoring the agency's performance in terms of each of these dimensions. Exactly who participates in each of these steps is not inherent in the technique used. The division of labor used in the decision analysis application discussed could, for example, be followed when applying one of the other multiattribute techniques.

If the relative importance of performance dimensions are already known, using any of these techniques to elicit weights would be superfluous. Similarly, if people have no opinion about the relative importance of different performance measures, none of these techniques could help. Of the four, decision analysis is the most complicated and the method least likely to be tolerated by those whose judgments would be elicited. The simplified multiattribute rating technique is the simplest and the quickest, but some people doubt the appropriateness of a linear, additive aggregating function.

Data Envelopment Analysis

Mathematical programming techniques can be used to combine multiple performance measures into a single indicator. The most recently developed technique in this area is called data envelopment analysis. Like the production function, data envelopment analysis allows comparisons of an agency's efficiency relative to that of other agencies. The technique synthesizes from the set of efficient agencies a piece-wise linear extremal production function.

Its proponents (Charnes et al., 1981) claim that data envelopment analysis has fewer of the limitations attributed to production functions. The method does not

(1) require specification of the functional form;

TABLE 10.1 Comparison of Multiattribute Techniques for Measuring Performance

Method	Policy Application	Who Identified Performance Dimensions	How Dimension Weights Were Set	How Each Alternative's Effect on Each Dimension Was Determined	Aggregating Function	Calculation of Overall Performance
DA	Police sector design	Consultant	Direct tradeoff by administrator	Consultant estimates based upon hypercube queueing model	Curve drawing derived from preferences of a citizen representative and a police representative using the lottery technique	For each plan, insert effect for each dimension into function and evaluate the function to calculate the overall utility
SMART	School desegregation	School board members	Average of Individual school board members' weights based on direct scaling of each attribute's importance	School district staff estimates, located on a 0 to 100% effectiveness scale	Linear, additive	For each plan, multiply effectiveness score for each attribute by that attribute's weight and sum the resulting products
AHP	Higher education	College-level teachers	Priority eigenvector developed from consensus reached on paired comparisons by teachers	Teachers, by consensus, assigned scores based upon paired comparisons	Linear, additive	Multiply matrix of alternatives' effect on dimensions by weight vector
SJT	Police handgun ammunition	City officials and other interested groups	Weights derived from regression analysis of ratings by city councilmen and other interested groups	Judgments from ballistics experts	Curve drawing derived from multiple regression analysis of ratings	For each bullet, insert its score on each dimension into regression equation to calculate its overall performance rating.

275

(2) require predetermined prices or weights for each input;

(3) assume the differentiability of frontier surfaces;

(4) assume that prices for the inputs and outputs are independent of their magnitude; or

(5) assume an absence of capacity restraints for inputs.

Data envelopment analysis has been applied to data generated as a result of the Project Follow Through experiment sponsored by the federal government (Charnes and Cooper, 1980). For each school included in the analysis, three output measures were used: reading scores, mathematics scores, and a self-esteem measure. In addition, five input measures were used: education level of students' mothers, occupation level of students' family members, number of times parents visited the school, time parents spent with students on school-related topics, and number of teachers at each school site. For the 49 Program Follow Through sites, relative efficiency ranged from 80 to 100 percent.

Production and Cost Functions

The production and cost functions developed mainly by economists constitute a third technique to aid in understanding the nature of operations in corrections agencies. Recent developments in the use of this technique — frontier cost and production functions — allow one to develop a single overall measure of effectiveness. In this subsection we discuss the concepts underlying cost and production functions, emphasizing important issues to consider when studying the activities of public bodies. In the next section we illustrate the use of these techniques in understanding the operation of various types of correctional agencies.

The economic constructs of cost and production functions were originally developed to analyze the nature of production in private sector, profit-maximizing firms, particularly manufacturing firms.[1] The production function summarizes, mathematically, the nature of technically efficient production. It indicates the maximum output attainable for any specified level of inputs, given the existing technology or state of the art.

An alternative way of looking at the productive relations of a firm is through the firm's cost function. The cost function indicates the minimum costs of producing various outputs, given input prices and the prevailing technology. Duality theory, which only became a well-integrated part of economic production theory during the 1960s, establishes the equivalence of the cost and production function approaches to understanding the nature of a firm's operation.[2] The equivalence of the two approaches makes selection of one rather than the other largely a statistical and empirical issue.

In developing their constructs of cost and production functions, economists originally made a number of simplifying assumptions that have since been relaxed. Originally, economists assumed that firms produce a single, homogeneous output. Actually, most firms have multiple outputs, and these are often of varying quality. A number of authors (Hall, 1973; Hasenkamp, 1976; Denny and Pinto, 1978) have explored, both theoretically and empirically, the nature of production in a multiproduct firm. However, work in this area is in its infancy and, as one might expect, the production process in multiproduct firms rapidly becomes quite complex.[3]

Even if a firm produces a single output, that output is rarely homogeneous. For example, although some automobile plants produce a single output (a certain model), this output is of highly variable quality (for example, an automobile with all accessories versus one with none). Researchers have adjusted for differences in product quality by introducing a number of quality indicators into production and cost functions. In applied research, many investigators have succeeded in avoiding the difficulties associated with analyzing a multiproduct firm by considering relatively similar products to be a single product of varying quality. We take this approach in our work.

Economists often find it necessary to drop the assumption that firms constantly seek to maximize profits. In a perfectly competitive market system, firms would be forced to attempt to maximize their profit in order to survive. A side benefit is that competition from other firms would force each firm to produce efficiently. However, when competition is not present, firms are free to choose a course of action other than profit maximization.

When one moves from the profit-making sector of the economy to the nonprofit-making and public sectors, the plausibility of profit making as a goal disappears. Consider the situation in public units such as a police department or a prison. The public provides such bodies with funds in order to produce certain goods and services, but these public services are not sold; they are supplied to all those eligible according to some set of guidelines. For example, police services are provided to all residents of a city, and correctional services are provided to all criminals with a certain type of sentence. This means that, to some degree, public managers do not control the type of product they produce or the conditions under which it is produced. Researchers studying production in public bodies suggest that the conditions of production and the type of product imposed on public managers by those providing funds be controlled when estimating cost and production functions.[4]

Because public bodies that do not sell their output do not receive revenue, they cannot maximize profits even if they wish to. Rather, the public often judges such bodies by their satisfaction with the services provided for tax dollars. While some public bodies seek to produce their services at minimum costs, many others do not, resorting instead to various alternative types of bureaucratic decision making, such as maximizing their budget or the size of their organizations.[5] In situations like this, efficiency cannot be assumed; actual production results probably do not indicate the maximum output attainable with the given inputs, and costs observed are not the minimum attainable.

When operating in situations where efficiency is not likely to prevail, researchers using economic cost and production functions must incorporate inefficiency in their models. Quite recently, economists have attempted to deal with the incorporation of inefficiency in cost and production functions. The new models developed have been called frontier cost and production functions.[6] Frontier cost and production functions do not assume that all observed productive units are producing efficiently. Instead, they seek to infer what might be possible with efficient production by examining the performance of the most efficient firms observed. To date, two different types of frontiers have been estimated — deterministic frontiers and stochastic frontiers. Deterministic frontiers[7] assume that for the most efficient firms' observed, output or costs are subject to no random effects. The observed productive relations for these firms (called the frontier firms) are used to construct the frontier cost or production

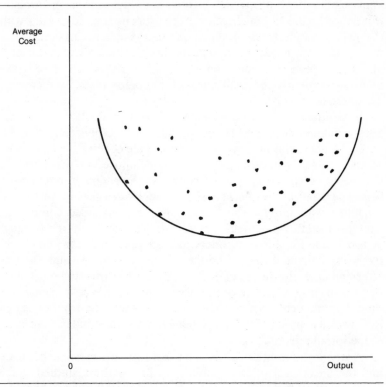

Figure 10.1   Frontier Cost Function

function generally, using linear or quadratic programming techniques. For example, a deterministic frontier cost function for the firms indicated by dots in Figure 10.1 would be constructed based on the experience of the firms with the lowest observed costs for each level of output. A deterministic frontier function is illustrated by the curve drawn along the lower boundary of the dots in Figure 10.1

Deterministic frontiers have two major problems. First, such frontiers are extremely sensitive to outliers. For example, consider the effect of an extremely low-cost firm on the frontier cost function in Figure 10.1. Such an outlier would pull the frontier cost function downward and might well cause the frontier to reflect poorly the nature of efficient productive relationships. Second, the parameters of estimated deterministic cost and production functions have no known statistical properties. Thus, although the deterministic frontier of Figure 10.1 might allow us to estimate how costs vary with the level of output for the production process under consideration, it will not allow us to say whether costs vary significantly with the level of output. Note that data envelopment analysis (discussed previously) was developed on the basis of the deterministic frontier work discussed above.

In contrast, stochastic frontier cost and production functions[8] allow random effects on firm output and costs to be reflected in the output frontier relationships. The essential idea behind the stochastic frontier model is that the error term is composed of two parts. A symmetric component permits random variation of the frontier across firms and captures the effects of such things as measurement error and random events outside the firms' control; a one-sided component captures the effects of inefficiency relative to the stochastic frontier. A zero value for this component indicates that the firms are effectively minimizing costs, while the size of a positive value for this effect indicates the degree of inefficiency for the firms studied. Figure 10.2 illustrates the nature of the stochastic average cost frontier for three hypothetical prisons. Note that the stochastic frontier varies from prison to prison (for example, due to riots, fires) but has the same shape for all prisons.

A stochastic frontier allows one to estimate the mean inefficiency and the mean cost of this inefficiency for all firms studied. Such estimates of inefficiency and the associated costs can be very useful both for correctional managers and executive and legislative groups that oversee their activities. For example, estimates of the costs of inefficiency may provide managers with incentives to pursue improvements. In addition, an estimate of these costs may allow executive and legislative organizations to set more realistic budgets. Further, by studying the factors related to relatively efficient production, managers and others may be able to suggest improvements that are likely to increase systemwide efficiency.

Recent work on stochastic frontier functions (Schmidt and Lovell, 1979; Jondrow et al., 1982) allows one to obtain efficiency estimates for individual productive units, as well as the overall measure of inefficiency discussed above. Information of this type is, of course, extremely useful for management decisions, as it allows the

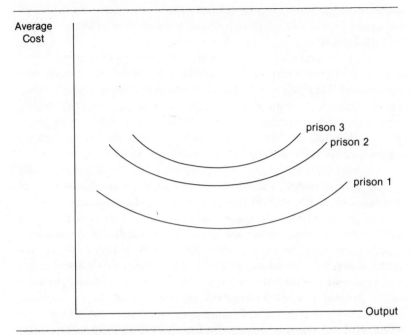

Figure 10.2 Stochastic Frontier Average Cost Function

manager to compare the relative performance of the units he or she supervises.

COST FUNCTION APPROACHES TO CORRECTIONS

In this section we illustrate the use of cost functions to analyze the operation of correctional agencies. We begin by developing a model of the nature of production in these agencies.

A Model of Production in Correctional Agencies

The development of a model of production for correctional agencies requires the researcher to make a number of simplifying assumptions and decisions. We begin by discussing the role of correctional agencies in the criminal justice system and how agency operation is affected by other executive branch agencies — the legislative branch and the judiciary.

As an integral part of the criminal justice system, correctional agencies, in cooperation with the police and courts, are charged with preventing crime when possible and with punishing offenders when crime does occur. Both of these services must be performed within legally defined constraints regarding due process and humane treatment. While society sees the criminal justice system as an entity with definite goals, most people familiar with the "system" know it to be composed of distinct agencies having only limited interaction and coordination. Indeed, ultimate decision-making authority for many of the agencies resets with different levels and branches of government. Although the actions of the agencies of each segment of the criminal justice system affect the agencies of other segments, these effects are rarely considered when the administrators of a particular agency make decisions. No single administrator is responsible for the efficient operation of the entire system, and thus it is not possible to think of the system as a productive unit seeking to produce justice effectively. From an economist's perspective, we would not seek to estimate production and cost functions for the system as a whole (at least as the system is currently structured in the United States); however, in seeking to model the nature of these relationships for individual segments of the system, it is important to understand the effects of segments other than the one being analyzed.

A number of researchers, mainly from operations research backgrounds,[9] have described the way in which police, courts, and correctional agencies interact. Figure 10.3 depicts these interactions, emphasizing the role of correctional agencies. The relationships among the components of the criminal justice system consist of a flow of individuals through the system, court surveillance of police and correctional activities, and the provision of evidence and other information by police and correctional agencies. As shown in Figure 10.3, interactions between agencies are many and complex, and the number of alternative paths open to offenders is large. Managers in most agencies of the criminal justice system are relatively free (barring court intervention) to make day-to-day (short-run) decisions about how their organizations should operate. For example, the administrators of a state prison system are relatively free to decide on

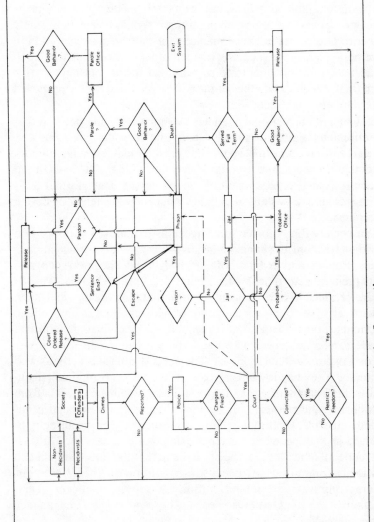

Figure 10.3 Flow of Offenders and Organization Interactions

SOURCE: Portions of this diagram were adapted from Blumstein and Larson (1976: 473).

283

the housing and care of inmates. Long-run decisions concerning the purchase of new capital equipment and buildings, as well as major changes in methods of operation (technology), are subject to both legislative and judicial review, but are largely made by agency managers or other executive branch personnel. Again, to use an example from corrections, correctional managers usually propose capital improvement plans to executive budget offices. These offices then decide which improvements to recommend to the legislative body, which finally decides whether funds will be provided for the proposed improvements.

Having put correctional agencies in perspective and decided that correctional administrators have substantial decision-making power, we need to determine the goals that correctional agencies pursue. Recall that we perceive correctional agencies as in the "formalization and control" stage of organizational development. Thus, formal goals and internal processes are of primary importance when considering performance.

Our society funds correctional agencies to impose restrictions on individual freedom as a punishment, to protect society by incapacitating the offender, and to deter both offenders (specific deterrence) and others (general deterrence) from committing future offenses. We also provide services to offenders and require that they occupy their time productively. We do this for a number of reasons. First, many believe that some services and some types of work serve to rehabilitate offenders. Second, work and other activity requirements often lower the costs of correctional agencies. They may do this indirectly, as well as directly. They can lower the costs of operating correctional agencies by direct payment (for example, Florida requires payments from probationers and parolees) or by providing maintenance and other needed activities. Occupying offenders' time may serve indirectly to lower the level of correctional supervision that is necessary. Third, at least some members of our society believe that the provision of such activities is morally right, because deprivation of liberty provides sufficient punishment and retribution for crime. In recent years, correctional agencies have also been asked to provide for and manage the payment, by offenders, of restitution to victims.

Finally, we would like all of these goals achieved as cheaply as possible and under conditions that we deem acceptable. Given this menu of often conflicting goals, it is not surprising that our correctional system has often seemed to lack direction or to change directions at fairly frequent intervals. Which correctional goals are emphasized has changed through time and varies from correctional agency to correctional agency.[10] Currently, the major goal of the majority of correctional agencies appears to be control, although rehabilitative programming continues.[11]

As noted earlier, most economic models of cost and production assume that costs are minimized. The above discussion should make it clear that cost minimization is, at best, one of many goals pursued by correctional administrators. Pressures on correctional administrators to minimize costs generally come from outside the correctional system. For the federal correctional system, the pressures come primarily, in the executive branch, from the Office of Management and Budget, and in the legislative branch, from congressional committees and the General Accounting Office. For state and local correctional agencies, pressures to minimize cost come from the department of finance or budget, speaking for the chief executive, and from various analysis offices and staff, speaking for the legislative body.

Our work in prisons, and in parole and probation offices, leads us to conclude that the assumption that correctional administrators minimize costs is tenuous at best. Yet the use of duality theory and standard statistical techniques (for example, ordinary or generalized least squares) requires this assumption. We attempt to deal with this dilemma in two ways. First, when interpreting results obtained using standard estimation techniques, we are careful to point out results that depend critically on the assumption that costs are minimized. Second, we estimate frontier cost functions that explicitly model the fact that administrators may not minimize costs. Briefly, we found that administrators do not minimize costs. Thus, our results, which use traditional estimation techniques, are best interpreted as behavioral equations rather than the cost curves of microeconomic theory. In the absence of cost-minimizing behavior, inferences about the nature of the production function from these results require the strong assumption that inefficient behavior neutrally transforms the cost curve (that is, shifts the cost curve up equally everywhere). However, we feel that the "behavioral" cost curves estimated are in many cases as important as the cost curves of economic theory. They provide insight concerning the actual behavior of correctional agencies and thus may be useful as economic cost curves in understanding the nature of production in these agencies and in projecting future behavior.

Our next task is to determine the productive unit we wish to analyze and the output that this unit produces. We have argued elsewhere (Witte et al., 1979) that the individual prison is the entity that most closely approximates the economic concept of a productive unit within the prison system.

Having decided on the productive unit, we must next decide what this unit is producing. As noted above, the dominant correctional goal currently appears to be controlling convicted offenders. Conforming to this outlook, we see the output of the correctional agency as a certain number of convicted offenders supervised for a certain period of time. However, we do not see this output as homogeneous, but rather seek to introduce a number of factors that will reflect different qualities and types of supervision. We also recognize that different correctional agencies work in different environments and with differing types of offenders.

Having developed a basic model, we must next decide whether to estimate this model using a cost or production function approach. As noted earlier, this is largely a statistical and practical issue. One should estimate a production function if one believes that the level of output is largely under the control of managers (that is, endogenous to the model), but a cost function if one believes that costs are under more control by managers than is output. Recall that our measure of output for a correctional agency is the number of convicted offenders supervised during any given period of time, which we will refer to as the "case load" for the sake of brevity. Correctional managers have little control over the size or composition of their case loads, because they are required to accept all convicted offenders directed to them by the courts or other agencies. Further, correctional managers have only limited control over the release of offenders from their supervision. While costs are not entirely within the control of correctional administrators, they are so to a far greater degree than output, particularly in the long run. Thus, we chose to estimate cost rather than production functions for the correctional agencies we studied. We began by estimating cost functions of the following general form for selected prisons, and for probation and parole officers.

$$\ln AC = a + b_1 y + b_2 \ln y + (\ln P)' \gamma + A'N + S'U + Q'\, F + \epsilon \quad [10.1]$$

where AC is the average cost of operating the correctional agency; y is a measure of the number of convicted offenders supervised; $\ln P'$ is the transpose of a vector of the natural logarithm of factor prices; a, b_1, and b_2 are parameters to be estimated; γ, N, U, and F are vectors of parameters to be estimated; A', Q', and S' are the transpose of vectors — measures of output quality, input quality, and the service conditions under which the agency operates; and ϵ is a vector of "disturbance terms" (or "error terms") representing random influences on average cost which we were unable to capture in our model.

One aspect of this model deserves comment. The mathematical form in which the output variable and factor prices were entered was dictated by our choice of a homothetic Cobb-Douglas production function to represent the operations of correctional agencies. We selected this form over other alternatives because we felt that while relatively simple, it imposed important technical restrictions (for example, diminishing marginal physical product for inputs). It also allows costs to vary with output in rather complex ways.

The Data

The data set contains information on Federal Correctional Institutions and was obtained from a number of different sources within the Federal Bureau of Prisons (FBOP) and the U.S. Department of Justice's System Design and Development Group. Federal Correction Institutions (FCIs) are generally the more modern and relatively smaller (as compared to federal penitentiaries) medium-custody institutions in the federal prison system. FCIs hold the bulk of federal prisoners, and administrators of the federal prison system are committed to replacing most penitentiaries with FCIs. Further, given FBOP's role as "a model for state prison systems," FCIs are likely to be a type of facility that is widely utilized in the future. Appendix 3 of Schmidt and Witte (1983) contains a detailed description of this data set. It includes monthly data for the period from October 1975 through June 1978 for all 21 FCIs that were operating.

TABLE 10.2   Variable Definitions and Expected Sign of Coefficients

Theoretical Variable and Symbol	Empirical Measure and Acronym for Prison Data Set	Expected Sign of Coefficient
Costs (TC) (dependent variable)	Sum of actual disbursements, increments, in accounts payable and nonfunded costs, changes in applied costs and normal depreciation during the period divided by the number of confined days (AC)	N.A.
Output (Y) (independent variable)	Number of offenders incarcerated times the number of days confined during the quarter and its logarithm (CD-ALL, LNCD-ALL)	? ?
Input prices (P)	Logarithm of the cost of capital proxied by a regional index of construction wages (LNCOST-C); logarithm of the cost of labor, proxied by average hourly wage and fringe benefits paid to institutional staff (LNCOST-L)	+, +
Product quality (members of the vector A)		
Security	Ratio of correctional officers to average confined population (SECURE)	+, +
Incidents	Sum of institutional escapes, inmate assaults, and violent inmate deaths (INCDNT)	+
Crowding; Deviations short run from planned output	Ratio of average confined population to institutional physical capacity and its squared value (CROWD, CROWD2)	−, +
Service condition (members of the vector S)		
Racial balance	Ratio of the percentage nonwhite in the correctional staff to the percentage nonwhite in the inmate population and its squared value (R-BAL, R-BAL2)	−, +
Auxiliary facilities	Percentage of confined days' output produced in an associated camp, female facility, or detention center (PC-OTH)	?

(continued)

TABLE 10.2 (Continued)

Theoretical Variable and Symbol	Empirical Measure and Acronym for Prison Data Set	Expected Sign of Coefficient
Labor Quality		
Staff type	Ratio of guards and other staff (RATIO-S)	?
Education	Average years of education (ED-S)	−
Race	Percentage of staff that are non-white (RACE-S)	?
Age	The average age of the staff (AGE-S)	?
Sex	Percentage of staff that are male (SEX-S)	?
Capital Quality		
Living area	Square feet of living area per bed (SQFPER)	?
Single beds	Proportion of design capacity housed in single-bed cells or rooms (SINGLE)	?
Sanitary facilities	Number of toilets and urinals per design capacity (SANPER)	?
Production quality and service conditions (members of the vector A and S), age	Average age of the inmate population in months and its squared value (AGE-I, AGE-II)	+, −
Racial composition	Percentage of the inmate population whose race is nonwhite (RACE-I)	?
Sexual composition	Percentage of the inmate population whose sex is female (FEMALE)	?
Occupation	Percentage of the inmate population whose longest job prior to incarceration was professional, technical, managerial, or in accounting (WCOLLAR)	?
IQ	Average Beta IQ of the inmate population (BETAIQ)	?
Sentence	Average length, in years, of the sentences of the confined population (LENGTH)	?

(continued)

TABLE 10.2 (Continued)

Theoretical Variable and Symbol	Empirical Measure and Acronym for Prison Data Set	Expected Sign of Coefficient
Crime type of offender	Percentage of the confined population sentenced for a crime against a person (O-PERS); percentage of the confined population sentenced for property offenses (O-PROP)	+, ?
Addiction	Percentage of inmates with a history of significant alcohol use (ALCOL); percentage of inmates with a history of significant drug use (DRUGS)	+, +
Previous record	Number of previous convictions resulting in periods of incarceration of six months or more (RECORD)	?
Marital status	Percentage of inmates who are married (MARRIED)	–
Rehabilitative activities	Number of rehabilitative activities provided during the period and its squared value and its value interacted with CD-ALL (IPRS, IPRS2, CD-ALL* IPRS)	?, ?, ?

Given our model specification (see equation 10.1) and data set, we next specified empirical measures for our theoretical constructs. Table 10.2 summarizes our choices.

Empirical Results for Prisons

We began our work by estimating a short-run cost function for each of the 21 federal correctional institutions, using the monthly time series data. The dependent and independent variables used are defined in Table 10.2. The results we obtained, which are reported elsewhere (see Witte et al., 1979; Schmidt and Witte, 1983), indicate that methods of operation at the 21 FCIs varied substantially. This means that when conducting an economic analysis of costs, we would not be justified in estimating a long-run cost function by pooling data for all institutions. Economic theory indicates that we can only learn important facts about a particular method of operation if we study groups of facilities that are using the same method.

We searched among the 21 FCIs for a group of prisons that appeared to be using broadly similar methods of operation; we were able to identify six such institutions.[12] We began by using ordinary least squares to estimate our long-run prison cost function, using quarterly data for these six institutions for the period beginning in the first quarter of 1976 and ending in the second quarter of 1978.[13] Results are reported in the second and third columns of Table 10.3.

We were able to explain a large portion (87 percent) of the variation in average costs with our model. However, only the coefficients of a few variables were statistically significant, due to extensive multicollinearity and relatively low variance in a number of the independent variables.

Desiring to rid our average cost curve specification of variables unrelated to costs, we selected two basic rules for reducing our specification. First, we retained the output and factor price variables, regardless of the significance of the coefficients on these variables, because both economic theory and intuition provide strong support for their inclusion. Second, we proceeded to drop other independent variables sequentially, beginning with the variables whose coefficient had the smallest t-ratio, until the coefficients associated with all remaining variables were significant at the 0.05 level of significance. We tested to see if we could accept the hypothesis that all deleted variables, when combined, were insignificantly related to average costs; we were able to accept this hypothesis. Results for the reduced specification appear in the fourth and fifth columns of Table 10.3.

Our work to this point had proceeded on the assumption that the correctional agencies that we studied were effectively minimizing costs. Both our own work with correctional agencies and the work of others with public and private entities led us to believe that this was not likely to be the case. To test this assumption, and to develop an overall measure of performance, we estimated a stochastic frontier cost function using a method developed by Schmidt and Lovell (1979).

Our specification for the frontier long run average cost function was identical to our reduced specification in Table 10.3, except that we reduced the specification by one variable by imposing the restriction that the factor shares had to sum to one. We did this to conserve both degrees of freedom and computational costs.

TABLE 10.3 **Estimated Long-Run Average Cost Curve for Six FCIs (ordinary least squares)**

	Initial Specification		Final Specification	
Variable	Coefficient	t-ratio	Coefficient	t-ratio
Intercept	51.680161	1.2933	39.150440	4.3261***
Output				
CD-ALL	9.3807×10^{-6}	0.2418	2.155835×10^{-5}	2.2922***
LNCD-ALL	−1.681052	−0.4607	−2.449731	−3.2825***
Factor prices				
LNCOST-L	−0.705843	−0.6858	−0.289815	−0.4740
LNCOST-C	−2.951293	−0.3530	−0.335975	−0.6408
Product quality				
SECURE	4.126519	0.6225		
Product quality and service conditions				
IPRS	-4.9511×10^{-5}	−0.4108		
IRRS2	-5.80347×10^{-4}	−0.0300		
CD-IPRS	6.424353×10^{-3}	0.3058		
AGE-I	−0.182319	−0.3024		
AGE-I2	1.730014×10^{-3}	0.1810		
RACE-I	−0.071175	−1.7084*		
BETA-IQ	−0.044039	−0.4459		
WCOLLAR	0.029246	0.7696		
LENGTH	0.162459	0.7699		
O-PERS	−0.086788	−0.8333		
O-PROP	0.028065	1.0395		
DRUGS	4.752206×10^{-4}	0.0193		
ALCOHOL	0.077491	1.3125		
RECORD	0.103382	0.3002		
MARRIED	0.016079	0.5384		
FEMALE	0.046490	1.9028*	0.018893	3.7500***
Service conditions				
R-BAL	−4.601240	−1.1431		
R-BAL2	1.214325	0.3213		
PC-OTH	−0.029699	−0.4496		
Labor quality				
RATIO-S	0.462797	0.3732		
AGE-S	−0.278803	−2.0947**	−0.176617	−4.8028***
ED-S	−0.036526	−0.2132		
RACE-S	0.066769	1.0285		
SEX-S	-4.0059×10^{-5}	−0.3333		
Capital quality				
SQFPER	−0.132315	−1.1588	−0.033156	−2.2100**
SINGLE	−2.931725	−0.7770	−1.573329	−5.2792***
SANPER	2.843853	0.9086	2.124388	3.1417***
R^2 (F-ratio)	0.8704	(4.61)	0.8126	(24.08)
N		60		60

*Indicates that the coefficient was significant at the .10 level, two-tail test.
**Indicates that the coefficient was significant at the .05 level, two-tail test.
***Indicates that the coefficient was significant at the .01 level, two-tail test.

Specifically, we estimated the following function:

$$\ln(AC) - LNCOST-L = B_0 + B_1 \, LNCD\text{-}ALL + B_2 \, CD\text{-}ALL + B_3 \, (LNCOST\text{-}C\text{-}LNCOST\text{-}L) + A'N + S'U + \psi \qquad [10.2]$$

where A' is the transpose of the vector of output and input quality measures in the final specification of Table 10.3, and S' is the transpose of the service condition variable in that specification. The random disturbance, ψ, is composed to two parts. One part is normally distributed with zero mean and a variance of $\sigma^2\nu$. The other is a non-negative, half normal, random variable with a positive mean and variance $\sigma^2\mu$.

The normal portion of the disturbance term captures random variations in costs between prisons that are due to factors such as weather, riot, and fires that are outside the individual prison decision maker's control. The half-normal portion of the disturbance reflects inefficiency. This portion of the disturbance is either zero or a positive number. A zero value for this variable indicates that the prison is operating efficiently — that is, it is a frontier prison. The size of a positive value for this variable indicates the degree of inefficiency.

We estimated our frontier cost function using maximum likelihood techniques. Results are reported in Table 10.4. Our frontier estimates indicate that costs will be at a minimum when the prison contains 1467 inmates.

The most interesting results of the frontier estimates were our estimates for the variances of two parts of the disturbance term. Note that the variance of the half-normal portion of this disturbance was quite large, indicating large differences in efficiency among prisons. We estimate that, on the average, costs in the six FCIs studied were 9.4 percent more than they would have been if the most efficient methods of operation had been utilized. Given Federal Bureau of Prison expected outlays of $327 million in fiscal year 1980, our results indicate that efficient operation could have saved approximately $30 million. While savings of this size seem unlikely to be realized, our results indicate that some savings may be possible.

Using a technique recently developed by Jondrow et al. (1982), we also estimated the extent of inefficiency at each prison in our sample

TABLE 10.4   Results of Estimating the Frontier Average Cost Function

Variable	Coefficient	t-ratio
Intercept	29.6038	4.09
Output		
CD-ALL	1.615E-5	−3.23
LNCD-ALL	−2.1480	2.02
Factor prices		
(LNCOST-C)-(LNCOST-L)	0.4305	2.56
Production quality and service conditions		
FEMALE	0.0123	3.11
Labor quality		
AGE-S	−0.1244	−5.16
Capital quality		
SQFTPER	−0.0196	−1.39
SINGLE	−1.2488	−4.73
SANPER	1.2230	2.50
Estimated variances		*Standard Error*
$\hat{\sigma}^2_{\psi}$ (the entire disturbance)	0.0204	0.0067
$\hat{\sigma}^2_{v}$ (the normal portion)	0.0066	0.0028
$\hat{\sigma}^2_{u}$ (the half-normal portion)	0.0138	0.0084
N	60	

for each quarter. Table 10.5 contains those results. Note that there is considerable variation through time in the level of inefficiency at any given prison. Indeed, the temporal variation in efficiency appears to be greater than the variation across prison units. The mean estimated inefficiency for the different prison units ranges only from 8.5 percent for prison 1 to 10.4 percent for prison 2.

Briefly summarizing, our analyses indicate that the average cost of incarcerating offenders at first decreases and then increases as prison population rises. According to our model, costs will be lowest when prisons are quite large (1000 to 1500 inmates), but not huge. We

TABLE 10.5   Estimated Inefficiency ($\hat{\mu}$) by Prison and Quarter

		Prison					
		1	*2*	*3*	*4*	*5*	*6*
	1	.08	.10	.06	.05	.08	.09
	2	.08	.15	.09	.21	.07	.30
	3	.06	.11	.08	.04	.06	.07
	4	.09	.02	.12	.10	.09	.07
Quarter	*5*	.08	.09	.07	.07	.10	.05
	6	.08	.09	.09	.10	.07	.07
	7	.05	.06	.10	.08	.09	.06
	8	.06	.06	.10	.08	.06	.08
	9	.08	.12	.03	.08	.06	.04
	10	.19	.24	.13	.07	.19	.19
	Mean Inefficiency	.085	.104	.087	.088	.087	.102

found further that the cost of operating these FCIs will be higher according to the relative cost of capital, the lower the proportion of female inmates, the older the average age of staff, and depending on whether inmates are housed in relatively large single cells but have limited sanitary facilities.

SUMMARY AND CONCLUSION

All three methods — multiattribute decision theory, data envelopment analysis, and production and cost functions — can be used to generate a single overall measure of agency performance. Data envelopment analysis and production and cost functions should probably be applied only to agencies having well-defined processes, for the reasons given below. Further, these two types of analyses generally provide estimates of only the efficiency aspects of agency performance, while multiattribute decision theory allows one to consider other aspects of agency performance, such as equity.

In the context of our work, production and cost theory provide more useful guidance when analyzing the performance of large-scale prisons than that of probation and parole agencies. In a related effort (Witte, 1982), we estimated cost functions for five probation and parole offices. The data set contained monthly information for a single calendar year. Production and cost analysis poorly described the operation of these offices.

As a whole, the work reported in this analysis of production and cost functions tends to support the conclusions of a number of other researchers who have analyzed the performance of other types of public agencies.[14] These researchers found that the economic constructs of production and cost functions were most directly applicable to public agencies that produce physical outputs (for example, water, electricity, refuse collection) with well-defined inputs and known technological processes. For other types of public agencies, production and cost functions mainly provide useful insights as to important variables to consider and possible functional forms to be used in analysis. Production and cost analysis appears to provide the fewest insights for public agencies that produce services requiring extensive interaction between public employees and the individuals receiving those services (that is, education and other social services). In such situations, individual skills are extremely important, and the exact way that the service is provided may vary substantially from employee to employee.

When processes are not well understood or vary as a result of employee discretion, multiattribute decision theory may be a more appropriate aid when generating an overall measure of agency performance. Further, multiattribute techniques allow researchers to consider aspects of agency performance other than efficiency. However, multiattribute decision analysis, unlike cost and production function approaches, provides little information concerning how agencies currently operate.

NOTES

1. See Fuss et al. (1977: 267-268) for a brief survey of recent work.
2. For a survey of duality theory, see McFadden (1978).
3. Some second-order approximations generalize readily to multiple output. Darrough and Heineke (1978) have estimated a multiple-output translog cost function for police services. Many exact functional forms, however, are intrinsically nonlinear, making estimation difficult and expensive. In addition, for both exact

functional forms and second-order approximations, the number of parameters to be estimated for multiproduct production processes quickly becomes very large if extremely restrictive assumptions are not made.

4. See Alesch and Dougharty (1971), Hirsch (1973), or Vernez (1976) for surveys of early work, and Witte (1980) for a discussion of more recent work in six areas (education, fire protection, hospitals, libraries, police protection, and large-scale prisons).

5. Orzechowski (1977) provides a review of this literature.

6. Such functions were first developed by Farrell (1957). More recent work has been done by Aigner and Chu (1968), Timmer (1971), and Aigner et al. (1977).

7. See Farrell (1957), Aigner and Chu (1968), and Seitz (1970) for examples. Carlson (1972) estimates deterministic frontiers for higher educational institutions.

8. See Aigner et al. (1976); Aigner et al. (1977); or Schmidt and Lovell (1979). The May 1980 issue of the *Journal of Econometrics* is devoted to the specification and estimation of frontier production, profit and cost functions. The lead article contains a survey of frontier work.

9. For an example of this work, see Blumstein (1975) and Chaiken et al. (1976). Blumstein and Larson (1976) provide an extensive survey of criminal justice models.

10. See Martin et al. (1981) for a survey.

11. See Minerva (1982) for a discussion of selected parole and probation offices. Witte et al. (1979) discuss the goals of large-scale prisons and provide detailed analyses of the federal and California prison systems.

12. These institutions are Ashland, Lompoc, Lexington, Oxford, Texarkana, and Alderson. We did two things to determine if these six institutions were using similar methods of operation. First, we conducted a generalized Chow test to determine if we could accept the hypothesis that the coefficients on all variables in the short-run cost function were equal across the six institutions. The value of the test statistic, which is distributed $F_{125,48}$ under the null hypothesis, was 1.979. We next ran three sets of simply specified long-run cost functions for subsets of these six FCIs. Specifically, we estimated cost curves for (1) the older versus the newer prisons in the group, (2) the more versus the less secure prisons in the group, and (3) the bigger versus the smaller institutions in the group. In each case, we accepted the null hypothesis that the six prisons were using similar methods of operation.

13. Appropriate statistical tests were performed to ensure that this pooling of time series data was justified. We pooled data around the third quarter of 1977, as detailed descriptions of the capital stock were available for that quarter when a complete physical plant inventory was conducted. The test statistic for the appropriateness of this time series pooling, which is distributed $F_{45,10}$ under the null hypothesis that pooling is appropriate, was 0.794.

14. For example, see Alesch and Dougharty (1971), Hanushek (1979), Summers and Wolfe (1977), Vernez (1976), and Witte (1980).

REFERENCES

AIGNER, D.J. and S. F. CHU (1968) "On estimating the industry production function." American Economic Review 58: 826-839.

AIGNER, D.J., T. AMEMIYA, and D.J. POIRER (1976) "On the estimation of production frontiers: maximum likelihood estimation of the parameters of a discontinuous density function." International Economic Review 17: 377-396.

AIGNER, D., C.A.K. LOVELL, and P. SCHMIDT (1977) "Formulation and estimation of stochastic frontier production function models." Journal of Econometrics 5: 1-17.

ALESCH, D.J. and L.A. DOUGHARTY (1971) Economies of Scale Analysis in State and Local Government. Santa Monica, CA: Rand.

ANDERSON, D.F. (1981) "A system dynamic view of the competing values approach to organizational life cycles." Public Productivity Review 5: 160-187.

BAHL, R.W. and J. BURKHEAD (1977) "Productivity and the measurement of public output," in C. H. Levine (ed.) Managing Human Resources: A Challenge to Urban Governments. Beverly Hills, CA: Sage.

BLUMSTEIN, A. (1975) "A model to aid in planning for the total criminal justice system," in L. Oberlander (ed.) Quantitative Tools for Criminal Justice Planning. Washington, DC: Law Enforcement Assistance Administration.

——— and R. LARSON (1976) "Models of a total criminal justice system," in L. R. McPheters and W.B. Stronge (eds.) The Economics of Crime and Law Enforcement. Springfield, IL: Charles C Thomas.

BODILY, S.E. (1978) "Police sector design incorporating preferences of interest groups for equality and efficiency." Management Science 24: 1302-1313.

BRADFORD, D. F., R. A. MALT, and W. E. OATES (1969) "The rising cost of local public services: some evidence and reflections." National Tax Journal 22: 185-202.

CAMERON, K. (1981) "The enigma of organizational effectiveness." New Directions for Program Evaluation 11: 1-13.

CARLSON, D. (1972) "The production and cost behavior of higher educational institutions." Paper P-36 of the Ford Foundation Program for Research in University Administration. Berkeley: University of California.

CHAIKEN, J. et al. (1976) Criminal Justice Models: An Overview. Washington, DC: Government Printing Office.

CHARNES, A. and W.W. COOPER (1980) "Auditing and accounting for program efficiency in not-for-profit entities." Accounting, Organizations and Society 5: 87-107.

——— and E. RHODES (1981) "Evaluating programs and managerial efficiency: an application of data envelopment analysis to program follow through." Management Science 27: 668-697.

COULTER, P.B. (1980) "Measuring the inequity of urban public services: a methodological discussion with applications." Policy Studies Journal 8: 683-697.

DARROUGH, and J.M. HEINEKE (1978) "The multi-output translog production cost function: the case of law enforcement agencies," pp. 259-302 in J. M. Heineke (ed.) Economic Models of Criminal Behavior. Amsterdam: North-Holland.

DENNY, M. and C. PINTO (1978) "An aggregate model with multi-product technologies," pp. 249-267 in M. Fuss and D. McFadden (eds.) Production

Economics: A Dual Approach to Theory and Applications, Vol. 1. Amsterdam: North-Holland.

EDWARDS, W. (1980) "Multiattribute utility for evaluation: structures, uses, and problems," pp. 177-215 in M. W. Klein and K. S. Teilmann (eds.) Handbook of Criminal Justice Evaluation. Beverly Hills, CA: Sage.

——— (1979) "Multiattribute utility measurement: evaluating desegregation plans in a highly political context," pp. 13-54 in R. E. Perloff (ed.) Evaluator Interventions: Pros and Cons. Beverly Hills, CA: Sage.

FARRELL, M. J. (1957) "The measurement of production efficiency." Journal of the Royal Statistical Society, Series A, Part 3: 253-281.

FUSS, M., D. McFADDEN, and Y. MUNDLAK (1977) "A survey of functional forms in the economic analysis of production," pp. 219-268 in M. Fuss and D. McFadden (eds.) Production Economics: A Dual Approach to Theory and Applications, Vol. 1. Amsterdam: North-Holland.

GRIZZLE, G. A. et al. (1982) Basic Issues in Corrections Performance. Washington, DC: National Institute of Justice.

HALL, R. E. (1973) "The specification of technology with several kinds of output." Journal of Political Economy 31: 878-892.

HAMMOND, K. R. (1976) "Externalizing the parameters of quasirational thought," in M. Zeleny (ed.) Multiple Criteria Decision Making, Kyoto 1975. Berlin: Springer-Verlag.

HANUSHEK, E. A. (1979) "Conceptual and empirical issues in the estimation of education production functions." Journal of Human Resources 14: 351-388.

HASENKAMP, G. (1976) Specification and Estimation of Multiple-Output Production Functions. Berlin: Springer-Verlag.

HATRY, H. P. (1980) "Performance measurement principles and techniques: an overview for local government." Public Productivity Review 4: 312-339.

HIRSCH, W. Z. (1973) Urban Economic Analysis. New York: McGraw-Hill.

International City Managers' Association (1958) The Technique of Municipal Administration (4th ed.). Chicago: Author.

JONDROW, J. et al. (1982) "On the estimation of technical inefficiency in the stochastic frontier production function model." Journal of Econometrics 19: 233-238.

JONES, B. D. (1981) "Assessing the products of government: what gets distributed?" Policy Studies Journal 9: 963-971.

KEENEY, R. L. and H. RAIFFA (1976) Decisions with Multiple Objectives: Preferences and Value Tradeoffs. New York: John Wiley.

LEVINE, V. (1981) "The role of outcomes in cost-benefit evaluation." New Directions for Program Evaluation 9: 21-40.

LINEBERRY, R. L. and R. E. WELCH (1974) "Who gets what: measuring the distribution of urban public services." Social Science Quarterly 54: 700-712.

MARTIN, S. B., L. B. SECHREST, and R. REDNER [eds.] (1981) New Directions in the Rehabilitation of Criminal Offenders. Washington, DC: National Academy Press.

McFADDEN, D. (1978) "Cost, revenue and profit functions," pp. 3-109 in M. Fuss and D. McFadden (eds.) Production Economics: A Dual Approach to Theory and Applications, Vol. 1. Amsterdam: North-Holland.

MINERVA, K. S. (1982) "Probation/parole operations." Working Paper 82-1, The Osprey Company, Tallahassee, Florida.

ORZECHOWSKI, W. (1977) "Economic models of bureaucracy: survey, extensions, and evidence," in T. E. Borcherding (ed.) Budgets and Bureaucrats: The Sources of Government Growth. Durham, NC: Duke University Press.

OSTROM, E., R. B. PARKS, S. L. PERCY, and G. P. WHITAKER (1979) "Evaluating police organization." Public Productivity Review 3: 3-27.

QUINN, R. E. and J. ROHRBAUGH (1981) "Competing values approach to organizational effectiveness." Public Productivity Review, 5: 122-140.

SAATY, T. L. (1980) The Analytic Hierarchy Process: Planning, Priority Setting, Resource Allocation. New York: McGraw-Hill.

SCHMIDT, P. and C. A. K. LOVELL (1979) "Estimating technical and allocative inefficiency relative to stochastic production and cost frontiers." Journal of Econometrics 9: 343-366.

SCHMIDT, P. and A. D. WITTE (1983) The Economics of Crime: Applications, Theory and Methods. New York: Academic Press.

SEITZ, W. D. (1970) "The measurement of efficiency relative to a frontier production function." American Journal of Agricultural Economics 52: 505-511.

SUMMERS, A. S. and B. L. WOLFE (1977) "Do schools make a difference?" American Economic Review 67: 639-652.

TIMMER, C. P. (1971) "Using a probabilistic frontier production function to measure technical efficiency." Journal of Political Economy 79: 776-794.

VERNEZ, G. (1976) Delivery of Urban Public Services: Production, Cost and Demand Functions, and Determinants of Public Expenditure for Fire, Police and Sanitation Services. Santa Monica, CA: Rand.

WILENSKI, P. (1980-81) "Efficiency or equity: competing values in administrative reform." Policy Studies Journal 9: 1239-1249.

WITTE, A. D. (1982) "Using production and cost functions to measure the efficiency of corrections agencies." Working Paper 82-9, The Osprey Company, Tallahassee, Florida.

——— (1980) "Economies of public service delivery systems." Summary of round table discussion of the Special National Workshop on Research Methodology and Criminal Justice Program Evaluation, Baltimore, Maryland, March 18.

——— et al. (1979) "Empirical investigations of correctional cost functions." Final Report to the National Institute of Law Enforcement and Criminal Justice on LEAA grant 78-NI-AX-0059.

ABOUT THE CONTRIBUTORS

ROBERT J. BURSIK, Jr. is an assistant professor of sociology at the University of Oklahoma. In addition to the study of recidivism, his ongoing work in community processes of delinquency includes a longitudinal analysis of changes in neighborhood delinquency rates. He is also involved in a cohort study of the dynamics of delinquency among early adolescents.

SIMON DINITZ is a professor of sociology at Ohio State University. He has authored or coauthored over a dozen books and numerous articles appearing in professional journals. He is a past president of the American Society of Criminology, a recipient of that organization's Sutherland Award, and a former editor of *Criminology*. His latest book deals with the careers of violent adult offenders.

SHELDON EKLAND-OLSON is an associate professor of sociology at the University of Texas at Austin. His current research interests include microstructural approaches to deviance and social control. His most recent publications have appeared in *American Sociological Review, Criminology,* and *Journal of Applied Behavioral Science.*

GLORIA A. GRIZZLE is an associate professor of public administration at Florida State University. She does research and teaches in the fields of policy development and implementation, evaluation, and budgeting. For the past several years she has concentrated on developing theory and methods for measuring performance in corrections, higher education, and social programs. Her current research projects include measuring the performance of probation and parole agencies and emergency medical services.

KENNETH A. HARDY is the director of the Social Science Statistical Laboratory of the Institute for Research in Social Science at the University of North Carolina at Chapel Hill. He is currently examining equity in case processing in a cohort of homicide cases processed through the North Carolina court system.

WILLIAM R. KELLY is an assistant professor of sociology and a research associate in the population research center at the University of Texas at Austin. His current research interests include the analysis of annual changes in U.S. fertility and modeling the determinants of temporal change in urban racial insurgency. His recent publications have appeared in the *American Journal of Sociology, Social Forces,* and the *Journal of Political and Military Sociology.*

JODY R. KLEIN is a graduate assistant in the Institute of Criminal Justice and Criminology at the University of Maryland, College Park. She is currently involved in research concerning determinants of dispute resolution by police officers in both domestic and nondomestic encounters.

BRUCE W. McCLEARY is a graduate of the University of Illinois and holds an M.A. in social psychology from the University of North Carolina at Chapel Hill. His main research interests are in attitude formation and research methods. He is currently involved in marketing research.

PETER K. MANNING is a professor of sociology and psychiatry at Michigan State University. He received his Ph.D. from Duke University. He is the author of three books, the latest of which, *Narc's Game,* is a comparative study of the issues, structures, processes, and constraints that shape the enforcement of drug laws in the United States. Additionally, he has written numerous articles and essays in the areas of medical, occupational, and theoretical sociology and criminology. He is currently on leave as a Visiting Fellow, Balliol College, Oxford.

MARY ELLEN MARSDEN is a research sociologist with the Center for the Study of Social Behavior of the Research Triangle Institute. She has directed a number of evaluations of criminal justice and energy information programs.

STEPHEN MASTROFSKI is an assistant professor of the administration of justice at Pennsylvania State University. He received his Ph.D. in political science from the University of North Carolina at Chapel Hill and has conducted research on the structure of police organizations and performance.

THOMAS ORSAGH is an associate professor of economics at the University of North Carolina at Chapel Hill. His research chiefly involves the application of the economist's paradigm to issues in crime control and the allocation of criminal justice resources.

ELINOR OSTROM is the chair of the political science department and a co-director of the Workshop in Political Theory and Policy Analysis at Indiana University. Her research interests lie in the areas of urban service delivery and the effects of institutional arrangements on citizens, elected officials, bureau chiefs, and street-level bureaucratic behavior. She is the author of *Urban Policy Analysis: An Institutional Approach,* and the editor of *The Delivery of Urban Services: Outcomes of Change.*

CHARLES DAVID PHILLIPS is an assistant professor of political science at the University of North Carolina at Chapel Hill. His research interests revolve around public policy toward crime and delinquency. He is the author of *Sentencing Councils in the Federal Courts* and has contributed to a variety of professional journals. He is currently involved in an analysis of the determinants and effects of aggressive policing.

DOUGLAS A. SMITH is an assistant professor in the Institute of Criminology at the University of Maryland, College Park. He received his Ph.D. in sociology from Indiana University in 1982. His current research is on the determinants of discretionary decision making by police officers, with an emphasis on neighborhood and organization constraints on police behavior.

MICHAEL SUPANCIC is a Ph.D. candidate in the department of sociology at the University of Texas at Austin. His current research activities include analyses of the impact of divorce and other relational disruptions, as well as an historical study of frontier law. He recently published an article in *Criminology.*

GORDON P. WHITAKER is an associate professor of political science at the University of North Carolina at Chapel Hill, where he also serves as the director of the MPA Program. He studies city agencies and the delivery of services, especially the organization and performance of local police.

ANN D. WITTE is a professor of economics at the University of North Carolina at Chapel Hill. She has published extensively in the areas of law and economics and has a long-standing interest in analyzing the performance of public organizations. Her most recent publications include a book (*The Economics of Crime: Theory, Methods and Applications*) and a series of papers on tax compliance and tax administration.

MARY ANN WYCOFF joined the Police Foundation in 1972 and since then has directed research on organizational change, the crime-effectiveness of police, the police role, and police supervision. She is completing her Ph.D. dissertation in sociology at the University of Wisconsin, Madison. Her areas of interest include socialization, supervision, organizational change, service delivery, and the measurement of attitudes and performance.